THE COMPLETE HISTORY OF CENTRAL EUROPE

Covering Austria, Germany, Poland, Switzerland, and Much More

By
ANDREW GREEN

© **Copyright 2021 - All rights reserved.**
The content contained within this book may not be reproduced, duplicated or transmitted without direct written permission from the author or the publisher.

Under no circumstances will any blame or legal responsibility be held against the publisher, or author, for any damages, reparation, or monetary loss due to the information contained within this book, either directly or indirectly.

Legal Notice:
This book is copyright protected. It is only for personal use. You cannot amend, distribute, sell, use, quote or paraphrase any part, or the content within this book, without the consent of the author or publisher.

Disclaimer Notice:
Please note the information contained within this document is for educational and entertainment purposes only. All effort has been executed to present accurate, up to date, reliable, complete information. No warranties of any kind are declared or implied. Readers acknowledge that the author is not engaging in the rendering of legal, financial, medical or professional advice. The content within this book has been derived from various sources. Please consult a licensed professional before attempting any techniques outlined in this book.

By reading this document, the reader agrees that under no circumstances is the author responsible for any losses, direct or indirect, that are incurred as a result of the use of information contained within this document, including, but not limited to, errors, omissions, or inaccuracies.

Table of Contents

The History of Austria: A Fascinating Guide to this Beautiful Country

Location, Location, Location 2

Prehistoric Austria 5
    The Dawn of Civilization 5
    The Copper Age and Otzi 7
    HALLSTATT: The Bronze Age and the Iron (Roman) Age 8

From the Romans to the Middle Ages 10
    The Holy Roman Empire Emerges 10
    Babenberg Rule 11
    The Hapsburgs Come to Austria 12

The Habsburg Dynasty – Power and Doom 13
    Simple Rules of the Dynasty 13
    The Long Line of Succession and Destruction 14
    Habsburg Origins 16
    Habsburgs as Holy Roman Emperors 17

Maximilian I (1459-1519) 18
    The Austrian Empire's Growth in the Middle Ages 18
    Young Maximilian 19
    Maximilian Takes Tyrol 21
    The Pan-Ethnic Empire of Maximilian 22

Protestant Reformation 24
    Charles V Can't Stop the Protestants 24

    Ferdinand I Takes Over in Troubled Times 25
    Ferdinand I's Division of Austrian lands: 60 Years of Chaos 26
    Ferdinand II and the Thirty Years' War 26
    Ferdinand III's Peace: the Austrian Baroque 28
    The Reign of Leopold I: Two Wars on Opposite Fronts 29
    Charles VI and the Pragmatic Sanction 29

A Side Trip to Salzburg 31

The Age of Empress Maria Theresa 34
    The Only Hapsburg Empress 34
    Maria Theresa Wins Hungarian Support 35
    Maria Theresa Reforms Taxes and Education 36
    Changing Alliances 37
    The Empress 38
    The Schonbrunn Makeover 39
    Maria Theresa's Vienna 40
    The Composers of Vienna 40
    The Death of Maria Theresa 43

Joseph II Begins the Habsburg-Lorraine Dynasty 45

The French Revolution and Napoleon 48

The Congress of Vienna 52
    Metternich 52
    The Biedermeier Period (1815-1848) 53
    The Truth Behind Metternich's Censorship 54
    Ferdinand I of Austria 55
    Why a Revolution? What Were the Results? 56

- The Era of Franz Josef I 57
  - Austria Leaves the German Confederation 58
  - The Creation of the Ringstrasse 58
  - Semmering Railway 60
  - Johann Strauss II (1825-1899) 61
  - The Austro-Hungarian Empire 61
  - A Renaissance of Art and Thought under Franz Josef 63
  - A Series of Tragedies 67
- A Visitor to Vienna 68
- World War I on the Horizon 70
- World War I 71
  - Austria Declares War Against Serbia 71
  - Vienna is Starving 72
  - The Last Emperor: Charles I 73
  - After World War I 75
  - Austrian Civil War: Fascism vs. Socialism 76
  - Anschluss 76
  - The Austrian Holocaust 77
  - Political Treatment Following World War II 80
  - Neutrality 80
- Modern Austria 81
  - Government 81
  - A Look at Austria, via the Modern World's Most Famous Austrian 82
  - Modern Vienna, the "Easternmost City of the West" 87
  - The Habsburg Family Today 91

Conclusion 93

Sources 95

History of the Czech Republic: A Fascinating Guide to this Wonderful Country in Central Europe

The History of the Czech Republic 98
    Origins 99
    Ancient Times.. 100
    Samo 101
    Medieval 103
    Charles University.. 104
    Jan Hus and the Hussite War 105
    Habsburg Rule 106
    The Thirty Years' War 107
    War Rages On 109
    Czech Republic After the Thirty Years' War............ 110
    National Revival 111
    World War I 114
    Czechoslovakia 117
    World War II 121
    Battle for the Sudetenland.. 122
    The Second Republic.. 127
    Operation Anthropoid.. 128
    Post-war and Inner Turmoil 132
    Communism... 134
    De-Stalinization 135

The Late 60s in Czechoslovakia.. 138

The End of Dubcek and The End of Communism....................... 139

The Velvet Revolution 140

The Czech Republic 142

The History of Germany: A Fascinating Guide to the Past, A Look at the Culture, and Famous Historical Events

Introduction.. 146

Humble Beginnings.. 152

The Middle Ages of Germany 161

Moving Forward 167

The Spark that Started the Fire 172

The Lasting Effects of the Protestant Reformation 180

The Age of Enlightenment in Germany 186

An Explosion of Prosperity... 192

A New Man at the Helm.. 201

Ushering in the Storm 212

Germany in World War I 214

Germany under Adolph Hitler... 217

A War Fought with No Weapons.. 221

Germany, Today 224

Conclusion 226

References 228

The History of Hungary: A Fascinating Guide to this Central European Country

Introduction 230
Early Days 232
The Arpad Dynasty and King Saint Stephen 235
The Vast and Varied Lines of Succession 238
The Elected King Matthias Corvinus 240
Hungarian Hussars 242
A Divided Hungary and the Habsburg Empire 243
The 12 Demands of Hungary: 1848 Revolution 245
The Austro-Hungarian Empire 247
The Growth of the Right 249
Hungary in World War II 251
The Age of Communism 253
The Revolution of 1956 255
The Era of János Kádár 257
The Fall of Hungarian Communism 259
The Modern Face of Hungary 261
    The Economy 263
    Tourism 264
    Technology and Science in Hungary 265
    Transportation 266
    Judicial System 267

    The military 267

The Demographics of Hungary 269

    Administrative Divisions 269

    Population 269

    Health 270

    Language 270

    Religion 271

    Education 271

Hungarian Culture 273

    Architecture 274

    Music 276

    Dance 277

    Literature 278

    Folk Art 279

    Porcelain 280

    Sports 281

    Baths 282

    Cuisine 283

    Cinema 284

Conclusion: Centuries of Conflict 287

Sources 289

The History of Poland: A Fascinating Guide to this European Country

Introduction 292

The First Days of Poland 299

The End of the Middle Ages in Poland 306

The Early Modern History of Poland 314

The Modern History of Poland 323

The Economy of Poland 336

The Demographics of Poland 344

The Politics of Poland 350

The Geography of Poland 361

Conclusion 368

References 369

The History of Slovakia: A Fascinating Guide to this Central European Country

Intro 371

Basis 373

Prehistoric Through Iron Age of Slovakia 378

The Era of the Roman Empire 385

The Communist Era of Slovakia 393

Slovakia 1990s Until Now 396

Important Artifacts 400

Geography of Slovakia 408

Recap 412

The History of Switzerland: A Fascinating Guide to this Wonderful Country in Central Europe

Introduction 418

Geography 420

Early History of Switzerland 421

    Prehistory 421

    Geographic Advantage 423

    The Gotthard Pass 424

    The Swiss Confederacy Responds to Habsburg Interference 425

The Warriors of Switzerland 427

    Origins 427

    The Pikemen's Square 430

    The Burgundian Wars 432

Swiss Mercenaries 434

    The Papal Swiss Guard 435

Defeat of Emperor Maximilian 439

Reformation in the Cantons 440

    Huldrych Zwingli 441

    John Calvin 443

    Battles, Spoken and Fought 444

Swiss Population Growth and the Peasants' Uprisings 446

The Thirty Years' War 449

The Renaissance in Switzerland..451

The Helvetic Republic 455

Switzerland as a Federal State 457

Under the Alps: the Gotthard Tunnel......................................459

World War I..462

Between World Wars...465

World War II..467

The National Redoubt...471

The Cold War 473

Switzerland and the European Union.....................................475

The Things She's Famous For 476

    The Swiss Cheese Empire..476

    The Fine Chocolatiers...481

    A Question of Time: Swiss Clocks and Watches.........................485

Modern Switzerland..491

    What is Direct Democracy?...491

    Citizenship in Switzerland..493

    Switzerland as a World Center...495

    Swiss Military Today 496

    The Swiss Economy 497

    Mysteries of the Swiss Bank Account 499

    Speaking in Switzerland..501

    Education and Sciences...502

    Energy and the Environment...504

    Culture, Media, and Entertainment 504

Sports 506
Life and Tourism in the Alps 508
Life in Switzerland's Great Cities.. 512
    Basel.. 513
    Geneva 514
    Bern 515
    Lausanne 516
    Lucerne 516
    Zurich 517
Conclusion 519
References 521

The History of Austria: A Fascinating Guide to this Beautiful Country

Location, Location, Location

Today, Austria is a small, East Alpine county in Southern Central Europe, composed of nine federated states. In its landlocked location, Austria borders eight other European countries.

Within its Modern Borders, Austria has three geographic zones:

1. The Alps in the southern portion of the country cover just under 63% of the country's land. This area is not widely populated. Above the Alps, the Danube River runs west to east across the land.
2. In its upper northern portion, Austria holds the southern section of the Bohemian Forest (this composes about 10% of the country's area).
3. Along the border with Hungary are the Pannonian lowlands, and the Vienna Basin (and the Danube Valley) stretches across the northern section of Austria. It is sandwiched between the Bohemian Forest to the north and the Alps to the south. These

geographic denotations make up a vaguely cockeyed U-shaped portion of Austria that is the most densely populated area because of its accessibility and climate. Its capital city of Vienna is situated in the far west of the country, right at the arc of our imaginary "U" shape.

Austria's location in the center of Europe and along the Danube River has pushed it to the forefront of history. Let's examine why this is the case:

- » It is centrally located between dozens of countries with ever-changing borders and affiliations.
- » Within Austria, the Alps made a nearly impenetrable barrier *but* Austrian territory also contains the gateways to the easiest passes through the Alps into Italy – if one knows where to look!
- » The Danube Valley and its river served as a major corridor of passage between Western and Eastern Europe. The Danube River, which cuts an invaluable swatch through the country of Austria, is Western Europe's longest river, flowing through ten countries from the Black Forest in Germany to the Black Sea in Romania. It is the only river in Western Europe that flows west to east, giving it a distinct advantage for trade.

Basically Austria, with its prime location in the middle of everything European and its huge section of riverfront property on the Danube, is located in a spot that is far too busy for history to ever have ignored the little area.

Until World War I, Austria was far larger than its own literal borders. It was for several hundred years the center of the mightiest, most far-reaching empire in the world, and for a millennium, it seated the glorious (and notorious) Habsburg family that held the power of the Holy Roman Empire and seemingly countless thrones throughout the European nations. One cannot separate the history of the Habsburgs from the history of Austria; they are one and the same.

To look at Austrian history is to look into a cauldron of mysterious, ever-changing ingredients and nearly constant warfare. Yet the history is also brilliant with artistic endeavors, intellectual advancements, and governmental reforms centuries ahead of its time. The region of Austria has always been a melting pot of cultures that produced incredible outcomes, for good or ill.

Prehistoric Austria

The Dawn of Civilization

The development of human society varies worldwide, and eras are not precise. Being further north and subject to a number of "little" Ice Ages, including climate change as recently as 10,000 years ago, means that the societal development of the Central European region does not precisely follow those in warmer areas like Northern Africa or South America. Civilization was rather slow to build in these colder climates. During our planet's last major Ice Age, the Alps were covered, so as was the case with most of Central European land. Relatively widespread human habitation did not begin in the Austrian area until the Middle Paleolithic era (from 300,000 to 50,000 years past).

The oldest traces of human existence that have been located in the Austrian region were left behind 250,000 years ago in the Repolust Cave of Styria (a Southeastern Austrian state). Here, stone and bone tools and pottery fragments were located along with the remains of mammals.

Remains from the Upper Paleolithic era (50,000 to 10,000years past) are far more commonly found in Austria, including the two oldest pieces of art known from the area. Both of these pieces portray women (the Venus of Galgenberg, 32,000 years old, and the Venus of Willendorf, 26,000 years old.) The pair of statues is usually displayed together in the Museum of Natural History in Vienna, where they are playfully called the "two old ladies." The oldest burial ground found to date in the region is a double infant burial site that is around 27,000 years old.

Human artifacts from the Mesolithic era reflect the general nature of that era worldwide - a transition from hunter-gatherer societies to agricultural ones, including the first rock shelters (Lake Constance and the Alpine Rhine Valley). The Neolithic era (in Europe, varying from about 8000 to 1000 years BC) saw the settling of the Austrian landscape as an agrarian culture.

Salt mining in the region now known as Salzburg was likely already in progress as long ago as 7000 years BC. Today, tours of the 7,000-year-old salt mine are available, showing the elaborate system used to transport salt brine out of the mines through pipes (the oldest of which are made from logs) to the towns in the Hallstatt region, where the brine was cooked down until only the salt remained.

One of the first known rural settlements in the region was at Brunn am Gebirge, a town which exists still in Mödling, a district of the state of Lower Austria. Artifacts from the area show it settled approximately

6000 years BC, putting the settlement of the region well in the timeline of some of the world's oldest continuously populated cities.

The Copper Age and Otzi

The Copper Age (about 4500-3300 BC) saw civilization forming around the hilltops of Eastern Austria and the Alpine lakes. The area was rich in minerals and raw materials.

Iceman Otzi (who lived sometime approximately between 3400-3100 BC) was discovered in 1991 on the border between Austria and Italy. Italy and Austria disputed his country of origin for some time, as each one wanted to claim this archeological marvel, but a survey showed him to be just a few kilometers on the Italian side of the border. He and his possessions are now displayed in Italy. This small figure from long ago has provided invaluable insight to the scientific community regarding life in the Copper Age. Scientific analysis has deduced an incredible amount of information about our old friend, including his clothing, regular diet, the two meals he ate prior to his death, his "job" (he is believed to have been a copper smelter) and various sicknesses he suffered in the months prior to his death.

Otzi carried an axe made of Mondsee copper; the Mondsee group were prehistoric lake-dwellers, recognized for their development and production of arsenical bronze, which they formed by smelting arsenic with copper. Arsenical bronze had certain advantages over copper and other alloys because it was stronger, harder, and easier to cast. Tools made from it were better for cutting and chopping. Worldwide, this method of smelting was discovered by independent cultures, probably because most copper is already contaminated, to a small extent, by arsenic.

HALLSTATT: *The Bronze Age and the Iron (Roman) Age*

This historical time period (about 3300-1200 BC) saw the beginning of fortifications built to protect the Austrian area's resources in mining, metal processing and metal trade. The commencement of salt mining in the Hallstatt region of Upper Austria ("Hallstatt" translates as "place of salt") gave way to the entire Hallstatt culture. Salt (which was used in the preservation of meat) was a profitable and influential resource for the Hallstatt area, the trade of which formed and maintained relations with Greek Colonies, Etruscans, and regions of Italy (all of which were under Greek influence at the time). Excavated gravesites in Hallstatt have yielded evidence of luxury goods purchased from areas as far away as Africa.

The Hallstatt Culture is fairly synonymous with the Iron Age in the Austrian region, but toward the end of the Iron Age, the La Tène (Celtic) culture spread throughout the area, giving rise to tribal and place names including Dürrnberg and Hallein (Salzburg), which were Celtic salt settlements.

The quality iron ore found in Styria and the Burgenland gave birth to trade-based cities such as Virunum, Kulm, Idunum, Burg, Linz and Braunsberg, all of which remain in Austria today, though most have been renamed. The Celtic tribes of Austria united under the kingdom of

Noricum, which became a province of the Roman Empire. Carnuntum (presently known as Petronell-Carnuntum) was a Roman legionary camp, then a capital city, and for almost 400 years, a home to 50,000 people. It served as the headquarters for the Roman Pannonian Fleet.

The remains of the ancient Hallstatt city now lie buried beneath a quaint and secluded tourist spot on the Danube in the Carnuntum Archeological Park, an area of almost 10 square kilometers. The secluded area served as a summer retreat for the Habsburgs, who enjoyed Lake Hallstatt, its beautiful views, and its population of elegant swans.

From the Romans to the Middle Ages

The Holy Roman Empire Emerges

The region of Austria was somewhat in flux following the fall of the Roman Empire, suffering invasions by Bavarians, Slavs, and Avars. Charlemagne conquered the area in 788 AD, introduced Christianity, and promoted colonization of the region. In about 800 AD, Charlemagne's area of rule solidified into what became the **Holy Roman Empire.**

The Holy Roman Empire was a group of approximately 300 principalities throughout Europe that united more or less under the practice of Christianity; today, the territories roughly encompass the areas of Germany and Austria. The Emperor was an elected position decided by seven electors. The Pope would then crown the emperor himself.

Babenberg Rule

East Francia, one of Charlemagne's three successor states, ruled the region until the area was bequeathed to the House of Babenberg for its loyal service to East Francian Emperor Otto I and his son Otto II. Leopold of Babenberg took control as Margrave in 976, and in the year 996, the name "Austria" was first found written in his records as *Ostarrîchi*. Modern Austria marks this year as the founding of their nation.

Leopold extended the reach of his rule down the Danube River by driving away the Magyars (Hungarians) in the region. Then, his sons Henry and Adalbert continued to expand the Austrian territory up to its present northern borders. Further descendants of Leopold promoted religious order in the area by establishing monasteries and then jumping to support the Crusades.

Emperor Frederick Barbarossa elevated Austria to the status of a Duchy in 1156 in a document called the *Privilegium Minus* and kept its control in the hands of the Babenberg dynasty. He did this as a royal favor in response to the Babenbergs releasing the power of Bavarian rule to atone for the upheaval of the first and second crusades and to reward his ducal allies. The Duchy of Styria was united with the Duchy of Austria in 1198. The Babenberg dynasty ruled over Austria until 1246.

The Hapsburgs Come to Austria

From about 1254 to 1273, the Holy Roman Empire (inclusive of the Duchy of Austria), without a ruler in the late medieval period, suffered an interregnum eventually ending with the accession of the House of Habsburg through Rudolf I's election as King of Germany. In 1282, Rudolf I acquired the Duchy of Austria as part of his kingdom.

Then, when Rudolf I bequeathed the Duchy of Austria to his sons, it established the duchy as part of the "Austrian hereditary lands" and dubbed the Habsburgs as the "House of Austria." Though the exact territories controlled by the Austrian monarch changed many times over the centuries, the core hereditary lands always consisted of most of the states of Austria and Slovenia as they are now, the county of Tyrol in Italy, the Kingdom of Hungary, and the Kingdom of Croatia.

The Habsburgs would rule Austria in its various forms throughout the next seven centuries. The history of not only the Austrian empire but of Central Europe is one of constantly changing borders, advantageous marriages, temporary allies, sworn enemies, skirmishes, and all-out war. The Austrian Empire had four major threats surrounding it: Prussia to the north, France to the west, Russia to the east, and the Ottoman Empire to the southwest. Hundreds of years passed, yet still the core of Austrian rule from Vienna and Habsburg powerhouse family sentiment remained steady.

The Habsburg Dynasty – Power and Doom

Simple Rules of the Dynasty

The Habsburg monarchy never shared a constitution or an organizational structure beyond its own court. The unification of all its territories was a unification of family affirmed through the monarch's identity. Often, the vast holdings of the Habsburg Empire were controlled by several or even dozens of family members, with less important members being given charge of small portions and allowed to conduct business by their own rules so long as they were faithful to the family power. This seemed to be motivation enough, for holding the Habsburg title guaranteed power, influence, and protection, all the way up to the Emperor himself. Their method became the standard practice of all monarchies in continental Europe.

The Long Line of Succession and Destruction

The Habsburg Dynasty is as complex a family tree as one might ever find because of an alarming amount of intertwined branches. The family quickly understood the way to gain territory and avoid conflict was to marry its members off to other royal families. Marriages account for most of the Hapsburgs' gains, for when it came to war (and there were dozens), they were either unsuccessful or their success was temporary. Territory was always at a premium, usually with more than two nations wanting control, resulting in alliances that lasted only as long as victory and breaking apart when a decision had to be made on how to divide the spoils. Seldom did a region acquired through battle remain in the possession of the victor for long. Marriage, on the other hand, solidified kings, queens, and holdings, and thus it remained until the 19th century, when a growing middle class suddenly revolted against monarchy altogether. But that was later. For a long time, the Hapsburg rulers enjoyed constant power.

The problem that arose was of the Hapsburgs' own making: over time, the seriously detrimental effects of inbreeding began to burn their dynasty from the inside out. Rather than risk another family gaining too much power, the Habsburgs married within their family, usually through cousins, double-cousins, aunts to nephews, and nieces to uncles. It was easily possible to have a mother who was one's own cousin. Paintings tell the tale as the Habsburgs all began to look remarkably alike, though not in a good way. The "Hapsburg jaw," the quite elongated jawbone clear in so many of the family's portraits, was a physical deformity that was first merely odd-looking and then became an actual handicap. Some of the later sufferers had such pronounced lower jaws that their upper and lower teeth could not meet, some could not chew solid food, and some could not properly close their mouths.

If the problems had stopped with physical deformities the Hapsburgs might have been all right, but inbreeding resulted in terrible neurological issues such as epilepsy and hydrocephalus, and many forms of "madness" that could not be diagnosed at the time. Many Hapsburg children failed to survive, many were severely mentally disabled, and a good number of the family members were infertile or impotent. This resulted in a number of the family lines simply dying out. Other Habsburgs were infamously odd or violent. Empress Maria Theresa, arguably the most effective Hapsburg ruler, managed to have sixteen children, fourteen of which survived to adulthood, probably because she married a man from a different family, introducing some much-needed genetic diversity.

While the Hapsburgs were in power throughout Europe, they seemed willing to wager on their royal issue, for certainly past a certain point it became obvious what the problem was. Still, if children could be produced from a union, hopefully some of them would survive and be mentally capable of rule. Of course, there was even then the double standard – if one is poor, one is crazy; if one is rich, one is merely eccentric. The Habsburgs had declared themselves appointed by God to rule the Holy Roman Empire – regardless of their madness, their jawline, or their inability to speak or think clearly.

Habsburg Origins

The Habsburgs' first territory was in the Holy Roman Empire territory of Switzerland (and it is the only country in Europe to have a town called Habsburg). The Hawk Castle, or Habichtsburg Castle (built in 1020 by their ancestor Radbot), gave origin to the family name.

In 1291, the people of Switzerland, in a force composed of little more than farmers, revolted against the ruling class and drove the House of Habsburg out of the country with surprising ease. The agile farmers, armed with mere stones and sticks, were able to overwhelm the heavily mounted Habsburg knights. The freed Swiss rejected the Holy Roman Empire and then formed the Everlasting League, which is still the basis of the Swiss Confederation.

The Habsburgs, who controlled several territories within the Holy Roman Empire, fled eastward along the Danube River. The Danube River at the time was relatively undeveloped, but the Habsburgs made their way to Vienna. Vienna in the late 13th century was a remote town at the edge of the Holy Roman Empire's frontier, its population a mere 20,000, and it was constantly under threat of invasion by Hungary or the Ottoman Empire. Here, the Habsburgs took up residence, building a castle upon the ruins of an older one, and here their base of power would remain for centuries to come.

Habsburgs as Holy Roman Emperors

Beginning in 1438 with the succession of Albert V of Austria as Holy Roman Emperor, whichever Habsburg served as Archduke of Austria would also be elected as Holy Roman Emperor. The only exception occurred briefly when Maria Theresa was the Austrian ruler, as women were not permitted to hold the position of Holy Roman Emperor, and the title was given to Charles VII of the House of Wittelsbach for a mere three years.

However, upon the death of Charles VII, the crown was then passed to Maria Theresa's husband, Franz Stefan (or Holy Roman Emperor Francis I). Maria Theresa and Franz Stefan's relationship was such a mutually companionable and supportive one that Maria Theresa basically held the position as decision-maker without officially holding the title. Maria Theresa will be one of the several highly influential Habsburgs we will discuss.

First, however, of the Hapsburg line during this era, no members were as widely influential as the beloved Maximilian I. His rule, though rocky in the beginning, set a precedent not only for Habsburg rulers to come but also for the overall spirit of European culture through the centuries.

Maximilian I (1459-1519)

The Austrian Empire's Growth in the Middle Ages

During the 14th and 15th centuries, the Duchy of Austria began to accumulate more lands under its rule, many of these acquisitions occurring through advantageous marriages.

In particular, the marriage of Maximilian's son Philip to Joanna the Mad brought previously unimagined territories to the Austrian Empire. Joanna, heir of Castile and Aragon, inherited Spain, and all of its Italian, African, and New World (American/Mexican) territories.

The Austrian Empire was in almost constant conflict with the Ottoman Empire, which was consistently attempting to spread its power into Hungary. Hungary was partially controlled by the Habsburgs as well thanks to their acquisition of the Bavarian crown. The Turks regularly invaded Styria, and Suleiman the Magnificent even attempted a siege of Vienna in 1529.

Young Maximilian

To discuss Maximilian I, we must back up somewhat to the year 1477 when the 18-year-old prince, son of Emperor Friedrich III, was married to Maria, Princess of the Dukedom of Burgundy. Maria's father had been quite recently killed in a battle against the Swiss Army. At that time, any rule delivered into the hands of a woman was immediately a target. Young Maximilian rushed from Vienna to her side to support Maria as she became monarch of Burgundy. In support of his wife, Maximilian stayed in Brussels, the capital of Flanders, and from her, Maximilian learned all he could about the language and culture of her people.

This marriage of Maximilian to Maria united the Habsburgs to the Burgundy's wealthy ports of North Sea, trading out of the Netherlands and Flanders (now Belgium). Merchants were making vast fortunes in trade. Flemish merchants, for a high price paid to the monarchy, were allowed to participate in the government, and this practice would in time influence Maximilian's style of rule.

The culture of Burgundy, spurred by its vast financial success, was undergoing an artistic renaissance, advancing rapidly in music and in artistic crafts (most particularly, wool weaving and tapestries). Music of the time was monophonic (one melody sung), but the Flemish had moved into polyphonic music (multiple melodies combined). Maximilian, a music lover, traveled with musicians in his entourage. Of note, when Maximilian eventually left Brussels, he returned to Vienna with Flemish polyphonic singers. In his love of their performances were the roots of the Vienna Boys' Choir, which he commissioned and promoted to use the polyphonic style.

Though his willingness to adopt their culture endeared him somewhat to the people of Burgundy, Maximilian's policies did not. He saw it as his duty to win back territories that had been taken from Burgundy after the death of Maria's father, and to fund his battles, he tried imposing taxes on items such as beer. These taxes were not happily accepted by the citizens, for taxes seldom ever are.

Maria died in 1482 after a fall from her horse. She left behind the two children she had with Maximilian, and according to the wishes of her will, Maximilian took over the rule of Burgundy as Regent until their son could inherit the territory. France, however, had been moving in secret against Burgundy and gaining allies among the discontented taxpayers, encouraging the citizens to rise up against the Regent.

Suddenly, Maximilian was put under house arrest in 1488 and his various aids and other assistants were executed in plain view of the windows. In this fearful state, Maximilian turned to his father, Emperor Friedrich III. The Imperial Army arrived three months later to put an end to the revolt, leaving Flanders under Habsburg rule entirely, with a changed, more fair-minded Maximilian in charge.

Maximilian Takes Tyrol

In 1489, in the southern Holy Roman Empire, a battle broke out between the territories of Tyrol and Bavaria. Archduke Sigmund of Tyrol had taken out a large loan from Bavaria, using Tyrol land as collateral. Now, Sigmund refused to repay the debt. Maximilian, being related to both countries, offered to mediate. The matter reached settlement in 1490 under the condition that Maximilian claim rule of Tyrol. However, he also must claim Tyrol's debt. Maximilian established Innsbruck as the capital and began developing much-needed economic reform policies that would pay back the loan. It was a tall order, for Innsbruck's government was notoriously corrupt, and there was no legal system.

Innsbruck lies directly north of Brenner Pass, well-known as the easiest route through the Alps to Italy. Tyrol was also rich in gold, copper, and salt mines. In six years, Tyrol's debt was mostly paid and the corruption corrected. Maximilian took great pains to work with the merchants of the country, resulting in many of them obtaining incredible wealth - and Maximilian had learned in Brussels that happy merchants are loyal, leading to increased trade, expansion, and a healthy economy. Wealthy merchants were also handy when it came to loaning the emperor much-needed funds, as Maximilian's grand plans could often not be financially supported from his own governmental funds.

The Pan-Ethnic Empire of Maximilian

Two important occurrences happened into Maximilian in 1493. First, Maximilian's father, Holy Roman Emperor Frederich III, died, and the Emperor's crown was passed on to Maximilian. Second, Maximilian married his second wife, Bianca, who was daughter of the Duke of Milan. This made Milan a part of Maximilian's empire - a region of Italy for which France was constantly vying against him.

In 1496, Maximilian's son Philip was married to Joanna the Mad, bringing all the Spanish-controlled territories under the Habsburg Empire. The Habsburg territories were now vast, stretching around the globe. Though Philip lived only two years after his marriage, his progeny and descendants ruled Spain and its territories until the 1700s.

Maximilian spent his life traveling his massive empire as best he could, from the far north shores in Burgundy to their southern territories in Italy. Maximilian held the various cultures of his empire in high respect and seemed to understand the best ways to combine their skills and resources without ever requiring a country to cede its language or heritage. He strongly encouraged the development of arts, architecture, and music. He had a particular passion for the artisanship of armor.

Rather than force a universal language on his empire, Maximilian took pains to learn their various languages and issued edicts and correspondence in numerous European tongues. As the empire grew, the number of different languages grew as well, and Maximilian embraced and learned to speak, read, and write in Latin, German, French, Spanish,

Italian, Hungarian, Czech, and Slavic. He found that learning a people's language was the way to secure their respect.

Maximilian abandoned the code of chivalry he had been raised to know in favor of joining his territories into a multicultural landscape in which the people of each region were respected for their own merits. He is responsible for the flourishing of a pan-ethnic nation. For centuries to come, his descendants followed the same relatively open-minded belief that multiple cultures working alongside one another can result in increased creativity and mutual benefits.

His rule was not without troubles, however, and as Holy Roman Emperor, he was forced to grant freedom to the Swiss Confederacy. He also had a long-standing struggle with France over territories controlled in the region of Italy (i.e. Milan). He also made a strong attempt to unite the three regions of Austria into one country, but the attempt was ultimately unsuccessful.

In a final ironic twist, a depressed Maximilian, alone at the end of his life, commissioned an elaborate gravesite for himself in Innsbruck, his tomb to be surrounded by statues of those who had influenced his life, including among them his family members, the legendary King Arthur, and even Archduke Sigmund. However, Maximilian died in 1519 while traveling and was buried outside of Tyrol. The tomb at Innsbruck was completed following his death but lies empty, now a cenotaph (that is, a memorial to someone who is buried elsewhere) to the emperor whose noble goals seemed often to exceed his grasp.

Protestant Reformation

Charles V Can't Stop the Protestants

Upon the death of Maximilian I, his grandson Charles V assumed rule of the Austrian Empire and the title of Holy Roman Emperor at a relatively young age due to the premature death of his father, Philip, and his mother Joanna's inability to rule alone due to her mental illness. He ruled for decades in a rapidly changing environment.

In 1517, just two years prior to Charles' ascension, the Holy Roman Empire had been challenged to its very foundations when Martin Luther posted his ninety-five theses on the door of Wittenberg's Castle Church. Protestant reformation moved through Habsburg territories with surprising speed, despite Charles' condemnation of Luther. Meanwhile, the Ottoman Empire grew in power, and the advancing Turks required Charles to seek help from Protestant princes. Despite his firm resolve to impose Catholicism, Protestantism could not be stopped, and the exhausted emperor eventually withdrew from politics altogether, abdicating his throne to his brother Ferdinand I and retiring in 1556 to the monastery where he died a year later.

Ferdinand I Takes Over in Troubled Times

Austrian lands remained Catholic, but non-Austrian provinces turned to Lutheranism. Upon taking the throne, Ferdinand I tolerated the Lutheran presence and wanted, in fact, to reconcile the religious differences of his people. It must be said that the Counter-Reformation of the Austrians (from 1545-1563) was far more tolerant than that of the Spanish (who, in the form of the Spanish Inquisition, "forced" Protestants into conversion back to Catholicism). The Counter Reformation of Austria was led by Jesuits and used persuasion, not force, as the process of reformation. Ferdinand I's more flexible view of the problem created a relatively peaceful coexistence on the religious landscape.

Meanwhile, Ferdinand I married into the Hungarian dynasty in 1521. Hungary, for almost two centuries, had been in conflict with the Ottoman Empire. Despite various treaties and borderlines being drawn through Hungary, splitting the country between the two empires, the hostilities and conflict would continue over the control of Hungary for two more centuries.

Ferdinand I's Division of Austrian lands: 60 Years of Chaos

The Habsburg tradition was to divide lands between children upon the death of a monarch, but this proved to be a mistake for Ferdinand I, who died in 1564. He divided Austria among his three surviving sons, which caused marked weakness of the Austrian Empire that it could ill afford considering the threat of the Ottoman Empire.

Still, Austria was divided by his command into Lower, Upper, and Inner Austria and remained divided for almost 60 years. The close relationship between the rulers of these three districts resulted in political maneuvering and several exchanges of power.

The Holy Roman Emperor succession proceeded through Maximilian II, Rudolf II, Matthias, and finally to Ferdinand II. During this time, conflict with the Ottomans was nearly constant, including the Fifteen-Year War (1593-1606), and the religious upheaval continued with many imperial connections feeling that Austria's handling of the reformation was far too lenient.

Ferdinand II and the Thirty Years' War

The Austrian lands remained more or less divided until the deaths of various lines resulted in Ferdinand II re-inheriting all Austrian lands in 1620 (except for Bohemia, which he invaded and took back from Frederick I). Ferdinand II put Upper Austria in the hands of his brother, Leopold V. Ferdinand II then aggressively moved to re-establish

Catholicism as the only religion for Austria, Bohemia, the Habsburg's portion of Hungary and, in effect, any other Protestant areas that fell under the jurisdiction of the Holy Roman Empire. His intolerance won him no popularity, immediately resulting in a strong opposition to his policies (as in, the Revolt in Bohemia) that led to the Thirty Years' War.

Within strictly Austrian territories, Ferdinand II did manage to bring Catholicism back, at least officially, but the feelings of resentment caused a severe reduction of the amount of power that other nations were willing to allow the Habsburgs. More and more outlying nations turned to their own governments and centers of power, unwilling to follow Habsburg rule and able to "mind their own stores," technically, because the Austrians were otherwise occupied with fighting a devastating war with constant interference from outside nations who strongly opposed the war on Protestantism.

Tragically, while the Hapsburg rulership on Austria tightened, the Thirty Years' war decimated the population, either through battle-related deaths or the stretching of resources to the breaking point. Famine was widespread. Some estimates of the Austrian death toll are as high as 50%. There is no doubt that Austria, returned to Catholicism or not, was seriously diminished.

Ferdinand III's Peace: the Austrian Baroque

Ferdinand II died in 1637, leaving the Hapsburg Empire to his son, Ferdinand III, in the position where he was forced to try making or repairing peace with the angered nations of Europe. To do so, and probably to save what remained of Austria, Ferdinand III gave independence to German states and generally increased the power of all the Austrian states.

An accomplished composer and musician himself as well as a patron of the arts, Ferdinand III led Austria out of economic and demographic hardship into the Austrian Baroque period. Baroque is a term that stylistically refers to great theatrical style in music, art, and architecture – baroque style is ostentatiously decorative and fancy, but there is a point behind its decorative intricacy. Baroque, in its theatrical nature, wishes to tell a story, and all of its trappings lead to that simple story, using heavy symbolism and typically illustrating the triumph of good over evil (at the time, God over the Devil, Catholicism over Protestantism, or whatever defined the current terms). The victorious side was heavily ornamented because it deserved to be.

Ferdinand III's son, Leopold I, took the throne in 1657, and Leopold I's reign lasted long enough for the rulership of Upper Austria to return to him when that separate line died out. Therefore, from 1665, Austria was at last reunited as one Archduchy.

The Reign of Leopold I: Two Wars on Opposite Fronts

Austria's Thirty Years' War had occurred at a time when the Ottoman Empire was luckily otherwise occupied. Therefore, though Austria was seriously vulnerable to attack on its eastern borders, the Ottomans made no earnest moves toward Austria until 1663.

At that point, however, they engaged in attacks on Austria and for almost thirty years sent invasions into Austrian territory. By 1699, Austria's victories resulted in most of Hungary being under Austrian control.

Meanwhile, the Habsburg line of the Spanish territories was coming to an end due to infertility. The War of Spanish Succession took place from 1701 through 1714, between the French and the Austrians. In the conflict, the Habsburgs made gains of formerly Spanish territories in the Netherlands, Milan, Naples, and Sardinia, but soon afterward, Emperor Charles VI would relinquish many of these lands in terms of territory, authority, or both for a special purpose of his own.

Charles VI and the Pragmatic Sanction

The Spanish Habsburgs were not the only line that was ending. Charles VI had only two surviving children, both daughters. He sought to abolish sole male inheritance. The Pragmatic Sanction strengthened the position of female inheritance while also providing that the Habsburg lands were inseparable. To ensure the recognition of the

Pragmatic Sanction, Charles gave the territorial and authoritarian advantages to other powers if they would recognize his daughter, Maria Theresa, as his heir, as well as his choice for her husband, Francis Stephen of Lorraine (i.e., Franz Stefan).

All the while, war continued almost nonstop through Europe, with small territories exchanging hands between France, the Turks, and Austria. Treaties to end wards usually saw Charles stipulating that in exchange for ceding land, France or Spain would agree to recognize Maria Theresa as his heir. By the time he died in 1740, Charles had largely ensured that, at least in theory, most European nations would accept Maria Theresa as his heir; the question was really whether her rulership could succeed in the pandemonium of the political climate. The Habsburgs' financial situation was precarious; their treasury all but depleted due to the constant waging of war.

A Side Trip to Salzburg

Salzburg was, for centuries, a territory under the Austrian Empire but also an independently ruled Prince-Bishopric. Since 1955, Salzburg has been one of the federal states of the second Republic of Austria. It should be noted that both the state and its capital city are called Salzburg. This territory was of significant importance throughout the history of Austria for its income-generating salt mining. It is, of course, also the birthplace of Mozart.

The importance of the salt mines in the area of Hallstatt were what gave Salzburg economic power from pre-history; salt was mined and then shipped down the Danube, then beyond. Salt was vital as a preservative prior to the use of refrigeration. Boats floated down the Danube and then were dragged back upriver by horses.

In the year 700, Salzburg's Bavarian rulers gave control of the town to the local bishop, who promised in return to defend Christianity in the area. Salzburg was an independent state for over 1000 years, led by Prince-Archbishops who combined both religious and political power. It remained independent up until the time of its surrender to Napoleon: it had a strong fortress and remained neutral in wars, it managed to avoid conflict until World War II. Old town Salzburg managed to survive World War II.

Prince Archbishop Wolf Deitrich was the most influential of Salzburg's rulers (circa 1600). He was from Rome and had close ties with the Medicis, and he wanted to turn Salzburg into "the Rome of the North." This is why visitors to the city of Salzburg now can see the strong Italian influence in the architecture. The series of interconnecting squares and the fountains that could just as easily be sitting on a plaza in Rome and landmarks replicate counterparts, such as the Triton fountain, which matches the famous Triton Fountain in Rome.

In the 13th century, Salzburg was outfitted with a canal system that channeled mountain streams through the town. The ingenious system kept the streets clean, powered factories through the use of watermills (some still in use until the 19th century), and also provided fire protection.

Because Salzburg was directly on an important Italian trading route, it was highly influenced by Italian style anyway. The Salzburg Cathedral is designed in high baroque style that, like all baroque, is highly symbolic and theatrical. Masses conducted featuring Mozart's music are popular Sunday events; Mozart was the church organist here for two years.

Much of the tourism is because of Mozart, who lived in Salzburg the first 25 years of his life. Both the houses of his birthplace and his later residence are popular tourist attractions with exhibits regarding the Mozart family. He moved to Vienna when he was 25.

Salzburg is famous for its live musical performances. Its summer musical festival is an extremely popular attraction, but throughout the year, there are live performances (over two thousand annually) in its palaces and churches. Mirabell Palace (home of the Prince-Archbishop) is a popular site both for such concerts and for its gardens.

The Hohensalzburg Fortress sits on a hilltop above the Salzach River. It is accessible to tourists through funicular cars. This castle was able to support a town of 1,000 and could be self-sufficient if necessary. The massive fortress was so forbidding that nobody attacked Salzburg; the fortress was never used in battle. Thus, as fortresses go, this one could be considered highly effective.

THE AGE OF EMPRESS MARIA THERESA

The Only Hapsburg Empress

Maria Teresa, born in 1717, was in many ways like her distant predecessor, Maximilian I, in her tendency to see the value in all cultures. As a child and against the wishes of her father, she sometimes stole into an all-male Spanish riding school in the Habsburg's Hofburg palace, where she trained in horsemanship; this would by no means be the only time she made her way in a traditionally masculine role. She was the only female ruler of the Habsburgs' dominion and considered one of the family's greatest and most successful leaders; possibly its finest.

Maria Theresa married Franz Stefan (Francis Stephen of Lorraine) when she was 18; only five years later in 1740 when she was merely 23, her father died of food poisoning and she was crowned as ruler of Austria. Strangely, though Charles VI had spent an incredible amount of time and effort to ensure his daughter's succession, he had done little in the way of training her to take on the role of empress.

At once, countries that had promised Charles VI their support of a female monarch began to chastise and mock the succession. Friedrich II of Prussia sent troops into Habsburg territory to seize Silesia; his success inspired similar attacks from Bavaria, Saxony, and France. This was the opening of the Austrian War of Succession, which would plague Maria Theresa for the first eight years of her rulership.

Maria Theresa Wins Hungarian Support

Maria Theresa, seeking allies, traveled down the Danube to Bratislava, Slovakia. This was the Hungarian capital of the Habsburg Empire. Wanting Hungary on her side for their strong cavalry, Maria Theresa decided to show them her horsemanship. She rode proudly into the town square of Bratislava on horseback, coaxing her horse stand on its hind legs - and from there, pointed her sword in the four directions, pledging that she would protect Hungary from all sides and all aggressors. The Hungarians, impressed by her valor and skill, agreed to enter the war of Austrian Succession on her behalf.

Before Maria Theresa took control, the Hungarian Army was made up of several cultures, and each followed orders from their own headquarters while largely ignoring the other factions. Maria Theresa abolished the cultural differences and established a general rule of armed forces training and rewards, to which the Hungarian army quickly adapted. Their combined skills made them a fierce ally.

Maria Theresa managed to maintain hold onto most of her Austrian territories, excluding the loss of Silesia and a few minor Italian holdings.

Maria Theresa Reforms Taxes and Education

Two obstacles standing in Maria Theresa's path to establish her true authority were the nobility and the church, and Maria Theresa dealt with both of these in problems in turn.

The multi-ethnic Habsburg Empire was a collection of kingdoms, each with its own nobility. These nobles were not shy about ignoring the Empress's authority (she was merely a woman, after all) and operating on their own. The nobles, for example, might decide to reduce or even refuse to pay their taxes to the imperial court. This, of course, made imperial finance unstable.

Maria Theresa set up a system of government that sent her own workers to work with the local nobilities with the goal of securing stable taxes. This brought the Habsburg treasury back to affluence. Like her predecessors, Maria Theresa was notably suspicious of the Jewish people and more than once suggested they be banished from certain places, but she was forced to admit the business prosperity that they generated. Her edicts to send them away were retracted because she needed their money.

As to education, the Habsburg family had deep relations with the Jesuits. The Jesuits had, therefore, dominated the religious education of the empire. Maria Theresa felt that they were getting of the way of modern education. She took their educational jurisdiction away from them and transferred the jurisdiction of censorship to her own committee so that books on the natural sciences were now made available for study.

To this point, Austria had trailed behind the other countries of Europe in the "Age of Enlightenment," but Maria Theresa was determined to bring her people into the modern age. She wanted education for the young in all social ranks. She imposed compulsory education but did not force the use of the German language. Textbooks were written in more than ten languages, and thus, anyone from farmers to city dwellers alike was able to get an education.

Changing Alliances

Wenzel Anton Kaunitz-Rietberg was to be a diplomat and statesman for the Habsburg Empire for nearly four decades. It was Kaunitz-Rietberg who suggested an Austrian alliance with France and Russia to help defeat the Prussian threat and win back Silesia. Kaunitz-Rietberg traveled to Versailles to form the alliance treaty, and a three-party alliance was established. War broke out in 1756, but after seven years of battle, the war ended with Silesia unreturned. Nevertheless, the Franco-Austrian Alliance and the alliance with Russia were political victories that established Kaunitz-Rietberg as a master diplomat. The Austrian Empire was now allied with France and Russian.

The Empress

In theory, and according to her father's Pragmatic Solution, Maria Theresa was expected to cede rulership to her husband Franz Stefan and her son, Joseph II, but she did not. Most importantly, she and Franz Stefan had a deeply respectful relationship toward each other and worked together to ensure the success of her rule. Franz Stefan aided his wife by hiring qualified advisors to help them make decisions regarding the empire. Maria Theresa's time in power was one of growth, industry, and artistic renaissance, with comparatively few battles fought against outlying lands. Maria Theresa would far rather arrange a marriage than fight a war.

While Maria Theresa was monarch of the Habsburg Empire, the Holy Roman Empire's crown went to Bavaria. Not quite four years later, when it returned to the Habsburgs, it was her husband, Franz Stefan, who received it. He, however, always showed his support to Maria Theresa. She was in charge of political issues. Whether or not the crown of the Holy Roman Empire ever rested on her head, she was its leader in spirit.

Franz Stefan died in 1765 of a heart attack. Following his death, Maria Theresa focused on the lives of her children, of which she had 14 that lived to adulthood, one of whom had become the French queen Marie Antoinette. Many conflicts were avoided as Maria Theresa married her children into other royal families, simultaneously expanding her own empire.

The Schonbrunn Makeover

In later years, with her popularity high and her treasury stable, Maria Theresa invested in the refurbishing of Habsburg palaces throughout the Austrian Empire along with the improvement of towns. She rebuilt towns across the empire to resemble Vienna, such as Maria Teresopolis in Serbia (today known as Subotica).

The magnificent Schonbrunn Palace, which might even rival Versailles as the grandest palace in the world, was the masterpiece establishing her monarchy. Maria Theresa had been given the palace as a wedding present. The exterior of the palace was baroque, the style of the times; inside the castle, Maria Theresa preferred Rococo style. Nevertheless, even her castle decorations were respectful of the many cultures beneath her rule. Huge murals dedicated to the working people from various countries decorate the ceilings, with a benevolent empress smiling on from her cloud on high, equivalent with a goddess. A zoo completed in 1754 on the palace grounds is said to be the oldest zoo in the world. The zoo was created by Franz Stefan, importing animals from around the world to show the public. Creatures as exotic as zebras and flamingos were kept there, and the people were bewildered by these previously unseen animals. Franz Stefan, like his wife, had a great interest in natural sciences.

Maria Theresa's Vienna

Under Maria Theresa's rule, Vienna underwent a cultural flourishing. It was the center of Europe, a gathering place for dignitaries as well as leading minds and talents of the day. Vienna accepted people of all cultures without barriers and therefore developed its own rather unique culture. Its population doubled to 20,000 people during her reign.

Maria was very interested in, and open to, foreign cultures. Ethnic backgrounds and languages did not matter. Opera was enjoying an explosion of popularity, telling stories from mythologies around the world. The surge of the musical arts in Italy had prompted the other European courts, of which the Habsburgs were no exception, to invite as many Italian musicians as they could get into their courts. These accomplished artists inspired a new generation of European composers. Austria's society, centered in Vienna, was so rich with its multicultural heritage that it seemed to be simply waiting for a special person to bring its own music to life.

The Composers of Vienna

Franz Joseph Haydn (1732-1809)

All of the nations within the Austrian empire had rich folk music histories. Franz Joseph Haydn was a remarkable musician who came onto the scene to incorporate the music from throughout the empire (like from Hungary, Slovenia, Moravia). He trained in music with an imported Italian master, Nicola Porpora. Haydn, working among Hungarian nobility (mostly for the Esterhazy family), was often invited to Vienna as Maria loved his music. He wrote his *Symphony 48 in C* for her. Haydn is considered the "Father of the Symphony" because of his development of the musical form; he is also credited with the evolution of chamber music like piano trios and string quartets. Haydn had a huge influence on Mozart as a mentor and paternal figure to the young musical genius. Haydn had a more antagonistic relationship with Beethoven, whom he tutored.

Wolfgang Amadeus Mozart (1756-1791)

Mozart was a native of Salzburg in the Holy Roman Empire. Acknowledged as a musical prodigy, he was engaged as a musician for the Salzburg Court before traveling to Vienna in search of better employment. He met Emperor Joseph II (son of Maria Theresa) and was given commissions and a part-time position in the court; he quickly became known as the finest keyboard player in Vienna. He became friends with Haydn, who was in awe of the young man's talent, and Mozart would in time dedicate six string quartets to the older composer. Yet while he was famous in Vienna (and throughout Europe), composing symphonies, operas, and concertos, he did not do well financially due to his own impetuous use of money. His performances were wildly popular, and he was known for booking unusual venues (ballrooms, restaurants, or apartments) in order to fit more audience members into the crowd. Audiences were delighted by his talent, enthusiasm, and the eagerness he showed for their enjoyment of his work.

Ludwig Von Beethoven (1770-1827)

German-born Beethoven's works transitioned over time so that scholars consider him to have gone through an "early," "middle," and "late" period in his composing career as he was working during a time when music was transforming from the classical to the romantic. It is well-known that by the end of his "middle" period, he suffered severe deafness.

By his 21st birthday, he moved to Vienna, which became his base, and studied with Haydn. At first, he was considered a musical successor to Mozart (who had quite recently died), and many of his early works have a distinct Mozart feel to them. Vienna proved to be a most successful location for Beethoven to work. He garnered support from several noble corners as he worked on his compositions and on his public performances.

Beethoven's increasing deafness prompted depression and difficulties with public performance, though he never stopped composing. He moved to the little Austrian town of Heiligenstadt, where he coped with his condition through writing and composing. When he returned to Vienna, he began what many call his "heroic" style (coinciding with this "middle" period"), longer and more dramatic and perfectly suited to the passionate romanticism that was sweeping music at the time. From 1802 to 1810, Beethoven worked in a Vienna that was under constant threat of siege by France. When Beethoven in 1824 wished to premiere his Ninth Symphony in Berlin, his Viennese admirers begged him for a performance at the Karntnertortheater, which he attended and conducted despite his deafness. He remained in Vienna or nearby for the rest of his life.

The fact that musical giants Haydn, Mozart, and Beethoven all worked within the same century and in the same city gives Vienna a reputation for being a bedrock of classical music influence; however, considering the scope of the Austrian empire and the fact that most well-known composers throughout the empire eventually landed in Vienna at least for a time, it is no wonder that Vienna and nearby Salzburg (which claims Mozart as its own) are mecca destinations for music lovers.

The Death of Maria Theresa

Maria Theresa contracted pneumonia in 1780. Before she died later that year at the age of 63, she wrote a request to her children that Schonbrunn – her beloved palace that she had renovated extensively - remain as it was. The amount of care she had taken in renovating the place is explanation enough for why. The massive grounds and palace make an obvious testament to the empress's benevolent hopes for her kingdom.

There is an interesting side note regarding Schonbrunn Palace: it remains unchanged and is of course a major tourist attraction, but also after World War II, some portions of the palace were converted to public housing. People are now allowed to rent rooms there, provided they undergo a strict screening policy. Similar arrangements can be made for offices at Hofburg Palace, which was the Habsburg "winter" estate in downtown Vienna.

JOSEPH II BEGINS THE HABSBURG-LORRAINE DYNASTY

The name "Lorraine" was added to the Habsburg Dynasty name because of the election of Franz Stefan as Holy Roman Emperor, in consideration of his own line combined with Maria Theresa's. With the death of Maria Theresa, their son, Joseph II, ascended as the first king in the Habsburg-Lorraine line and took over the rule of the largest realm of Central Europe with aspirations that can only be described as magnanimous, at least in intention.

Joseph II was a paternal ruler who wished for his people to be content and for his empire to be modern. His desire was to "keep up" with the progression of France and Prussia. He was open-minded in his selection of officials, appointing people for their merit rather than their heritage or background. Joseph II also made German the official "business" language, reformed the legal system (abolishing the death penalty), hired auditors to reform the taxing, financing, and expenditures of the Austrian empire, tried spreading religious tolerance, and put an end to censorship in the arts. He wanted to reform taxes to decrease the pressure of taxation on the peasantry. He continued his mother's emphasis on education for children of all classes.

The only real problem was that Joseph II, in his ambition to create a society of such fairness, overreached, moving too quickly to make change tolerable to those under his rule. He was opposed by the most powerful sections of society who saw his mandates as an end to the source of their wealth and power or at least a serious curbing of these things. His church reforms set the Catholic leadership strongly against him. Surprisingly, he was opposed by the lower classes as well for bringing radical change about too rapidly for a peasant class thoroughly set its ways. Additionally, some of his reforms were quite particular and odd, such as a ban on gingerbread (which he believed was bad for the stomach). Under these circumstances, no one was happy with their king's behavior. Joseph died in 1790, and most of his reforms were stopped or reversed, if not before his death then immediately afterward.

Not all of Joseph II's efforts were for naught. His push for medical centralization in Vienna resulted in the city becoming a preeminent place for medical study (at the Allgemeines Krankenhaus, or the Vienna General Hospital) for the following century. Though his reforms were introduced poorly, his successors continued working on his widespread ideas for societal improvement, and Joseph II's vision is now seen as having provided a foundation for later important reforms of the 20th Century.

Joseph II died in 1790 and was for two years replaced by his brother Leopold II. Leopold worked quickly to undo the mess his brother had left behind and end the many revolts and threatened revolts that had arisen. Leopold II restored some calm to the empire.

Yet, outside of the Austrian Empire, serious threats were rising, especially in the case of the French Revolution. Leopold II (who was the brother of Marie Antoinette) did what he could to avoid war with France, but the French revolutionaries were incensed by the monarchy of not only France itself but by what they saw as Austria's support of the monarchy. Leopold died in 1792 after only two years of rule. The throne was taken by his son Francis II, and the French revolutionaries declared war on the Austrian Empire almost immediately.

The French Revolution and Napoleon

Francis II may have only been 24 when he succeeded Leopold II, yet his reign would last 50 years and oversee a dramatic change in the political lines of Europe. One of the first events of his reign was the shocking assassination of his aunt, Marie Antoinette, in 1793. The French Revolution (1792 to 1802) swept across Europe not only physically but also psychologically, striking up similar feelings of rebellion in nations under monarchies. Austria too feared its citizens would join in the sentiment of the revolutionaries. This upheaval was immediately followed by the Napoleonic Wars, from 1803 to 1815. The nearly non-stop warring is divided into seven segments by historians, some of which had little to do with Austria, and some of which were right on Austria's doorstep, as follows:

1. France declared war on Austria in 1792, and it lasted until 1797 (**The War of the First Coalition**). At first, the French armies were disorganized, but after this initial inexperience,

the motivated French overran their enemies. Austria lost their part of the Netherlands (Belgium) to the French. Meanwhile, Prussia and Austria on the opposite side of the nation fought over the partitioning of Poland. The French gained momentum with the leadership their brilliant young Corsican General, Napoleon Bonaparte, whose relentlessness forced the enemies of France into relinquish to French demands or be overrun. Fighting stopped in 1797, but the short-term peace lasted barely a year.

2. **The War of the Second Coalition** (1798-1801) emerged over disagreements between France and Austria concerning the terms of their first truce. Napoleon was unstoppable it seemed, and, even an alliance of Austria with Russia, Britain, and Naples, could not withstand the force of the French Army. One by one, the nations were forced to make peace with France. By 1802, the Holy Roman Empire was reorganized by the French. This meant that territories and free cities of the Holy Roman Empire that had been most friendly toward the Habsburgs and the House of Austria had, by French reorganization, ceased to exist. Between the Wars of the First and Second Coalition, the Austrians suffered over 750,000 casualties.

3. When Napoleon crowned himself Emperor of the French Empire in 1804, Francis II decided he would become "Emperor of Austria," in addition to being Holy Roman Emperor. The threat of Napoleon's imperial title was a

strange one to the Habsburgs, for the existence of a second emperor meant that Habsburg possession of the Holy Roman crown was no longer a guarantee. (They seemed to have forgotten that such an arrangement had never been meant as a "guarantee," though they had long since assumed the emperor's crown was their God-given right). Napoleon, however, had other aspirations. **The War of the Third Coalition** (1805) continued to shuffle borders and territories. It seemed that most of the lands that had once fallen under the Holy Roman Empire were distributed now to Napoleon's states, and the Holy Roman Empire, after a millennium of holding power over Europe, was dissolved.

4. By maintaining peace with France, Austria managed to spend a few peaceful years and avoid **the War of the Fourth Coalition.**

5. However, in 1809, the Habsburgs went once more into **the War of the Fifth Coalition**, quite foolishly, with no allies but the United Kingdom. They had assumed they would find support in Germany (they did not) and with Russia (which was allied with France). Napoleon had taken Vienna, and Austria was defeated once more in a bloody fight that even cost Napoleon more than he had expected. Peace was negotiated through the Treaty of Schonbrunn, which stripped Austria of almost all its remaining land and left it little more than a state of France.

6. With Austria putting up a front of being a good French ally now, **the War of the Sixth Coalition** (1812-1814) began. At first, Austria sided with France (for what else could it do?) as Napoleon invaded Russia. However, when Russia drove him back and Prussia joined Russia's cause, Austria saw opportunity to escape its situation. Perhaps the pain of being relegated to a simple state had stirred up Austrian fighters to new heights of ferocity; Austria declared war on France and joined the Russians and Prussians, and its participation in the war was integral to victory. Napoleon (acting as the voice of France) was unwilling to compromise, so Austria and its allies fought and eventually forced him to withdraw completely into France, and soon afterward, into exile in Elba.

7. Napoleon had one more war in him: **The War of the Seventh Coalition**, a hundred days during which Napoleon attempting to restore his hold. Here, he was famously defeated at Waterloo. We will let French history take over Napoleon's part of the story completely, and we return to...

The Congress of Vienna

Technically, the War of the Seventh Coalition would occur during the Congress of Vienna. Regardless, this 1815 gathering convened as a great social event inviting heads of all the European states together to make some sense of a confused European community that had been juggled and rearranged by war for the past 20 years. Here, the Concert of Europe was developed, which redrew, once more, the political map and established a power balance. The Habsburgs would never again have their claim over the Holy Roman Empire; however, the German Confederation was created as one of the four circles of power in Europe, and Francis II of Austria was given presidency of this entity.

Metternich

Klemens von Metternich had worked in Austrian diplomacy most of his life, spearheading complex relationships with France from the marriage of Napoleon to Austrian archduchess Marie Louise to signing the Treaty of Fontainebleau that sent Napoleon into exile. Throughout the various Coalitions of the French wars, Metternich's service to Austria was indefatigable. He led the Austrian delegation at the Congress of Vienna. He was awarded the title of Prince for his service to the country.

Within Austria, Metternich held the post of Austrian Chancellor from 1821 until 1848. He served under Francis I and Ferdinand I.

The Biedermeier Period (1815-1848)

From a social standpoint, the Biedermeier period of Central Europe saw the growth of the middle class, a growth that changed the artistic styles of decor, painting, and literature. Industrialization promoted a sort of "new" class, the urban middle class, who were, in turn, a "new" audience for art. Artists and writers therefore began to move their focus on domestic matters, taking a sentimental view of the world and portraying it realistically. Landscapes, courtyards, family life, and country life were popular subjects.

However, the underpinnings of this movement were also heavily influenced by censorship. Artists were wise to avoid political subjects, and therefore, focus on the "everyday" subjects such as country life and historical fiction that were the safer and more profitable options.

Physically designed objects (furniture, architecture) focused on clean lines and utilitarian function, designed to emanate a non-fussy, airy feel. Admittedly, the middle class coming into its own money had its own thoughts: they relished the fussy baroque styles that had always, in the past, signified wealth. Regardless of their splurges, the era is known for practicality and functionality in its design, and the style evolved fairly naturally into the Victorian styles of the second half of the century.

Musically, the period was of interest because of a new focus on making music "at home." Arrangements of operas and symphonies that could be performed in the home were published, so that families or friends could play fine music in their own drawing rooms without the need of professional training. This is an amusing and clever precursor to what we might call "home entertainment" and, because it required a certain amount of skill, professional or not, it also sounds like quite a worthwhile way to spend time together.

The Truth Behind Metternich's Censorship

The true nature of Austria during this time is far darker than its lighthearted artistic movements suggest, though it can be surmised from the fact that artists so carefully avoided political topics. From 1815 through 1848, Austria entered a strange police state during which expression and communication was seriously censored. Metternich kept the government, and people, firmly under his thumb. He was a staunch conservative who was determined to keep peace and order using policies strictly against rising nationalism and liberalism. Metternich believed only that conservatism and the church would keep the country out of war or conflict.

Conflict was rising regardless, as the burgeoning middle class brought with it that burgeoning liberalism and nationalism. When the people of Austria revolted in 1848, it deflated Metternich. He went into exile for some years before returning in an advisory position to Franz Josef I. Metternich was blamed for Austrian unrest for the remainder of the 19th century, the feeling that if he had only allowed Austrian society to follow its natural course, much catastrophe (maybe even World War I) could have been avoided. Today, historians are more forgiving of his methodology, seeing it as a natural reaction to the chaos of the previous 50 years and an honest attempt, perhaps, to calm down the confusion throughout not only Austria but also most of Europe.

Ferdinand I of Austria

While Metternich fought to keep a changing Austria on a short leash, Ferdinand I of Austria took his father's throne in 1835.

It seemed that all of the disasters of inbreeding had come to fruition in poor Ferdinand, who was so severely disabled by maladies that rule was impossible for him. He suffered a speech impediment, epilepsy, and hydrocephalus and numerous other neurological problems, and ultimately proved impotent and unable to produce an heir. Though his intelligence is under serious doubt (he is rumored to have been an "idiot"), he was able to keep a legible and coherent journal. Yet bearing up to twenty seizures daily, he simply could not coherently rule an empire. His father, Franz II, before leaving the empire to his son, strongly encouraged Ferdinand to let Prince Metternich be his guide. In fact, during Ferdinand's rule, the government was mostly controlled by the Regent's Council, which was composed of Metternich, Archduke Louis, and Count Kolowrat.

In 1848, Austria was seized by revolution. Metternich and Emperor Ferdinand I were both forced to resign, and the emperor's nephew, Franz Joseph, replaced him.

Why a Revolution? What Were the Results?

Franz Josef I came into power after the revolution of 1848 put him there - but why had it happened? The purpose behind the revolution seemed to be the desire to promote a united Germany out of the German Confederation as nationalism continued to rise in strength. The truth was, however, that no consensus had ever been reached on what a "United Germany" actually meant. Would it be all Germanic territories united under Germany? Under Austria? The answer would not come for another eighty years.

The Era of Franz Josef I

Franz Josef ascended the throne at the age of 18 and ruled for 68 years. He was always known as a strictly regimented man who kept his routines and a fairly simple personal existence despite the wealth that surrounded him. He worked 10 hours a day out of his office, retired at 8 p.m. each night to sleep in a simple iron bed, and then rose at 4 in the morning. Hunting was his only diversion - over 1,500 hunting trophies decorate their country lodge. He was deeply in love with his wife Elisabeth but they were seldom together, owing to her frequent journeys taken for the sake of her health. She spent about eight months out of the year away, mostly in Hungary, where she was quite popular with the Hungarian people.

During the first years of Franz Josef's reign, the countries of Europe were in continued discord. As France, Prussia, Russia, Sardinia, and Serbia stretched and tested the limits of their powers and territories, the various nationalities within the Austrian Empire began to show discontent. Following 1848 revolution, at the end of forced labor, freed peasants made their way to the cities of Austria for work. This increase of larger numbers of people into smaller areas resulted in mixed feeling of racism and nationalism. The Magyars of Hungary declared independence and rose in revolt against Austria. Franz Josef's first act as Emperor was to quash the Hungarian Revolt in 1848. He executed over 100 who had taken part in the uprising, a harsh judgment that left the Hungarians deeply resentful. Five years later, a Hungarian nationalist tried, unsuccessfully, to assassinate him.

Austria Leaves the German Confederation

In the fifteen years following the revolution, the confusion and fighting seemed only to grow worse, and Franz Josef's reign continued to be plagued by the confusion of a Europe no longer held in check by the Holy Roman Empire. Austria refused to give up its German-speaking territories to a German Empire, and so, following the rebellion, Prussian King Friedrich Wilhelm IV became King of the German Empire. Austria sided with Prussia against Denmark to secure the Schleswig and Holstein duchies; when they could not decide how to divide the land, Austria fell into the Austro-Prussian war in 1866. After being defeated by Prussia at the Battle of Koniggratz, Austria left the German Confederation entirely.

The Creation of the Ringstrasse

While his country was engaged in numerous conflicts outside, Franz Josef made concerted efforts to improve Vienna as had many Habsburgs before him. In 1857, Franz Josef undertook the redesign of Vienna by tearing down its ancient fortress walls, filling it its moat, and then selling the land to common investors. He used the money for the creation of important buildings on a "ring boulevard" or the Ringstrasse, as it is still known today in its fame as one of Europe's most magnificent roads. The great Ringstrasse is about three miles long and arcs around the center of Vienna. It is generally where one will find the most important buildings in the city. Because the buildings were all built after the creation of the Ringstrasse, their styles are all "neo," but each is built in a style that seems appropriate to its purpose:

- » The Austrian Parliament is built in the neoclassical style because democracy came from Greece.
- » The City Hall is neo-gothic, a nod to the age when city merchants ran the government.
- » Museums are neo-renaissance, in the spirit of discovery. The Museum of Art History (completed in 1881) is in the Italian Renaissance style.
- » Vienna's court theater is neo-baroque because it of its place in the age when opera and theater flourished.
- » The Vienna State Opera House (constructed in 1869) is renowned throughout the world, a leading opera house offering about 300 performances each year. It is the pride of the city. Most of this beautiful structure had to be rebuilt after the war as it was bombed and burned. This top opera house has one of the largest stages in Europe, about the size of the interior of St. Stephen's cathedral.

» The Volkstheater and the Volksoper were developed for entertainment more suited for the "common" folk, and popular entertainment was represented by the "operetta."

Semmering Railway

Also in 1857, Franz Josef appointed his brother, Archduke Maximilian, to control Milan and Venice, the territories Austria held in Italy. This was Austria's gateway to the Mediterranean. Venice and Italy are separated by the Alps, and Franz Josef ordered that a railway through the Alps be built to connect the two. Twenty thousand workers and engineers were brought together to accomplish this incredible task. Semmering Railway (constructed in the Semmering Pass) was the first railway to cross the Alps.

Archduke Maximilian suggested they offer the Italians autonomy, but Franz Josef thought doing so would lead to more rebellion. Maximilian was relieved from his job by his brother and, because he was unwilling to go back home; he was not given a new assignment. He spent the rest of his life at one of the many Habsburg castles along the Danube. Like many Austrian territories, Italy would see its way to independence as Austria continued to lose skirmishes with other nations and a growing middle-class public that wanted independence.

Johann Strauss II (1825-1899)

While discussing Austrian music, it is essential also to mention Johann Strauss II, the "Waltz King" of Austria. He may be the first composer to begin a "dance craze." Strauss the Younger, as he is sometimes called, was the son of Johann Strauss I, who also was well-known for Austrian waltzes. It was Strauss the Younger who distinguished himself with famous works such as "The Blue Danube" and several waltzes dedicated to Emperor Franz Josef I. Strauss the Younger was born in St. Ulrich near Vienna; throughout his life, he would tour the world with his orchestra.

The Austro-Hungarian Empire

In 1867, the Austro-Hungarian Compromise (the "Ausgleich") happened when Franz Josef granted significant autonomy to Hungary, allowing it to become a "dual monarchy" which would share the same emperor. He and his wife Elisabeth were crowned monarchs of the country. Elisabeth was extremely popular in Hungary, though Franz Josef was not (due in no small part to his violent reaction to their rebellion of less than 20 years earlier).

This may seem like a strange turn of events, considering that the first act of Franz Josef's reign had been to crush the life out of Hungarian rebellion. Why would the Emperor now turn around to give autonomy to the country he had tried to keep in stranglehold?

Recall, however, that Otto Von Bismarck, the Prussian Chancellor, had worked hard to exclude Austria from the German Confederacy, decided in June 1866 to declare war on Austria (the Austro-Prussian War), and kicked Austria out of the German Confederation. This left Austria on the verge of collapse and gave Hungary the idea that this might be the perfect time to gain its own independence.

Rapidly, Franz Josef moved to keep Hungary within Austria's territories. In accordance with the "Austro-Hungarian Compromise," foreign affairs, defense, and finance were controlled by the sovereign, but the governments of the two countries operated separately. There were numerous ethnic groups in Hungary, including Italian and Romanian communities as well as various Slavic groups (including Croats, Czechs, Poles Rusyns, Serbs, Slovaks, Slovenes, and Ukrainians). Even so, the Magyars came to dominate the government.

This wildly varied melting pot was difficult to rule at a time when nationalist movements were on the rise, but Austrian government did the best it could to respect the variations of its people. National groups were allowed to use their native tongues even in governmental capacities and schools for the various ethnicities were also permitted. The simple fact may be that, regardless of Hungary being given its own government, it was still ruled by monarchy that left the middle and lower classes and minorities without what they felt was adequate representation.

After this arrangement was made, the Czech people felt that Bohemia should have the same rights as Hungary and asked for a triple-monarchy arrangement. At first, Franz Josef was agreeable, but the Magyars and the Germans of Bohemia disagreed, the German majority worrying about disappearing in the tide of minorities that were currently building up power in Austria.

Note that this Germanic resistance to minorities is only the beginning, and that at this time, and for a century to follow, the desire for a united German country would affect both politics and sociology of the countries. German Austrians felt that their national character had been stripped from them. Members from all social circles were reeling from the Austrian exclusion from the German Confederation. They wore colors of the German flag and the favorite color of German Emperor William I to show their displeasure at their multi-ethnic culture. They made clear that they wanted the Austro-Hungarian Empire to collapse, if only it would afford Austria the chance to be annexed by Germany.

A Renaissance of Art and Thought under Franz Josef

Franz Josef allowed the Jewish people to move freely through the empire, own property, and to vote, assimilating themselves into the empire. Many famous and influential people of the time were Jewish. For example:

» **Sigmund Freud** (1856 - 1939). Freud was born in the Austrian Imperial territory of Monrovia. Most students of psychology know Freud as the father of psychoanalysis, the iconic system of mental therapy involving the ongoing dialog between patient and therapist. Freud's methodology was innovative, and even though his various behavioral theories are now debated as to their true accuracy, particularly considering their tendency toward sexism, he changed the face of psychology and brought on an entirely new concept of the treatment of mental illness. He lived and worked in Vienna until he fled Nazi persecution in 1938, and he died while in exile in the United Kingdom the following year.

» **Gustav Mahler** (1860 - 1911). Mahler was an Austro-Bohemian composer but, during his lifetime, was better established as the leading conductor of his age, at the height of which he served as director of the Hofoper (the Vienna Court Opera). He converted from Judaism to Catholicism, in fact, to secure the job. Even so, he was subject to criticism and hostility, and his own compositions went largely ignored. He was well-known for his skill in bringing the operas of other composers (such a Wagner and Mozart) to the stage, and he was so occupied with conducting operas that his career as a composer resulted in relatively few created pieces when compared to other composers of his era. Though Mahler's music was banned throughout Europe during the Nazi era, after 1945 his compositions were rediscovered, and he is now widely recognized as a great composer.

» **Franz Kafka** (1883-1924). The Bohemian Kafka was born in Prague while it was still a part of the Austro-Hungarian Empire. He became an important figure in 20th century literature by combining fantastical elements with realism, normally putting lone characters into frightening situations of guilt, alienation, and bizarre, inexplicable circumstances. Not much of his work was published during his life, and those stories that were published by magazines were mostly ignored by the public. In fact, Kafka, who died quite young from tuberculosis, instructed his executor to destroy all of his unfinished work. His executor fortunately did not follow that instruction, and Kafka's work became greatly influential in the 20th and 21st centuries. The term "Kafkaesque" has become an identifier for a story told about the overpowering of an individual by a surreal, disorienting power (likely a governmental entity), leaving the protagonist confused and helpless; but outside of literature, the term has come to mean any incomprehensibly complex situation, which might make it apply fairly well to the history of the Habsburg Dynasty.

» **Gustav Klimt** (1862-1918): After training at the Vienna School of Arts and Crafts, Gustav Klimt broke with convention and developed his own controversial style of painting using golden and ornamental backgrounds in his paintings and shamelessly employing heavy sexual symbolism. He was a prominent member of the Vienna Secession movement (a group of artists who resigned from the Association of Austrian Artists to protest its support of traditional styles).He was also a favorite artist of Emperor

Franz Josef and commissioned to paint several ceilings and murals in important Viennese buildings. Still, the rather shocking nature of his work made him a target of criticism. Klimt, after a time, refused to accept commissions and simply carried on with his distinctive work, influenced by Japanese art and his own perfectionism. His most famous works are his brilliant golden paintings such as *Portrait of Adele Bloch-Bauer I, Judith and the Head of Holofernes,* and *The Kiss,* but his body of work is long, influential, and highly valued.

» **Ludwig Josef Johann Wittgenstein** (1889 - 1951). Philosopher Wittgenstein was born midway through Franz Josef's rule; during World War I, he volunteered for the Austrian Army where he won many medals for bravery. Though his parents were both Jewish and Wittgenstein was both baptized as and buried as a Catholic and claimed to see every problem he considered through a religious viewpoint, he made no commitment to any religion during his lifetime. Wittgenstein moved to Cambridge in 1929. He was a highly influential figure in the field of philosophy with a general theory that all philosophical problems come from the source of misunderstandings in the "logic of language." He made a serious study of the way our language influences the way we think.

A Series of Tragedies

Later in his life, Franz Josef lost his son Rudolf and his wife Elisabeth to strange and terrible circumstances.

In 1889, Rudolf, only 30 years old, was involved in a murder-suicide pact with his lover. Though the "official" story tried to cover the sordid details, saying first that it was a hunting accident, second that it was a heart attack, the truth soon became known because Rudolf had left letters to his friends and his mother, though none to his father. Rudolf's death resulted in Franz Josef's nephew, Franz Ferdinand, being promoted to the position of Archduke and heir to the throne.

In 1898, while traveling, Elisabeth was assassinated by an Italian anarchist. In recent years, Elisabeth has attained a certain celebrity status as people compare her with Princess Diana. She was a beautiful empress, extremely devoted to preserving her appearance with strict dieting and grooming. After bearing four children, she still had a twenty-one-inch waist, but as soon as her age began to show, she almost never allowed herself to be seen in public, always hiding her face behind a fan. Franz Josef, while sporting an emperor's usual string of mistresses, was still remarkably devoted to his wife, writing letters to her almost daily when she would take her months-long trips away from Vienna. He seemed always to gravely miss her presence. Her death was a terrible blow.

Franz Josef was left alone to rule his empire in an oncoming sea of troubles.

A Visitor to Vienna

In 1907, a 19-year-old Austrian man from Linz named Adolf Hitler came to Vienna to study art. He applied twice to the Academy of Fine Arts Vienna but was rejected both times. The director suggested Hitler should apply instead to the School of Architecture, but the young man did not have the needed credentials. Later in his life, Hitler would say that architecture was a passion of his and, indeed, he had in mind many fantastically large architectural projects, but these were not realized before his political career was cut short.

Hitler both loved and hated Vienna. An artistic soul, he loved the city's buildings, its opera (which he attended often, seeing repeat performances of his favorites), and the vast museum collections from the Habsburgs' long imperial history. He romanticized the classical imagery that surrounded him, seeing himself perhaps as a hero in a Wagnerian drama.

Unfortunately, he was also a poor man forced to live in homeless shelters or a men's hostel, earning money as a day laborer or sometimes from selling his watercolor paintings. The real Vienna demanded a certain financial independence, an importance of rank and birth, for an individual truly to enjoy its pleasures. Resentment burned in him as he saw others enjoying the things to which he felt entitled, which he felt he too could appreciate due to his artistic understanding. He had not yet developed the self-confidence he would later gain from his involvement in political movements and so was left isolated and unhappy, watching the life he envied from the outside.

In 1913, Hitler received a small inheritance and moved to Munich. He was conscripted for the Austro-Hungarian Army but deemed "unfit for service." Instead, when World War I began, Hitler voluntarily enlisted in the Bavarian Army.

Hitler would not return to Vienna until over 20 years later, after entering Austria Branau with troops and panzerwagens in March of 1938, to declare the country was annexed by the Third Reich.

World War I on the Horizon

For some time prior to WWI, Austria suffered domestic conflicts caused by the government's adoption of minority demands for the same rights as the German majority. In a country with as many minorities as Austria, this led to considerable confusion. For example, in Parliament, nine languages were allowed, but no translators were provided. Members of parliament, should they desire, could completely stop the work of parliament by filibuster, speaking endlessly in a language that many of their fellow diplomats could not understand.

In 1913, the German faction blockaded Bohemian Parliament. Bohemia was the homeland of the Czechs, so in rebellion, the Czechs stalled the Austrian Parliament. Out of frustration, Austrian Prime Minister-President Count Karl von Surgkh put the whole of Austrian Parliament "on hold," and they were not in session for three years. During that time, Austria was governed by emergency decree. One might note that those years would include the dawning of World War I.

WORLD WAR I

Austria Declares War Against Serbia

In 1914, Franz Ferdinand and his wife were assassinated by a young Serb in Sarajevo, which was at the time still a part of the Austrian empire. The young assassin was a member of a terrorist organization called the Black Hand. Emperor Franz Josef threatened war against Serbia, setting out demands that Serbia must meet to prevent this. Germany, allied with Austria-Hungary, took its side. Russia sided with the Serbians, and at that time, Russia was bound in the Triple Entent with Britain, France, and Ireland.

On July 28, 1914, a month after the assassination, Austria-Hungary declared war on Serbia with Germany's backing. Germany, however, went on to declare war against Russia and France only a few days later. German troops marched on France, taking a route through Belgium. Britain had pledged to maintain the neutrality of Belgium so was required to declare war on Germany. The countries seemed to fall into the war like dominos, as one after another joined in to support one side or the other. Ultimately, 135 countries took part in the "War to End All Wars."

Vienna is Starving

The war, so far beyond the intentions of Franz Josef, was devastating within the borders of Austria - not because of fighting but because of the sudden lack of supplies or food. They discovered almost at once that there were not enough trains to transport troops toward the war and food toward the population. War took precedence, therefore the population suffered. Out in the countryside, tons of grain and coal waited for transport but were never picked up. Large numbers of farmers were conscripted as soldiers, so agriculture suffered additional setbacks.

The situation in crowded Vienna, which relied on train transport of goods, became dire. Imports were not an option because of the Allied Blockade of the Mediterranean. By 1918, the Austrian economy shrank by 40%; almost half of the deaths in Vienna were due to starvation or malnutrition. Hungary was extremely unhelpful about sending food transports, offended by and dismissive of the Austrians asking for help during a war they essentially initiated and implying that if Austria did not have the capability to survive a war, they should not have started one.

Hunger riots commonly broke out in Vienna as five hundred thousand people lined up daily for supplies. The situation only worsened as years passed. Vienna was demoralized and its population desperate, many of them homeless, starving, and resorting to theft with no reliable security in charge. Enraged and hopeless, the German Austrians had ceased to care about the minorities at all, and in fact, hate crimes toward minorities were frequent.

Two years after declaring war, Franz Josef expressed terrible regret at the destruction his actions had wrought. On November 21, 1916, Franz Josef passed away from pneumonia in the middle of the war at the age of 86.

The Last Emperor: Charles I

Almost from the start of his ascension, Charles I (a/k/a Karl I), a deeply religious man, tried to stop the war, which he viewed with horror. He entered secret peace negotiations with France outside of the knowledge of Germany, Austria's supposed ally. But the war had become so much larger than the relatively simple conflict between Austria and Serbia that, despite his efforts, it was out of his hands to put a stop to the fighting.

Two years later, the Imperial army surrendered and the Austro-Hungarian Empire no longer existed. In April of 1919, the last Emperor, Charles I, was dethroned upon the formation of the Republic of German Austria. He fled into exile in Switzerland. Charles attempted to restore the monarchy for the remainder of his short life, but he died of respiratory failure in 1922 while in his mid-30s.

Charles's story does not end there, however. History has vindicated his brief rulership by noting his strong Christian faith, which he strived to put first in his decision-making. Pope John Paul II recognized his peace-making attempts in the final years of World War I in a beatification ceremony held in October 2004. Hereafter, the last emperor became known as Charles the Blessed.

Subsequent support of his cause for canonization has Charles the Blessed making his way toward sainthood. His cause has passed through the opening steps of the process:

1. He was declared a "servant of God" in 1954.
2. In 1972, his tomb was opened; there, his body was declared "incorrupt" (in that it had undergone little or no decomposition).
3. In 2003, he was given the title of "venerable" because of heroic virtues as declared by the Vatican's Congregation for the Causes of Saints.
4. In 2003, he also was credited with his first miracle, which occurred in 1960, when a nun who prayed for his beatification was cured of a debilitating condition.
5. In 2008, after a 16-month investigation, a Church tribunal recognized a second miracle they will attribute to him, when a woman claimed she was cured by prayers of recent converts to Catholicism.

The second miracle is required for canonization and sainthood. The canonization of Charles the Blessed to sainthood has not yet taken place.

After World War I

Austria struggled with its identity following the unforeseen horrors of World War I. Now, for the first time in centuries, the country was small, alone, and without territories or an empire.

Following World War I, the Austro-Hungarian Empire was dissolved, unable to organize under the many unsolved ethnic problems within the territories. What was left of Austria constituted a rump state that called itself "The Republic of German Austria." This sudden dissolution of the Austro-Hungarian Empire left over 3 million Austrians living as minorities in newly formed states such as Czechoslovakia, Yugoslavia, and Hungary.

The desire for unification with Germany (annexation of Austria to Germany) was already a popular public sentiment, and German Austria's quickly formed government declared itself to be integral to the German Reich. However, Allied powers forbade the unification of Germany to Austria, so the "Republic of Austria" was created and lasted until 1934.

The Republic of Austria suffered economic depression and right-wing violence. Inflation devalued Austria's national currency, the Krone. In 1922, Austria was granted a loan by the League of Nations, which was meant to stabilize the country and prevent bankruptcy, or, in simpler terms, to allow the country to get back on its feet. However, it also effectively put Austria under the control of the League of Nations. The country did enjoy a brief respite from economic hardship from 1925 to 1929, when Black Tuesday caused its economy to crash and worldwide repercussions of the Great Depression.

Austrian Civil War: Fascism vs. Socialism

Within Austria, two major political parties bitterly opposed one another. The fascists identified with Italy, whereas the socialists identified with Germany. In 1933, Austria was taken over by the Fascists, led by Chancellor Engerbert Dollfus, and the socialist's army was declared illegal. Illegal or not, it continued to function, and civil war broke out across the country. The February Uprising (1934), or the Austrian Civil War, saw Austrian fascism emerge victorious against socialism. The Fascists ultimately retained power, though Dollfus himself was killed in a coup. His successor, Karl Schuschnigg, wanted Austria to remain independent of Germany and attempted to announce a referendum concerning Austria's Independence. This would occur on March 13, 1938.

Anschluss

However, and doubtless not coincidentally, on March 12, 1938, the Nazi panzerwagens rolled into Austria, and no military action was taken against them. Many Austrians stood and cheered as they did so. Hitler came to Vienna to declare, to an overjoyed audience, that the small country was now annexed to Germany as part of its Third Reich. Austrian-born Hitler announced the "reunification" of his home country with the German Reich on Vienna's Heldenplatz. He received a hero's reception for the reunification of the German People.

On March 13, 1938, the *Anschluss* of Austria made it a part of Nazi Germany. Austria was now a province of the German Reich and renamed "Ostmark." Because Italy and Germany had become allies in 1936, this meant basically that Austria lost Italian support, and there was no opposition to the conversion.

On April 10, 1938, Parliamentary elections were held, the vote taking the form of a single question, asking whether voters approved a) a Nazi-party list of the Reichstag and b) the annexation of Austria. The results, likely tampered with, were overwhelmingly in favor, but even without interference, generally Austrian support for the unification was quite strong. Many felt that this combining of Germany and Austria was long overdue. The wish to unite with Germany stretched back at least as far as 1848, when the revolution had taken place and reignited again in 1867 when the Austro-Hungarian Empire left those of German descent feeling significantly slighted.

The Austrian Holocaust

The Austrians, under the same social stressors as their German cousins, were no less susceptible to the tide of hatred and megalomania Hitler brought forth. Soon after the takeover, Jews, Communists, and other opponents began to suffer severe public mistreatment. Almost 200,000 Jews lived in Austria when the *Anschluss* took place. Many subsequently fled the country (about 140,000 in 1938 and 1939) – and, well, they should have, because the violence against them was sudden and abrupt. Many Jews, not seeing a way out, committed suicide rather than suffer what they were certain was coming.

On November 9 and 10 of 1938, dubbed, "The Night of Broken Glass," Jewish shops were plundered on a massive scale, with many Jewish people murdered in the streets and many more sent to concentration camps. The nightmarish Mauthausen concentration camp, a major camp in charge of over a hundred sub-camps throughout the country of Austria, including three large camps at Gusen, was located near Linz in Upper Austria. It would be the last concentration camp to be liberated by the allies.

Over 65,000 Austrian Jews would die in the Holocaust. The Austrian population made up 8% of the Third Reich, but 13% of the SS members and 40% of the staff at extermination camps were Austrian. Many highly prominent and notorious Nazis were Austrians. Aside from Adolf Hitler himself, there were such criminals as:

» **Ernst Kaltenbrunner:** Kaltenbrunner was considered the leader of the Austrian SS. He was the highest ranking SS officer to be put on trial at Nuremberg and was sentenced to death for war crimes and crimes against humanity.
» **Arthur Seyss-Inquart:** Seyss-Inquart served as Chancellor of Austria for two days before Anschluss - following that, he served as governor of the newly formed Ostmark. He was Reichskommisar of the Nazi-occupied Netherlands, where he subjected the Dutch to forced labor and sent a majority

- **Franz Stangl:** Stangl was an SS commandant of the Sobibor and Treblinka extermination camps. Many years after the war, he was arrested in Brazil and tried in Germany for the murder of nine hundred thousand people. He was sentenced to life imprisonment but died soon after the trial.
- **Odilo Globocnik:** A high-ranking SS leader, Globocnik was responsible for organizing the murders of over 1,000,000 Polish Jews. Globocnik committed suicide after his capture by British soldiers.

A Last-Minute Change of Heart

While Austria provided troops and support to Germany throughout the war, Austria itself was well protected by its position on the map and saw very little in-country conflict. Austria was physically removed from the warfront, separated by Germany from all the Allied Nations and particularly Russia.

When Germany broke its treaty and invaded Russia, Austrian sentiment began to change. After Germany's defeat in the brutal Battle of Stalingrad, suddenly Austria rethought its alliance, in effect, recognizing the warning signs when it came to the tumbling Third Reich. It may seem excessively convenient that Austria expressed such doubts, hedging its bets with the winning side.

[Note: The page begins mid-sentence with "Dutch Jews to their deaths. He was convicted for war crimes at Nuremberg and sentenced to death." preceding the Franz Stangl entry.]

Vienna fell on April 13, 1945, to the Soviet's Vienna Offensive, and by April 27, party leaders in Austria had withdrawn the country from the Third Reich, setting up its previous constitution (from 1929) to the approval of Joseph Stalin. Afterward, the other allied nations entered Austria, balancing the country's future between liberation and sanction.

From 1939 to 1945, Austrian military deaths are estimated at just over a quarter of a million people.

Political Treatment Following World War II

Following World War II, Austria was divided similarly to Germany, into American, French, British, and Soviet Zones. The Allied Commission for Austria took over the government. Vienna, unlike Berlin, was not divided, and Austria, unlike Germany, was not forced to create a divide between Western and Eastern governments. Austria was treated more as a country that had been invaded by Germany and liberated at the hands of the Allies.

Neutrality

Austria regained full independence on May 15, 1955, by concluding the Austrian State Treaty alongside its four occupying powers. Once the occupation troops were entirely gone, Austrian parliament declared the country's "permanent neutrality." This date, October 26, is now celebrated as Austria's National Day.

Modern Austria

Government

The Austrian head of state is the Federal President, elected by popular majority vote. As of September 2020, the President is Alexander Van der Bellen. However, the presidential role in Austria is ceremonial. The real power of the head of the government is held by the chancellor, who exercises executive power. It is roughly the same official position as that of a prime minister. Austria's present chancellor is Sebastian Kurz. The highly controversial, right-wing Kurz was previously chancellor from December 2017 through May 2019, when he was ousted from the office by the National Council and then reinstated in January 2020.

Austrian Parliament is determined by vote every five years. The political system mostly divides Austria's decision-making by grand coalition between the Social Democratic Party and the Austrian People's Party, the two most popular political parties in the country. However, important interest groups are well-represented by chambers (rather like unions of workers), and most legislation passed reflects a general consensus.

Austria became a member of the European Union on January 1, 1995, by the decision of a two-thirds majority. Austria participates actively in the peacekeeping efforts of NATO's "Partnership for Peace. It is also a member of the Organization for Security and Cooperation in Europe, which means that its international commitments are subject to monitoring under the Helsinki Commission (an organization, in highly simplified terms, dedicated to the improvement of international relations, peaceful resolution to disputes and the equal rights of people).

A Look at Austria, via the Modern World's Most Famous Austrian

Arnold Schwarzenegger was born July 30, 1947, and is likely the most famous and beloved Austrian in the world today, a man who came from humble beginnings and through willpower, self-confidence, and discipline tempered by a joyful nature and an inner warmth became a success in every venture he tackled. His birth so soon after the Second World War gives his life an interesting parallel to the movement of Austria through the years since that conflict.

Schwarzenegger was born in the town of Thal in Allied-Occupied Austria, close to Graz, Austria's second-largest city after Vienna. Gustav, his father, was the local police chief, and his mother, Aurelia, was a homemaker. Gustav Schwarzenegger was previously a member of the Nazi party, though he was never linked to any atrocities and wounded at the Battle of Stalingrad. He was a strict, difficult father who demanded hard work and discipline from Arnold and Arnold's older brother Meinhard, and he impressed on his sons the value of physical fitness and athleticism.

His participation in sports has influenced Schwarzenegger throughout his life because it taught him discipline, camaraderie, and the ability to achieve more through hard work. Austria's mountainous terrain in the Alps make skiing, snowboarding, and ski-jumping extremely popular sports and vital to the Austrian tourism economy. In Austria, football (soccer), hockey, basketball, and horseback riding are popular sports.

Schwarzenegger was captivated also by movies and newsreels about the United States. He did not, however, know how a poor Austrian farm boy would be able to make it to a new country and find success.

At the age of 15, he attended a gym session where he became obsessed with bodybuilding, which made him not only feel great but also might be a way to gain fame: he felt it could be a way to get into the movies. He began to win junior bodybuilding contests, which improved his self-confidence. He soon performed his one-year service in the Austrian Army. Requirements have changed since Schwarzenegger's time. Presently, all fit young men of 18 are required to serve six months of military service, but both men and women 16 and older are eligible for voluntary service.

After his military service, Schwarzenegger moved to Munich in 1966 to work with professional bodybuilders. He won contests like "The Best-Built Man in Europe" and "Mr. Europe." At the age of twenty, he became the youngest Mr. Universe in the history of the contest.

He was invited to the United States to participate in the American version of the competition, his airfare paid by a sponsor company. In the United States, he even took ballet classes to learn grace in his posing and enrolled in business courses. He even started his own health-product business. He got an early movie role (*Hercules in New York*) that was critically panned. It would be another seven years before he had a chance at a film role. Nevertheless, between those roles, Schwarzenegger did continue to dominate the bodybuilding circuit. He retired from the bodybuilding sport after winning the Mr. Universe and Mr. World contents seven times. His prize money was well-invested, and he had made his first million only eight years after coming penniless to the United States. Austria, too, has been an active player economically, particularly in the area of Eastern Europe and building strong economic ties in the European Union.

He began to apply the same discipline to his acting career that he applied to bodybuilding and soon after got a second chance at being in films. In 1977, he won a Golden Globe for "Best Newcomer." Shortly thereafter, he met Maria Shriver and fell, as he says, in "love at first sight" despite their different political ideologies. Schwarzenegger was a republican, and Maria Shriver was practically part of democratic royalty as the niece of John F. Kennedy. Modern Austria is a quite conservative nation, with most of its politics taking a distinctly right-wing slant.

Schwarzenegger was never at rest. He got his first big role as Conan the Barbarian the same year he got his business degree. Soon after that, he tried out for the role of the "hero" in *The Terminator,* however, it was soon obvious to its director James Cameron that Schwarzenegger was perfect for the Terminator role. This would become his franchise standard and the film made a major star out of him; it is still considered a science fiction classic and continues to produce sequels as recently as 2019. Five of the six *Terminator* franchise films have included Schwarzenegger.

Life became even busier for Schwarzenegger when he finally married Maria Shriver and they began a family (they would have four children together). Schwarzenegger became a United States citizen. He also decided he wanted to make comedies in addition to major action films. His success in *Twins,* directed by Ivan Reitman, made him more publicly accessible and family-friendly. By the late 1980s, he was the most popular movie star in the world. He was able to invest in his own film projects such as *Total Recall.* He had the time to become involved in charity work that benefited children and in political rallies for the Republican Party. George Bush Sr. made him the head of the President's Council on Physical Fitness.

In 1997, (he was 49 years old) Schwarzenegger had elective heart surgery to repair a defective valve. Within a month, he was well enough to promote his next film, *Batman and Robin*, in his homeland of Austria. While on this trip, he also opened the Arnold Schwarzenegger stadium in Graz (which is only two miles from his hometown of Thal). Austria has also acknowledged its most famous son with the Grand Decoration of Honour for Services to the Republic of Austria (in 1993) and the Honorary Ring of the Federal State of Styria (in 2017).

In 2003, Schwarzenegger followed up success in bodybuilding, business, and film with politics. California was in a situation that made election easier for him; the state had a deficit and general dissatisfaction with their democratic governor. The state held a "recall," something that has only happened once before, with over 130 people on the ballot. Schwarzenegger entered the race at the last possible moment under the promise to "clean house." With the help of Maria Shriver and automatic publicity available for him, Schwarzenegger was able to take the election. Within the next couple of years, he demanded his name be removed from the stadium in Graz when Austrian officials condemned his decision to grant clemency to a death row inmate in his role as California governor. Awards given to him in later years suggest he is on better terms with his native country now.

Schwarzenegger has also acknowledged that climate change is an issue for which we must take responsibility. Modern Austria is extremely ecologically responsible, relying on hydropower, wind, solar, and biomass power plants for over half its energy resources. Its biocapacity is twice the world's average and, per capita, it runs at a biocapacity deficit meaning that, more or less, little Austria is undoing a bit of the damage caused by other nations.

Schwarzenegger served as the governor of California until 2011. Then, he returned to acting. Since that time, he has continued to produce and star in films and promote sports competition. He has quite recently appeared in a film promoting the wearing of facemasks during the COVID-19 pandemic.

A master of every career path he has chosen with a net worth of approximately $400 million, Austria's most famous son continues to inspire people around the world to better health and physical safety.

Modern Vienna, the "Easternmost City of the West"

The city of Vienna exists in a bizarre, halfway place; what was once the mighty cultural epicenter of the world's greatest empire is now an extravagant jewel in a small, modest, landlocked country, with a population of only about 9 million people, which seems ill-fitted to support it.

How did it come to be this way? Very much like Austria itself, Vienna's status has depended highly on its position. It went through a number of phases through the centuries:

1. In Roman times, it was Vindobona, with the Germanic barbarians just beyond.

2. In the Middle Ages, it was Europe's last stand against the Ottoman Turks.
3. During the Cold War, Vienna maintained freedom through neutrality, though it was surrounded by communist-dominated states.
4. Now, with many of those Eastern Bloc nations joining the European Union, Vienna is sitting once again in the middle of Europe.

The Congress of Vienna both stabilized and provided shape for 19th-century Europe, and this is really the era that shaped our view of Vienna now as a place of grand architecture, music, art, and a milieu of "good living."

As has always been the case, Vienna supports a multi-ethnic melting pot culture of descendants from all over the Habsburg Empire: Hungarian, Czech, Slovak, Poles, Slovenes, Jews, Serbians, Romanians, Italians, and many others. Its personality is now comfortably laid-back with its status of no longer being a superpower, and the population seems devoted to living well.

In the 1970s, Vienna dug a canal parallel to the Danube River that was ostensibly to be a flood barrier. The design also created a twelve-mile-long island in the middle of the Danube that is now a beloved "island" park, grassy and traffic-free. Locals and tourists alike use this long stretch of land as a regular park for simple pleasures such as barbecues and ice cream carts, swimming, fishing, and casual games of football.

Austrians, not just in Vienna but also throughout the country, have a knack for hometown spirit and liveliness shown most obviously in their beer gardens, where the townspeople gather for food, beer, and music. The word "Gemutlichkeit" is used to describe the feeling of coziness in a group of friendly townspeople enjoying themselves.

Of course, Vienna has long been Europe's music capital. It was a destination for musicians as early as the 12th century, and of course, the Habsburgs were serious supporters of the musical arts, many of them composers and musicians themselves. Vienna as a city is as well-decorated as its museums, galleries, and opera houses. For example, the buildings throughout the city are decorated with Vienna's own brand of art nouveau (curvy decorations painted or sculpted on the outside of buildings) called *jugendstil*, and examples can be found throughout the town, painted, carved, or embossed brightly on the facades facing the street.

Tourism is a major industry of the city (tourism money amounts to 9% of Austria's gross national income). Within Vienna now are more than 1,700 acres of vineyards and accompanying Heurige taverns where locals gather to drink "young" wines. The Habsburgs began the tradition by allowing vintners to sell their wine tax-free, giving rise to a traditional business. This has given way to a happy local tradition of gathering for a buffet-style dinner and careful wine sampling. Young wines, the Venetians joke, are hard to distinguish from vinegar.

Franz Josef's *Ringstrasse* is still the best place to see the finest of Vienna's history in its many museums and castles. Still, there are many sights to see outside of the famous ring.

- » The Belvedere Palace is another point of Viennese pride. Originally, it was the home of Prince Eugene of Savoy, Austria's conqueror of the Turks and a great Austrian military hero. Because he died without an heir, the state inherited his palace. Emperor Josef II in the 19th century converted the palace to Austria's first public gallery of art where Austria's 19th and 20th century art is housed. The museum features an impressive collection of respected Austrian romantic painters, Egon Echiele and Gustav Klimt.
- » The Museum of Nature and the Museum of History and Fine Arts face each other in the Maria Teresa Square. These hold the Habsburg family collection, which includes art created in Habsburg territories of Austria, Germany, Spain, Belgium, the Netherlands, and Italy.
- » The Kunsthistorisches Museum is a great collection of art from throughout the Austrian realm of circa 1500; many excellent examples of Italian works of the Renaissance are held here. Art from the southern realms (i.e., Italy) is rampant of gods, angels, and Madonnas; art from the northern realms preferred imagery of peasants, landscapes, and food.

- » The Hofburg is the Habsburgs' Central Vienna palace (or, their winter palace). This complex has been there from the 13th century. Through the centuries, it has grown along with the empire, and the last wing was opened just before World War I. The palace is now used for the offices of the Austrian president and government officials. It also has a Spanish Riding School and the Vienna Boys Choir and even a butterfly garden ("Schmetterling Haus").
- » St. Stephens is Vienna's gothic cathedral, heavily damaged during World War II but now mostly restored, and the elaborate tile roof is symbolically owned by the citizens (one tile apiece) who donated to rebuild the burned roof.
- » The Wauchau Valley, between Vienna and Melk, is the most romantic stretch of the Danube, where its terrain is at its most beautiful, little villages, pubs, magnificent castles, and cruise ships take tourists down the river.

The Habsburg Family Today

The current castle home of the Habsburgs is still in Tyrol, Austria, occupied by their descendants, the Enzenberg Family. Its most valuable treasure is the Habsburg family tree painted on the walls of the Habsburg Hall. The tree was painted to honor Maximilian I, connecting the family from 1300 to Maximilian's succession as Holy Roman Emperor.

The current head of the Habsburg Family is Karl of Austria, or Karl Thomas Robert Maria Franziskus Georg Bahnam von Habsburg (born

1961). He was a member of the European Parliament for Austrian People's Party for three years. Currently, he is involved in numerous committees and organizations advocating the protection of cultural heritage, humanitarian law, the protection of ethnic minorities, and the rights people have for self-determination.

In March of 2020, Karl Von Habsburg was the first known royal person to contract COVID-19 and thankfully recovered from the virus after three weeks of quarantine but now encourages people strictly to follow safety measures.

Conclusion

Separating the little country of Austria today with the bulging and overextended Austrian Empire of the past is not as simple as reducing its size in our imagination. It has always been hostage to its location and its landscape, chosen to be the center of the world's power for a time because a ruling family was driven out of Switzerland and simply traveled as far west on the Danube as they could make it before settling into an old castle. The Habsburg Empire and the Austrian Empire may have been one and the same, a far-reaching, nebulous power of marriages upon marriages; Austria, however, was a real place with a real population that paid the price again and again for the desires of the dozens of rulers and countries that surrounded it.

This small, landlocked country stands as a quiet example of dignity after hubris; after a time of reaching halfway around the world to claim territories as its own, little Austria is now content, even strict, about maintaining its identity as a peacekeeping nation. It is not always with the friendliest of intentions, either, that Austria "keeps the peace," as Austria closes its borders or refuses aid when it deems such actions necessary. Austria is the only Western European country with a right-wing government led by its Chancellor Sebastian Kurz; it has a hardline against immigration and an even harder one against Islamic terrorism. After a history of constant invasion, unreliable treaties, and untrustworthy allies, perhaps it is not unthinkable that Austria would tighten into itself.

Austria, conservative though it may be, has not relinquished the idea of its neutrality, and it continues to act in a role that supports peaceful resolutions to world problems.

Over a thousand years of history, Austria rarely had years when the empire was not at war, and conflict after conflict has peppered its ever-changing landscape. Perhaps the most recent horrors of World War II, with the added carnage of genocide haunting its population, put the final resolve in Austria to cease hostilities. Hopefully, the ongoing neutrality of Austria, even as it keeps a secretive hold on its inner resources, is its way of showing a more restful national spirit that is striving to come into its own identity. An identity not as the head of one empire or the state of another but as a country devoted to promoting a lasting peace for the first time in a long time.

Sources

Articles

Richter, Duncan J. "Ludwig Wittgenstein". Internet Encyclopedia of Philosophy

"Schwarzenegger terminates name on stadium." December 19, 2005. Associated Press. Nbcnews.com

Videos

"Arnold Schwarzenegger." The History Channel: Biography. 2003.

"Ask a Maestro: Why are so many composers Austrian?" Willcwhite. May 3, 2016. Via YouTube.

"Austria During World War 1" October 22, 2018. *The Great War.* Via YouTube.

"Austria during World War II - From Anschluss to Vienna Offensive (1938 - 1945)." *History Hustle.* July 20, 2019. Via YouTube.

"The Birth of Austria-Hungary" November 10, 2019. *Look Back History.* Via YouTube.

The Habsburg Empire (Episodes 1-3) "Under the Double-Headed Eagle - Birth of a Pan-Ethnic Empire"; "The Glory of Baroque - Vienna of Maria Theresa"; "The Beautiful Blue Danube - The Maturing Twilight." (2008) Directed by Kumiko Igarashi.

Hitler: A Career. (1977) Directed by Joachim Fest, Christian Herrendoerfer.

"How Did World War 1 Start?" May 5, 2018. Kidsconnect. Via YouTube.

"Salzburg and Surroundings". (2006) *Rick Steves' Europe.*

"Sebastian Kurz's Austrian conservatives bring far right into government." December 16, 2017. Reuters. Via YouTube.

"Top 10 Unbelievable Facts About Europe's Bizarre Habsburg Rulers" August 23, 2020. *OMG Facts.* Via YouTube.

"Vienna". (2006) *Rick Steves' Europe*

"Vienna and the Danube". (2008) *Rick Steves' Europe.*

"What was the Role of Austria as part of Germany in WW2?" July 5, 2020 *Knowledgia.* Via YouTube.

Websites

Aboutvienna.org.

Wikipedia.org: "Arnold Schwarzenegger"; "Austria"; "Biedermeier"; "Chancellor of Austria" "Charles I of Austria." "Ferdinand I of Austria"; "Franz Kafka"; "Graz"; "Gustav Klimt"; "Gustav Mahler"; "Habsburg Dynasty"; "History of Austria"; "Johann Strauss II"; "Maria Theresa"; "Mauthausen Concentration camp"; "Maximilian I"; "Metternich"; "Salzburg"; "Sebastian Kurz" "Sigmund Freud";

History of the Czech Republic: A Fascinating Guide to this Wonderful Country in Central Europe

The History of the Czech Republic

Nestled into Europe is the small country of the Czech Republic. Burrowed deep in the continent next to Germany, Austria and Poland, the Czech Republic is a hilly land filled with steep tradition, proud people and a way of life that has persevered for centuries.

Once known as Bohemia, the Czech Republic was ruled by various other nations for much of its early history and experienced eras of conflict and tumult. Like other parts of Europe, multiple rulers stormed through the country looking to take hold of anything they could. It found itself in the midst of numerous conflicts that threatened to make the Czech people pawns in other peoples' wars for years to come.

The strength and determination of its people and several prominent leaders allowed the Czech Republic to flourish and grow and remain a safe haven for its people for generations and while there were many rough patches ahead, the road to peace and prosperity loomed large for the land and its people.

The Czech Republic is a country that has survived numerous wars and major tensions, a country that has seen itself and others around it fall to the rule of ruthless leaders. It is a country that has become a developed and advanced nation in the modern age and has grown into one of the most peaceful countries in Europe.

The Czech Republic has often been a major player or witness to history.

Origins

There is an ancient legend among the Czech people, one that credits its founding to two brothers. The brothers, Čech and Lech, were out hunting in the wilderness when they spotted different prey. Lech headed in one direction to find his animal while Čech took a different path. The brother Lech would go on to found Poland while Čech would of course end up settling in what would later become the Czech Republic.

This story shows the deep tradition and pride that the people of the Czech Republic feel for their homeland. Those are some of the attributes and attitudes that have helped carry the nation along for so many years through so much strife.

In reality, the creation of the Czech Republic and its people had a much simpler origin. Like other countries across the globe, scientists debate a specific date and timelines but much has been made clear about the beginning of this historic country.

Researchers have uncovered archaic tools in the Czech countryside that date back to 800,000 BCE. That isn't the only historical artifact found in the Czech Republic. The Venus of Dolni Vestonice figure, which is the oldest ceramic creation in history, was discovered in the Dolni Vestonice area in south Moravia.

Stone tools and other objects have been uncovered in parts of the Czech lands, suggesting that it was home to several long, lost tribes like much of the rest of Europe. The Stone Age was a busy time in that region of the world and the hilly and mountainous countryside of the Czech Republic likely provided much game and shelter for the early people. However, they had no idea what that barren landscape would morph into: a modern land with modern people and a rich, diverse history.

Ancient Times

Like the rest of the world at that time, the Czech Republic remained a relatively quiet place with diversified and separated tribes and people dotting the landscape and doing their best to survive the cold nights and various predators.

There have been discoveries that suggest the Linear Pottery culture made their way into the Czech lands around 5500 to 4500 BCE. They were a wide-ranging group of people who began to create simple pottery such as jugs, bowls and cups. The Linear Pottery culture marks a major moment in the history of human evolution, a time when early people grew substantially and both the past and the future merged together to set the course for the rest of human civilization.

The area began to take on a stronger identity around the 5th century BCE, when the Celts arrived.

The Celts took to the Czech lands and named it Bohemia. The Celts would reside in the area until the second century BCE and began to assemble tiny towns across the countryside, merging and breaking apart as old tribes did. There was not much unity in the area; that would come much later. At the time, the land that would later be called the Czech Republic was filled with nomadic and stray tribes. But until then, it was many different smaller regions with different names and one fledgling identity.

The Slavic people made their way into Bohemia in the 6th century. They populated the countryside and more and more flooded in, giving the fledgling area some semblance of culture. Their culture would be tested - and improved - years later with the arrival of Samo.

Samo

Samo was a common merchant who came from modern-day Germany and would go on to become a great leader who assisted and guided the Slavic people populating Bohemia, the modern-day Czech Republic.

During the seventh century, the Avar people came to the Bohemia in hopes of taking it over. Conflict ensued and the Slavic people living in the area were at risk of being overrun and defeated. Every year the Avars would arrive and would steal away wives and daughters and forced payment from the Slavs.

The Slavs were forced to live this way for years, experiencing nonstop violence and misery at the hands of the Avars. In 623, they revolted against their oppressors despite having inferior numbers and less training.

Samo came to their defense with his group of soldiers and he rallied the Slavs to continue fighting back against the Avars. They would prove victorious, thanks to the leadership of Samo. A few years later, Samo would again defeat another group, the Franks, who were invading the Bohemian lands from the west.

The Slavic people would take Samo as their leader, who integrated himself with them and married multiple Slavic women. He would go on to have twenty-two sons and fifteen daughters and it is said he ruled the land for 35 years.

Samo's empire would continue to grow and much of his history has been lost to time. But his importance to the region was massive and it was the first instance of a true identity of the people. It brought them closer together and created something that felt like a nation.

Medieval

The first major state in the area was known as Moravia, or the Great Moravian Empire. It was created by the Serbs, Poles, Czechs (at the time they were still referred to as Bohemians) and Slovaks and revolved around the Morava River.

The timeline for Moravia is murky, as is much documentation from that time period, but it seems that it thrived most in the mid-to-late 800s with a collapse estimated to be around the years 902 to 907.

The proper Moravia era didn't last that long but it was a hugely influential period for the Czech lands. Moravia would see the first taste of Slavic culture, including the Old Church Slavonic language and expansion of Christianity throughout the region. In the 860s, the Glagolitic alphabet, the first Slavia alphabet, would be created.

Moravia would have multiple kings, most notably King Rastislav, who communicated with the Byzantine Empire and asked them to send teachers to the area to educate his people. The influx of teaching at the time was a major boon to the Moravian people.

The area of Moravia would split and fall apart as the empire began to collapse and from it came the Duchy of Bohemia, also called Czech Duchy. It was a principality of the Holy Roman Empire and was formed in the 870s.

This would be a time of conflict for the area, with multiple kingdoms and countries trying to take over and hold control of the latter-day Czech

Republic. While it was a time of great change and constant conflict among various rulers, the people living in the area would use that time to become more educated and enlightened. Many consider this time to be a golden age for the region when population and education boomed. It put the territory into the forefront of the world and became a cultural mecca for many.

After the fall of the Moravian Empire, the Holy Roman Empire swept up the area and incorporated it into its vast wealth. Prague was transformed into an independent center of the area and a cultural hub that provided education to many and set the tone and feel for the population for years. In fact, Prague became the capital of the entire Holy Roman Empire during this time.

Bohemia, the Czech state, would reach the height of its powers in the 1300s when its leader Charles IV became Roman Emperor.

Charles University

During his reign, Emperor Charles IV saw the potential of Czech area and wanted to continue to encourage great growth among his people. Because of this, he knew more education would be key to long-lasting success in the area.

Charles requested that his friend Pope Clement VI establish a proper university and the Pope agreed to it. Therefore, on January 26, 1347, Charles University was founded.

The world of art and expression bloomed under the rule of Charles IV. True enlightenment through not only education and art but also commerce drew great success to the expansive territory. The gold and silver mines of the Czech land were rich and were bringing in great sums of money, which only furthered the advancement of the Czech region.

But there were dark times ahead for the modern-day Czech Republic.

Jan Hus and the Hussite War

Jan Hus was a Czech philosopher and theologian who found himself in the middle of a major conflict that would lead to countless numbers of deaths and destruction throughout the region. He was so influential that an entire war was named after him: The Hussite War.

Hus was a preacher and dean at Charles University, which was seeing great success during his term. However, there was a massive dispute going on in the Catholic Church, one that would find its way into Charles University and alter the course of Christianity and the Czech people.

In the late 14th century, the church was incredibly powerful and its reach was felt all over the globe. However, great debate raged inside the inner workings of the mighty institution.

Two different men claimed to be the true Pope and leader of the Catholic Church. Many nations and people were divided between the two prospective leaders, which lead to a call for reform. One of those reformers was Jan Hus. Hus and his followers would butt heads with the church and King Vaclav IV, who eventually had Hus and his supporters expelled from Prague University in 1412. From there, Hus would wander the country preaching and amassing more followers even though he was then excommunicated from the church for what they called heresy.

In time, the Holy Roman Emperor Sigismund promised Hus safety despite his charges. But he changed his mind and had Hus put to death. Jan Hus was burned to death in July 1415 and his supporters were furious. Multiple conflicts ensued between the church and king and the Hussites.

It would lead to all-out war.

The Pope called for a mighty crusade against those in opposition to him and the Hussite War began. The war would last for years and see much bloodshed as the fate of the church and the Czech region was at stake. In the end, the Catholic Church would begin diplomatic relations with most of the Hussite followers and the war would come to an end in the 1430s. The impact of Jan Hus was felt for generations and his views on religion and social order can be seen in some aspects of Catholicism today. At the conclusion of the Hussite War, the church in Bohemia was a Hussite one. In many ways, the Hussites had won.

Habsburg Rule

More conflict and strife awaited the blossoming Czech region in the years and decades ahead.

The Habsburgs were a massive and ultra-powerful family that ruled many countries in Europe and were looking to expand their grip on the region. In 1526, Habsburg Ferdinand I took control of their empire including the Czech territory.

After so much bloodshed and war with the church, the province had become a mostly Hussite population. But Ferdinand I was a strict Catholic who forced the land to adhere to strict central rule once again. His tolerance of the Hussite Church diminished after a while and he had many priests executed. He also called upon the Jesuits to convert the people to Catholicism.

Luckily, Ferdinand's son Rudolf II was a kinder leader who was much more tolerant of those who thought differently than him. He was also a true believer in the power of the arts and under his rule, the region once again began to produce ample amounts of revolutionary pieces of culture.

But Rudolf's reign did not last long. In 1611, he abdicated the throne and handed off control to his brother Matthias. Matthias would then name his strict and conservative cousin, also named Ferdinand, as the heir in 1617. This caused a massive rebellion among Protestant Czechs and laid the groundwork for a traumatic and bloody conflict between them and the Catholics called The Thirty Years' War.

The Thirty Years' War

Ferdinand II continued to upset Protestants and non-Catholics in the Czech areas and attempted to force all citizens to convert to Roman Catholicism.

The response to that was drastic.

One of Ferdinand II's representatives was thrown from the window of Prague Castle by Bohemian nobility in 1618. It was a blatant rebellion and the beginning of all-out war.

The Bohemian regions had the support of other countries, such as Germany, Sweden and Denmark. These other countries joined the war to defend their allies. For his part, Ferdinand II called upon his Catholic nephew, King Phillip IV of Spain and the war ballooned into an even larger conflict.

The battle raged on across different countries. The vast Ottoman Empire joined in the fray and fought alongside the Bohemians as the Poles joined in on the side of the Habsburg Empire.

More nations would join on both sides as the entire continent became embroiled in a vast battle that cost millions of lives in dozens of nations.

In 1630, Sweden threw its support behind the Protestants and took the fight to the Catholic legions. With the help of Sweden, the Bohemians and other Protestant allies were able to push back their enemies and this led to many more major successes on their side. It would only last for a few years, however. After the death of their leaders, Swedish troops lost their resolve and much of the ground they gained was conquered again by Catholic forces.

War Rages On

In 1635, a treaty called the Peace of Prague was signed. However, it was a short-sighted deal that left out protection for areas in present-day Austria and the Czech Republic. The war continued on as neither side was satisfied with the results of the ill-fated Peace of Prague.

Ferdinand II passed away in 1637, nearly twenty years into the massive clash. But the war continued on without him as his son Ferdinand III now led their forces.

Other notable battles would take place after the change of control, especially since France joined the fighting as well.

The war started to wind down in 1647 when Swedish forces captured Prague Castle from the Holy Roman Empire and Habsburg forces. This left the Habsburgs with only Austria in their arsenal. Despite this, they would to continue running Bohemia after the war's conclusion. In fact, the Habsburgs ruled for hundreds of years more.

In 1648, a series of treaties called the Peace of Westphalia were signed and the Thirty Years' War essentially came to an end. The impact of the war cannot be overstated. It changed the entire way Europe operated, weakening nations while granting more autonomy and power to others. It established fixed boundaries for many of the countries involved in the brutal war and cost the warring nations 8 million lives. It was an insurmountable loss that would be felt for decades to come.

Czech Republic After the Thirty Years' War

The Czech Republic, still called Bohemia back then, was absolutely devastated at the conclusion of the Thirty Years' War. The nation's population was horribly reduced and much of the country was left in complete disrepair and damaged beyond repair.

Perhaps most pressing was the fact that Bohemia was now a Catholic state and Protestant citizens were persecuted and challenged. Additionally, the nation was now part of an empire along with Hungary and other countries. This led to a loss of the once-vibrant Czech culture.

Germanization is the spread of the German language and culture throughout a region and was something that Bohemia and the Czech people suffered from intensely after the Thirty Years' War since the Austro-Germany dynasty ruled the region after the war concluded. This was one of the major reasons why so much of the Czech culture was lost, it was swallowed whole by the empire that ran Bohemia.

Much of the world was hurting after the Thirty Years' War ended but Bohemia was possibly hurting more than most because it not only lost so many citizens, it also lost a lot of its heart and soul.

This time was referred to as The Dark Ages by the Czech people. But the painful transitional period wouldn't last forever. In fact, there were brighter times ahead for the Czech region.

National Revival

Maria Theresa was the ruler of the Habsburg dominion from 1740 until her passing in 1780. During this time, Bohemia saw a great resurgence in its culture and destiny.

Maria Theresa was much kinder and sympathetic to the Czech people and treated Bohemia much nicer than her predecessors did. This sort of rule led the nation to feel more comfortable celebrating themselves and their cultural norms. This would lead to the Czech National Revival, a major turning point for the country and the people in it.

The National Revival was fueled from the inside of the Czech regions, including modern-day Czech Republic. The population had lost so much during the war, including things that most people take for granted such as language and historical facts and legends. Many of the history books and lessons from previous centuries had been lost during The Thirty Years' War and the Czech people took it upon themselves to begin rebuilding their culture.

Starting in the early-to-mid 1800s, Czech citizens across Bohemia began to research and publish work that was related to the development and growth of Czech language and culture. Josef Dobrovsky published a Czech grammar book in 1809 while Josef Jungmann published a massive, five-volume Czech-German dictionary. This work required a lot of research and creation of new words since much of the Czech language had been lost since German became the predominant language.

Jungmann's work also developed much of Czech's scientific terminology and language. This allowed scientists in the region to begin work on more substantial scientific research and development.

At the center of the early days of the revival was The National Museum. The Museum was a paramount part of this national movement. Part of the Museum's efforts to restore the Czech culture was the Matice ceska, a Czech publishing house that released multiple essential works as part of the Revival.

The Bohemian Museum was another major asset to the Czech people during this time. It was a journal that allowed educated Bohemian scholars to publish their work about Czech language, science and history.

It wasn't just scholarly pursuits that were strengthened thanks to the National Revival. Artistic works in the region also blossomed tremendously during that period of the 19th century. Folktales, paintings and music became much more popular during the Revival. Age-old traditions that had been forgotten were suddenly remembered and given new life and there was a strong emphasis on the beauty and charm of the Bohemian countryside, which found its way into numerous pieces of art at the time.

The National Revival was a much-needed time of success, strength and healing for the Czech people. There was a chance after the end of the Thirty Years' War that Bohemia was going to forever lose much of what made it special, including major things such as language and history. It built a stronger sense of national and cultural pride and began building a new generation of Czech that valued education.

During this time, the population of Bohemia nearly quadrupled while many peasants moved from the countryside into the cities to work in manufacturing centers and factories.

There were many successful Czech residents who began to invest in new industrial enterprises, which both gave their fellow residents steady jobs and also laid the groundwork for Bohemia to take part in the upcoming industrial revolution that would sweep across the globe.

It is hard to overstate the importance of the Czech National Revival. Without it, the people could have lost so much of what made them so special. There was a good chance that entire Czech people could have faded away and become something else entirely if it weren't for the National Revival that came from the ashes of the Thirty Years' War and its aftermath.

In the years following the National Revival, the Czech lands and people would demand autonomy as Austria-Hungary, their ruling nation, was split into two counties. Sadly, this was not granted to them. At the same time, industrialization grew throughout Bohemia and many multiple industries exploded in popularity, such as coal mining and textile factories. Engineering became a national cause and the country gained thousands of more hard workers weekly. The working class of Bohemia grew and the population continued to expand as Bohemia became a strong industrialized nation with a booming culture and proud population.

Of course, bad times were once again right around the corner. War was waiting.

World War I

Like the rest of the globe, the Czech people were caught up in the chaos and fear that surrounded World War I. That major conflict that started with the assassination of Duke Frank Ferdinand had paralyzed the entire world and it seemed that everything stopped aside from the war.

Being deep within Europe, Bohemia was in the middle of the unrest. However, the nation and its people were reluctant to join the fight. They didn't want to pledge allegiance to either the Austrians or Magyars. They also didn't want to throw their weight against the Russians and many Czech soldiers surrendered to their fellow Slavs on the eastern front.

Inside the nation's boundaries, another battle was brewing: a battle of ideas. The thought of Bohemia striking out on its own, no longer run by the Habsburg or any other nation or group, was growing. Since the National Revival and the successful industrial boom that was sweeping the region, many Czech wanted a unified and independent nation for them and their families. While millions battled for the fate of World War I, including legions of Czech soldiers, politicians and intellectuals back home were plotting the next step for their people.

One of the people leading that plan was Tomas Garrigue Masaryk. Masaryk was a Czech politician who worked within the Young Czech Party and then the Czech Realist Party. These parties were seen as radical to some, including the ruling class that was dictating the fate of Bohemia. Their aim was to found Bohemian independence for his people and create a truly autonomous state that was free of overlords. They argued that the Czech people and the nation of Bohemia and its satellite countries had for too long been beholden to other nations and interests. The time was now, Masaryk said, for true independence.

As the war raged on, Masaryk took solid aim at Austria-Hungary, the nation that owned and operated Bohemia. Masaryk saw the war as a great opportunity to seek out true independence since Austria-Hungary was deep in battle. The political leader thought that if Austria-Hungary had to go through some growing changes because of the war, perhaps they would be willing to let Bohemia and its people go.

He needed support. He couldn't do it alone. So, Tomas Masaryk created a group called the Czech Committee Abroad, later renamed the Czech National Committee. His organization was a place for others to show their ideas and support for a free Bohemia. In 1914, Masaryk devoted himself to the cause full time and sent his daughter Olga into hiding. They traveled the world and began organizing Czechs and Slovaks abroad. He made the connections he would need if he were to succeed and reach his goal. He was laying the groundwork for a future free nation that would be home to Czechs, Slovaks and any free people who wanted to call Bohemia their home.

Masaryk proved his allegiance to the allies during the war, using his network of revolutionaries to provide crucial intelligence against the Germans and Austria-Hungary. Through his inside sources and spies, Masaryk's committee did much for his cause and the international cause of the allies.

One of the things that Masaryk did for the allies was help uncover a plot that would later be called the Hindu-German Conspiracy. It was an illegal plan formulated between 1914 and 1917 by Indian separatists and German officials that sought to start a rebellion against the British Raj across the globe. Eventually, British authorities cracked down on the planned insurrections and their rule was not disturbed. Members of Masaryk's crew were some of the people who helped discover and reveal the plan. Their help was greatly appreciated by British officials and assisted their goal of establishing international relationships friendly to their pro-Bohemian causes.

Masaryk also established some positive bonds with high-ranking officials in the Russian army, relationships that would prove fruitful as he fought for a truly free state for his people.

In 1914, the Russian high command authorized a battalion of Czechs and Slovaks in Russia. The unit was meant to see heavy battle on the frontlines of the war. It would take some work and political wrangling but Masaryk was eventually able to form a strong and growing group of Czechs and Slovaks ready to fight. He had Russia recruit POWs who had been captured while fighting for Austria-Hungary. With their assistance and a legion of other Czechs and Slovaks who resided in Russia, the First Division of the Czechoslovak Corps in Russia grew to 40,000 members by 1918.

During this time and because of his commitments to the Russian military, Masaryk created strong connections with some of the biggest names on Russia's side.

His fame and respect grew and soon Masaryk was seen as a world class diplomat from people all over the globe. He traveled to the United States in 1918 in hopes of convincing President Woodrow Wilson to support the cause of a Bohemian state without the rule of Austria-Hungary. Upon his arrival on May 5, more than 150,000 Americans greeted him in Chicago. He was joyfully referred to by fans as the future president of the Czechoslovak Republic, a title that honored him even if he found it premature.

On October 18, 1918 after years of making connections and fighting hard and politicking at the highest levels of power, Tomas Masaryk and his allies published the Czechoslovak Declaration of Independence, also known as the Washington Declaration since it was drafted in Washington, DC. The signing came hot on the heels of Austria-Hungary Empire's demise at the end of the war. Their collapse meant the end of the Habsburg's centuries-long hold on Bohemia and a chance to finally create a free state that Masaryk and others had dreamed of for so long.

Czechoslovakia

Upon the signing of the Czechoslovak Declaration of Independence, America immediately came out swinging for the cause. U.S. Secretary of State Robert Lansing proclaimed that all of the allies from World War I were on the sides of the Czechs and Slovaks and that they had the right and to govern themselves as a free nation, nothing less would be accepted. This forceful speech further drove nails into the coffin of the Austro-Hungarian coffin.

On October 28, Czech officials took over control of Prague. The country of Bohemia was now known as Czechoslovakia. Their new, free country was born.

Many of the rights written into their Declaration of Independence are similar to what you see in the American constitution. There is a promise of freedom of speech, freedom of religion and the press too. The document went even further than other countries, though, with its calls for universal rights for women and minorities. There was also heavy emphasis on shared prosperity for all Czechoslovakians and the right to own land and create your own destiny. The constitution also focused a lot on the crimes prosecuted against Czechs by the Habsburgs during their generations of rule.

The new nation of Czechoslovakia was going to be a representative democracy, with citizens voting in elected officials who would then represent them in their form of parliament. It was a strong form of democracy for that part of the world and drew praise from other countries across the globe, most notably America, which claimed

Czechoslovakia as an ally from the very beginning and repeatedly came to the nation's defense in its early fledgling years.

To no one's surprise, Tomas Masaryk was elected president of the newly-formed Czechoslovakia on November 14. He would be re-elected three more times in 1920, 1927 and 1934.

Despite calls for equality across all citizens of the new country, there were immediate issues in Czechoslovakia related to race and ethnic diversity. The greatly different views and religions and cultures of the Czech and Slovak citizens caused a lot of troubles in the early days of the country. It required that the new government continually tweak its approach to finding harmony amongst all the diverse people living in the nation. New progressive reforms were passed to bring about that promised equality, including workers' rights, social security and more.

Czechoslovakia was off to a strong start in terms of industry. With a population of over 13.5 million in 1918, the nation was in control of nearly 80% of all the industry in the former Austro-Hungarian empire. In fact, it was proclaimed to be one of the world's ten most industrialized countries at the time. However, even in that success there was cause for concern. While many of the Czech businesses and industries prospered, many Slovakian areas of the country were far less industrialized and a gap was already growing.

Czechoslovakia was a land of many different types of people. Of course, there were many Czechs and Slovaks but there were many other ethnicities too, including Hungarians, Poles and a large number of

Germans. In fact, at the time Germans were one of the largest minorities in the countries and took up a great amount of Czechoslovakia's population. It was yet another group that was attempting to live together harmoniously and was finding great difficulty doing so.

There were so many vastly different types of people living in one nation, attempting to work past everything and create the country they had dreamed of. However, this valley of differences between all the citizens of Czechoslovakia caused political leaders to find solutions to stop the growing chasm between their people. One of the solutions would be to divide into four territories: Bohemia, Moravia-Silesia, Slovakia and Carpathian Ruthenia. Rules were passed for the entire nation that would adjust the laws and provide special protection to minorities, such as the ability for people to speak their language if their ethnic group constituted for 20% of the population in an area. These attempts were seen as a way to heal the rifts growing but they also came across as short-sighted and unsuccessful to the cause at large.

The structure of the nation and the fact that the government was run by Czech politicians and few if any Slovaks or people from other groups was causing anger among the people of Czechoslovakia. This led to some political parties rising from the frustrations, including the Slovak People's Party. The party called for Slovak independence and was a far-right organization that favored some authoritarian and extreme views. Though the party never seized power, it certainly had an impact on many residents of the young Czechoslovakia.

The nation was finally free but it was experiencing many of the growing pains and inequalities that other nations suffer from. Despite this, Czechoslovakia was proving itself as a booming European nation. It was making its presence known immediately after its creation.

Of course, one of its biggest challenges was right around the corner as a determined and hellbent leader from Germany gathered his forces and cast his eye on all of Europe.

World War II

Adolf Hitler had risen to power in the 1930s and by the end of that decade, it had become apparent that he was intent on expanding his reach across the continent and, frankly, across the globe. He would accept nothing but complete control and saw Germany's future as one that was absolute and filled with countless nations within its rule.

Czechoslovakia was just one of the many countries that Hitler considered rightfully his and it was definitely one of his goals to annex it along with many, many other nations.

As the war really ramped up and began to spread like a cancer, the crisis lay at the feet of Edvard Benes, the second president of Czechoslovakia.

Like his predecessor, Benes was an advocate for a free and independent Czechoslovakia before it was announced as its own nation. He spent much of his time before and during World War I charting the globe and looking for support from others. It was his major cause and drive in life. Born the son of a peasant family, Benes had come a long way from the farm fields of his youth and was now one of the leading Czech politicians. He had risen so much and had learned a lot in his years of service.

All of that would be tested during World War II.

Battle for the Sudetenland

Part of the issue was that there were so many Czechoslovakian citizens with German heritage living in the country as World War II began. They essentially had their own country inside of Czechoslovakia and their own political party, the Sudeten German Party, also known as the SdP. Right from the beginning of Hitler's reign, this political party and its followers wanted to once again be a part of Germany.

The party's leader, Konrad Henlein, met with Hitler in 1938, where he was instructed to push back against President Benes and the Czechoslovakian government. That is exactly what he did. The SdP released the Karlsbader Programm on April 24, 1938. The statement was a declaration demanding autonomy for the German Czechs living in the Sudetenland region of the country. The goal was to be cut free from Czechoslovakia and then align with Hitler and become a part of Germany.

Hitler echoes the sentiments in a speech, saying: "I am simply demanding that the oppression of three and a half million Germans in

Czechoslovakia cease and that the inalienable right to self-determination take its place."

Surprisingly, there were many other nations that insisted that Czechoslovakia give into Germany's demands and allow part of its country to be gifted to the Nazis. Many, including British Prime Minister Neville Chamberlain, thought that perhaps Hitler's desires for rule were limited and that he would stop if he was given some of what he wanted, including the Sudetenland region of Czechoslovakia.

President Benes resisted, he didn't want to give Hitler anything and would not concede part of his country to the dictator. He was still pressured by the other countries to give in but Benes instead went the opposite route and created a partial mobilization in a section of Czechoslovakia in order to push back against a possible invasion from Germany. There is speculation that the mobilization was the result of faulty information from an allied country saying that a Nazi invasion was imminent. Whatever the reason, the sign was clear: Czechoslovakia was not giving into Nazi demands even though other countries insisted they do.

The British government informed Czechoslovakia that they wanted the young country to request a mediator between them and Nazi Germany. Not wanting to upset his allies even more, Benes agreed. At Chamberlain's request, Britain appointed Lord Runciman as the mediator and he immediately instructed Czechoslovakia to find a deal that would make the German Czechs happy. In fact, the SdP received nearly all of their requests short of full independence and the ability to join Germany.

Surprisingly, this did not please the Sudeten Germans living in Czechoslovakia. Instead, they pushed back harder than ever. They held demonstrations throughout their region, demanding more from Benes and the government. In September of 1938, the Sudeten Germans ended negotiations completely with the Czechoslovakian government and their leader, Konrad Heinlein, flew to Germany. It was there that he publicly called for a German takeover of the Sudetenland area of Czechoslovakia.

Things were not going according to plan. Neither the allies like Britain nor Czechoslovakia itself were happy with the path ahead and the possible major conflicts that awaited them.

Britain, still desperate to avoid a widening conflict, actually met with Hitler at this time to hear his demands. They were simple, he said. He wanted the Third Reich to rule the Sudetenland. He claimed that the Czech government was torturing and killing Sudeten Germans and that they belonged under the rightful rule of their homeland. Prime Minister Chamberlain conferred with his government and his allies in France and when everyone agreed to it, they told Hitler they would insist Czechoslovakia give up the Sudetenland.

President Benes and his government refused to give in that easily and claimed that the nation's economy would be left in shambles if they were to allow Hitler's plan to come to fruition. Benes also did not trust Hitler's intentions and believed that if he was given the Sudetenland, he would soon come for the rest of greater Czechoslovakia as well and that in time the complete nation would be his to own and rule.

But the allies continued to push back against Benes, insisting this was the only way to stop Hitler's march to more domination. The British and French gave Czechoslovakia an ultimatum and depended that they accept Hitler's terms. Czechoslovakia did on September 21, 1938. Of course, Hitler was not a man of his word. Just a day after getting what he wanted from Czechoslovakia, he added new demands to the agreement he had worked out. He now wanted Poland and Hungary as well.

The response from Czechoslovakians was swift outrage. They were furious and felt sold out. Mass demonstrations poured into the streets and there were calls for a great military reaction, a defense that would keep the nation intact and safe from Nazi rule.

The Czech military was cutting-edge at the time, one of the most advanced in the world. They were mobilized thanks to a new cabinet assembled following the protests from Czech citizens. This military mobilization heightened tensions and raised the possibility of Czechoslovakia entering full-out war with Germany. For their part, Russia threw its support behind the country and told Czech leaders that they would have their full and unwavering support if they decided to battle against Germany. Benes, terrified of defeat at the hands of the Nazis, refused to move forward without support from the West.

Hitler continued to make his play for part of Czechoslovakia and swore repeatedly that if he was given this goal, his plans would be complete and no other takeovers in Europe would happen. He assured Prime Minister Chamberlain that the Sudetenland in Czechoslovakia was "the last territorial demand I have to make in Europe."

Without Czechoslovakia's knowledge of presence, France, Italy and Britain met with Hitler on September 28, 1938. They then signed the Munich Agreement as a way to appease Hitler and avoid an all-out war. One of the demands was that Czechoslovakia give Germany the Sudeten territory like they had long requested.

Their hands were tied and the outcome was inevitable. On September 30, Czechoslovakia capitulated and gave into demands. The Sudetenland territory was Germany's and Nazi occupation of the region would be completed in just a few weeks, overseen by allied forces.

Benes resigned as president of his nation on October 5, 1938 as he saw the writing on the wall: a complete takeover of Czechoslovakia was inevitable. He hadn't given up on his country yet though and would continue to rule in exile throughout the rest of the war.

By November 1938, Czechoslovakia was split into multiple nations. Germany had taken their claim while Italy and Hungary and Poland took other parts as well. This left Czechoslovakia as a fractured country. But the borders were murky and not set in stone and the nations continued to creep further and further into territory that wasn't there. The newly-formed regions lost 40% of their land to Germany.

The state of what was once Czechoslovakia was in total disarray. Fleeing Germans and Czechs funneled into what remained of Czechoslovakia. Nearly 150,000 refugees filled the increasingly-smaller country.

Meanwhile, the Sudetenland was falling deeper and deeper into Nazi hands. Just a few years earlier it was part of Czechoslovakia but by later 1938, it was one of the most pro-Nazi regions in the world.

Since its inception, Czechoslovakia had come a long way. Thanks to Hitler and World War II, it had fallen a long way as well.

The Second Republic

Czechoslovakia was now known as Czecho-Slovakia thanks to the deals made with the Nazis and the great fracturing of the country. It was now officially three different autonomous units: Slovakia, Ruthenia and the Czech lands (which included areas such as Moravia and Bohemia).

The war was in full swing now and by 1940, President Benes and his shadow government in exile was recognized by the United Kingdom, giving him the power and support he needed to plot the course ahead for his nation, if he were ever able to return to it.

Back in the country that once was Czechoslovakia, Czech troops fought proudly among other allied nations. Benes worked overtime to find peace with nations such as Russia. They signed a treaty in 1943 that allowed greater cooperation between the two nations.

Meanwhile, the Czechs were planning a secret operation that they hoped would shake the Nazi regime to its core. With the assistance of the British government and the oversight of President Benes, Operation Anthropoid was created.

Operation Anthropoid

Reinhard Heydrich was one of the more fearsome Nazi officials during World War II. He was one of Hitler's most loyal officers, and was dubbed the "Protector of Bohemia and Moravia." Essentially, he was in charge of overseeing Nazi rule of most of what was Czechoslovakia. He was also one of the chief planners of the Final Solution, the Nazi term meaning the heartless killing of all Jews.

Heydrich had been running operations in the former Czechoslovakia since 1941 and was known as being a harsh leader who would stop at nothing to appease Hitler and secure ultimate Nazi rule across the world. He was referred to by many as The Butcher of Prague and The Blond Beast.

To show his confidence and belief in his rule, Heydrich was known to drive around his territory in a convertible without much protection. This would end up being his downfall.

On December 28, 1941, seven Czech soldiers who had undergone vigorous training were parachuted into Czechoslovakia. Two of the soldiers then put their plan into motion. After first toying with the idea of assassinating Heydrich on a train, they planned to take him out on his way home from work.

That is exactly what they did. After months of waiting, the plan went into effect. On May 27, 1942 two of the top-secret Czech soldiers ambushed Heydrich's car as his driver took him home. The first soldier attempted to fire but his gun jammed. A second soldier threw a grenade at the open-top car but it landed *next* to the vehicle. The explosion was still immense and greatly injured Heydrich. The soldiers fled on foot, chased by Heydrich's driver and Heydrich himself. However, the Nazi superior could not make it far because of his injuries and he collapsed shortly thereafter.

Reinhard Heydrich would die days later because of the injuries caused by the grenade.

The response from the Nazis was intense and brutal. At first Hitler wanted to slaughter a countless number of Czechs in revenge for the death of his friends and star disciple. In the end, he settled on killing "only" several thousand residents. The only reason Hitler decided to spare some of the Czech residents was because that area of the continent was vital to the Nazis and supplied them with a lot of industrial supplies, they needed the hard workers.

The Nazis set out for their revenge and completely destroyed the towns of Lidice and Ležáky. It was a huge blow to Czechoslovakia and a truly awful act of war by the Nazis. Britain's prime minister, Winston Churchill, was outraged and vowed to level three German villages for every Czech village destroyed. However, the allies did not follow through with that plan.

The assassination of Heydrich was a success but it was met with a heavy cost for the people of Czechoslovakia. It would end up being the only successful assassination of a top-ranking Nazi in all of World War II. That was quite the feat considering how strict and regimented the Nazis were.

There was another consequence of Operation Anthropoid. The plot and its aftermath completely soured Britain and France to the multiple deals that led to Czechoslovakia's dissolution at the hands of the Nazis. They vowed that if Germany was defeated, Czechoslovakia would be restored to its former state. This was a huge win for President Benes and his allies. It assured them that their country could become whole again, thanks to their hard work and commitment to the cause.

More success would come for Czechoslovakia forces. In 1944, Benes signed a deal with Russia that any Czech regions liberated by Soviet troops would be given back to Czech control. This was great news because Russia was a force to be reckoned with, an army that could put up a fight and actually overtake Nazi soldiers. If anyone could free Nazi-held lands, it would be the fierce Russians.

That is exactly what happened. Czechoslovakia was liberated by Soviet Troops and the Romanian Army, aided by Slovak and Czech support troops, in September 1944. The allies also took part in liberating parts of Czechoslovakia. Along with a major civilian uprising, these major defeats to the Nazis were signs that the tide of the war was changing. President Benes watched eagerly as the Nazis were forced out of his country and back into Nazi-owned territory.

Soon, the war would be over, Hitler would be dead and the Czechoslovakian people could get back to the business of running their country and remaining industrialized power in Europe.

In June 1945, a treaty was signed handing over Carpatho-Ukraine (formerly known as Ruthenia) to the Soviet Union. The treaty also called for the expulsion of Sudeten Germans to Germany. It was a treaty that was made possible because of President Benes' hard work while commanding the country from exile.

The expulsion of the Germans from Czechoslovakia became a painful part of the nation's history. The expulsions started in May 1945. They were initiated and carried out mostly by local, armed forces with the assistance of the army. Nearly 1.6 million ethnic Germans were expelled during the time and thousands died in the process, some from violence and many more from hunger and illness. A rough but reliable estimate says that about 270,000 Germans perished in the expulsions.

There were multiple instances of German massacres during the process and internment camps were created by Czechoslovakia as well, which led to nearly 7,000 deaths.

The Czechoslovakian government would eventually show regret for the actions during that time.

Post-war and Inner Turmoil

Now that the war had concluded, President Benes and his allies got hard at work to restore Czechoslovakia to its former state. They had a lot of work cut out for them. This time in the country's history would be referred to as the Third Republic. After a meeting in April 1945, the new government convened and was led by three socialist parties - the Czechoslovak Social Democratic Party, the Czechoslovak National Social Party and the KSC. Other former parties such as the Slovak Popular Party were banned after it was declared that they collaborated with the Nazis during the war. In fact, multiple political parties were limited in their abilities as the new government got on its feet.

The Soviet-friendly KSC party worked with President Benes to avoid much conflict between politicians. While KSC was favorable to working closely with Russia and other Soviet countries, Benes envisioned Czechoslovakia as a "bridge" nation that would work with both Democratic and Communist countries.

However, his desires were met with the sharp reality that the Soviets were very popular in Czechoslovakia following the war. Much of the liberation at the conclusion of the war was because of Russia and in much of Czechoslovakia, they were seen as heroes. At the same time, many Czech residents felt burned by the democracies of the west because of the lead up to the war and the way they felt they had been sold out to Germany. A growing majority of Czech nationals started to favor the KSC party and their allegiance to the Soviets. The KSC made their case even stronger by organizing labor unions across the country, assisting workers with gaining equal rights and benefits. In just over a year, the KSC membership exploded from 27,000 to 1.1 million.

The 1946 elections saw the pro-communist parties grab hold of more power in Czechoslovakia. They used this newfound support to suppress noncommunist opposition and place more of their party members in place of great power. This purge of non-communists would continue over the next few years as the KSC and communist allies made further ground in Czechoslovakian government. They would eventually claim the position of Prime Minister with the appointment of Klement Gottwald.

The KSC would also soon make moves to control much of the media in Czechoslovakia and did their best to ignore or silence non-communist voices. This caused great conflict within the government, especially with President Benes who was hoping to have a cabinet full of non-communists and communists alike. But he was being outnumbered and the communists put pressure on others to resign unless they agreed with them.

Benes would eventually cave to the pressure and install a government that was mostly full of communists or communist sympathizers. On the surface, it seemed that his government was full of a wide variety of politicians but in reality, they were all either communists or working with communists. This resulted in the effective communist takeover of Czechoslovakia.

Communism

On May 9, 1948, the National Assembly of Czechoslovakia, now a fully-communist organization, passed a new constitution. It wasn't a fully communist document but was laying the groundwork for a conversion from democracy to communism.

President Benes refused to sign off on this new constitution but his hand was forced when the people voted for a more pro-Communist approach to governing in late May. President Benes resigned on June 2 and Klement Gottwald became Czechoslovakia's new president on June 14, 1948.

With Gottwald in control now, the country took an even stronger shift towards Communism. The teachers of Marx and Lenin permeated through the culture and the government and the entire education system was taken over by the state, along with other features of everyday life. Private ownership was eliminated in Czechoslovakia and a planned economy was introduced. Anyone seen as a "dissident" was arrested and silenced as Czechoslovakia essentially became an extension of Russia, a satellite country that was adhering to communist views and politics smoothly.

Communists had complete control over the government by the end of the 1940s and as the 50s began, President Gottwald fought to purge anyone who opposed him and Communism as a whole. This results in thousands of Czechoslovakians being blacklisted and families and friends being torn apart. Because of this, the country started to see some fleeing from Czechoslovakia for West Germany, Austria and other anti-communist nations.

The country continued its complete conversion to Communism in the weeks and months ahead, all while President Gottwald's health failed and his relationship with Russian leader Stalin grew stronger.

Gottwald was suffering from syphilis, heart disease and alcoholism. It all caught up with on March 14, 1953 when he passed away and was succeeded by Antonin Zapotocky as President and Antonin Novotny as the leader of his beloved KSC party.

Stalin was effectively running most communist countries in Europe, including Czechoslovakia. He had a heavy hand and interest in all the proceedings happening in any nation favorable to him. However, he was also suffering from great paranoia during this time and was convinced there were enemies working against him in every region. Mass arrests and trials commenced, including many in Czechoslovakia. Anyone who even seemed like they could be against Stalin or could possibly hold any pro-west views was tried and usually convicted. It was a dark time for the country, one in which many hard-working people were sent to prison - or worse - for views they didn't actually hold.

De-Stalinization

In the years ahead, Communism thrived in Czechoslovakia because it had no competition. The clamp down of the ruling party grew stronger still and soon there were few rights that were not dictated and decided by the powers that be. The nation became a driving force of industrialized labor in Europe, producing heavy machinery and investing in coal mining. Its industrial growth in the 1950s was huge but all that hard work was tough on employees and factory workers who had to put up with long hours and draining weeks of labor. It started to hurt the morale of the nation, who saw no end in sight.

While the production output for Czechoslovakia was strong at that time, the quality of the products released was not. In fact, Czechoslovakian quality was rather poor during this time of booming economic growth.

This all came to a head in the early 1960s, when the economy of Czechoslovakia officially stalled. As other nations, even Communist ones, were beginning to move past Stain, Czechoslovakia held tight to their beliefs and loyalty to the former Communist leader. However, this did nothing to help their economy, where industrial growth was now the lowest in all of Eastern Europe.

There was pressure coming from all over for Czechoslovakia to let go of the past, let go of Stalin, and move forward for the sake of their economy and their people. Russia continued to persuade Czechoslovakia to move forward and fall in line with de-Stalinization, which was a method of purging the world of Stalin while still remaining communist. Russia's new leader, Nikita Khrushchev, was attempting to have all communist countries perform well on the world stage and he knew that wasn't possible if they were stuck in the past and clinging to Stalin. He needed Czechoslovakia to join Russia and other nations.

Eventually some Communists inside of Czechoslovakia started to look to reform the nation and update their standards and way of life and side with Russia and other communist countries.

While the KSC was still in control and they showed much resistance to any change, eventually some change would come. By the mid-60s, they were now starting to talk about the powers and benefits of democratic centralism. Their power was more limited and more emphasis was placed on the ability of the people and their choices. Regional committees and governments were given more autonomy and production would be focused on the market and not the will of the government.

Czechoslovakia was leaving Stalin behind and was becoming much more modern. Economists and experts called for more freedom in order to keep the country strong but Novotny and his allies still yearned for central control by the government and hesitated giving it up. But they had no choices as the people of Czechoslovakia started to push back in major ways.

Protests broke out because of Novotny's rule and the people seemed intent on supporting his opponent, Alexander Dubcek, who wanted to run the ruling KSC party. Novotny got no help from Russia, who wanted no part in the conflict arising from within Czechoslovakia. When Novotny was officially defeated and lost his power within the KSC to Dubcek, it marked the end of true Stalinism throughout the government.

Many who still supported Novotny and Stalin were purged from inside the government and a more democratic-minded form of Communism continued to grow.

The Late 60s in Czechoslovakia

Dubcek continued to push Czechoslovakia in a new, modern direction while still vowing support to Russia and Soviet causes. By the late 60s, he was pushing a form of new socialism that was both democratic and nationalist.

Some pro-Soviet party members and supports grew concerned in the following years as anti-Communist sentiment spread a bit more within Czechoslovakia. New parties were forming and their views were different from the KSC and its pro-Soviet stance. Dubcek tried to walk a fine line between pushing back against his opponents and censorship, something he promised would be left in the past.

This was not making pro-Communist officials in other countries happy. They saw Dubcek as being too relaxed about opposition and those pushing against Communism. They felt his "new form of socialism" was failing and would lead to full-on democracy. Dubcek requested to speak with the Soviet Union in order to show that he was still committed to the cause and would not tolerate the loss of Communism in his country. Tensions ran high and some communist countries wanted to intervene with their militaries to put down opponents and dissidents. They needed to know their way of life would be safe in Czechoslovakia and that the nation would crumble and fall into the hands of anti-communist sympathizers.

In August 1968, Czechoslovakia was just one of the many countries that signed the Bratislava Declaration. It committed the countries to the Marxist-Lenin philosophies and allowed the Soviet Union to intervene if a pluralist system of political parties was ever established. This went a long way to appease the Soviets and keep Czechoslovakia in their good graces.

The End of Dubcek and The End of Communism

Dubcek remained in office until April 1969 and the road to the end of his term was met with many problems and crisis after crisis.

In 1968, politicians in Czechoslovakia attempted to make a bid for power within the government that could lead to even more liberal policies that veered further away from the Communist views. As promised, this led to Soviet troops flooding into Czechoslovakia in a bid to keep the peace and keep their Communist country intact. They were immediately met with resistance. Troops expected to be in Czechoslovakia for just four days but remained there for eight months due to the uprising of the people.

This was more than the Soviets expected, they were surpassed by the steadfast determination of the people and their desire to keep the little rights they had been given in the last few years.

Many analysts have later claimed that the Soviet invasion of Czechoslovakia was a sign that Communism was on the way out. Though it would be many years until the Soviet Union collapsed, this was a sign that there were people inside of Soviet-friendly nations who were growing tired of the governments they had. It showed that eventually the people would rise up for something more democratic. It was also a sign that it would cost a great deal of money and manpower to keep citizens in line and could stretch the Soviet army very thin.

When Dubcek did step down in 1969, he was replaced by Gustav Husak. This started the process of "normalization," which was officially called a "restoration of continuity with the pure reform period." It was a return to form and a much stricter governing style that felt absolute and strong. The country suffered for it, including the humanities and sciences. Many were silenced and imprisoned once again and the Communist way of life became stronger than it had been in years. In the years ahead, the nation would stay in this state with little changes. The economy began to suffer and as Czechoslovakia entered the 1980s, the country was in a period of severe economic stagnation and low country morale.

The Velvet Revolution

The anti-Communist revolution that would free Czechoslovakia from its rulers was started in late 1989. It all started with a protest.

A group of students was having a peaceful pro-democracy protest when police arrived and violently broke up the assembly. This caused a nationwide outrage and multiple groups formed to push back against the state and fight for civil liberties. It seemed like the people had had enough.

Millions of Czechs soon supported the Civic Forum, which was a pro-democracy group that was fighting against the ideas of Communism and complete state control. The amount of popularity that the Civic Forum had overwhelmed the Communist Party in Czechoslovakia. They were met with a force they could not fight back against and soon the Communist Party completely collapsed inside of Czechoslovakia. Husak stepped down and shortly thereafter, a new government was put into place.

By June 1990, the first free elections in Czechoslovakia since 1946 took place and 95% of the population participated. More changes at the state and local level were enacted to give citizens true freedom in the voting booth. These events led to certain groups in Czechoslovakia, most notably the Slovaks, calling for more autonomy and freedoms.

After much in-fighting and negotiations, the Czechoslovakian parliament was able to divide the country along national lines to give Slovaks more freedom and retain Czech nationality as well. This created two different states: the Czech Republic and the Slovak Republic. The separation was complete on January 1, 1993.

The Czech Republic

The first president of the Czech Republic was Vaclav Havel, the popular Czech writer and dissident who was known for his gorgeous prose and outspoken political opinions. He would serve as president of the country from 1993 to 2003.

Since its creation, the Czech Republic has once again become a point of pride for Eastern Europe. It is a nation of laws and culture that values personal freedom. And since its split from the Slovak Republic, the Czech Republic has consistently been named one of the safest and most peaceful countries in the world.

The Czech Republic has joined the European Union, OECD, the Council of Europe and NATO. It has also formed and held strong relationships with the rest of the world, including America and Britain.

The Czech Republic's economy has remained strong throughout most of its existence though it has experienced its fair share of problems, especially during the financial crisis of the late 2000s. They are mostly known for their car manufacturers and oil exports.

Because of their rough history related to religious persecution, much of the Czech Republic refuses to declare their official religion or claim no religion at all. In fact, nearly 75% of the country says they are undeclared or atheist. That is the highest percentage of atheists in the world, only behind China and Japan.

The Czech Republic is known for their fine taste in arts and culture too. They have a fine sense of music, film and cuisine. The country has become one of the premiere tourist destinations in Eastern Europe because of their eclectic selection of sights to see and places to explore and foods and events to enjoy. The influence of many cultures can be felt in much of the Czech Republic but everything has a decidedly Czech look and feel too. The people have truly found an identity all their own.

The Czech Republic, now also referred to as Czechia by many, has come a long way from its beginnings. It was once a land full of various tribes without a true solid identity and since then has crafted a solid core with various different people and beliefs learning to exist side by side. It has suffered multiple wars and tragedies and painful growths and decline. Like all nations, it has seen its fair share of both ups and down.

The perseverance of the Czech people and their insistence on having a unified home for themselves is what has kept them strong after all these years. There were times when it seemed that the country would collapse or be swallowed whole by forces larger than itself. But the people pushed on and stayed true to their beliefs and their rights and their desire for true freedom of religion and speech. They have undergone some heavy resistance and have always come out on top.

Thousands of years later, the Czech Republic stays strong despite and because of all the struggles they have endured. They are now seen as a fully-formed and peaceful, safe nation that is the pride of much of

Europe. It wasn't an easy road for them, but the Czech people now have a homeland that is undeniably theirs.

The History of Germany: A Fascinating Guide to the Past, A Look at the Culture, and Famous Historical Events

Introduction

It truly is a journey to see how a country can go from being either a safe-haven or a newly discovered or conquered land to being a modern powerful nation. To trace the lines, lineages, and lessons that carved a nation creates a greater respect, or in some cases, a greater conundrum as to how it got to where it is. In some cases, countries that began on a slow, tedious trajectory are now swinging in full motion, fueled by the energy that their vast history reveals. Other countries have slowed considerably since their grand or tedious beginning. To gain a better understanding of what a country must possess in order to achieve success, the success of the nation must be delineated. For example, in the United States of America, success was achieved when the first settlers were able to worship God, free from the dictates and unrestricted taxing of England. For other countries, that success has been achieved through dictatorships that governed them since their inceptions. And still, there are countries that began as places of a free society but have since seen that freedom evaporate either from a takeover or the entropy of the original government.

In viewing the history of a nation, it is important to remember that one cannot simply judge the history of the nation through the eyes of current context. Arguably, there are tendencies, behaviors, and culturally accepted actions present at these countries' founding that today would repulse a nation. Only when the context of the nation's history is examined can judgment truly be passed on these nations. One country that saw its history begin through a takeover is Germany, once a member of the mighty realm of Julius Caesar. In fact, history credits Caesar with being the first to name Germany, originally naming the land mass Germania so as to avoid mixing up the unsettled land with his other conquered territories. At the time of Germany's founding, Rome had become the mightiest power on Earth. Julius Caesar influenced his troops mightily, resulting in an army that was truly a super power. But Germany would not fall under the hand of Rome; rather, after the reign of Julius Caesar, Germany fell under the power of the Franks who effectively divided the country into West Francia and East Francia. Today, the powers of East Francia are regarded as Germany while the powers of West Francia formed into modern-day France. Germany would achieve notoriety under its first Holy Roman Emperor, Otto I.

In looking at the history of Germany, it is easy to see how Germany has constantly been at the crux of many world-altering moments. For instance, in 1517, Martin Luther nailed his *Ninety-Five Theses* to the door of a church in Germany, igniting the Protestant Reformation and causing several of the states in Northern Germany to defect from the Roman Catholic Church and embrace Protestantism as their religion.

This revival would sweep across the world, that small ember in Germany slowly igniting into a roaring fire. One hundred years later, the world would watch as Germany became embroiled in a civil war of types called the Thirty Years War. Aptly named, the war would be contentious from 1618 until 1648. After the war ended with the monumental and revered Peace of Westphalia, the devastation to Germany's population would be revealed. Nearly 25% of the total population of Germany met their end during the war while a staggering 50% or more of the males in Germany were killed during the war. While the Peace of Westphalia was monumental in that it is still revered today as a document of hope, it also helped to quench the Holy Roman Empire and allowed Germany to finally exist as its own country.

Not all of Germany's horrors died with the Peace of Westphalia, however. In the mid-1800s, socialism began to seep in under the guise of new government and equality. Socialism was accepted by most Germans yet failed to gather traction until the early 20th century. A little after one decade into the new millennium, Germany was led into World War I, a war it would lose miserably at the hands of the Allied Powers, notably the United States. While this war was being lost throughout Central Europe, a young man was watching and seething the whole time. This man loved his country and was determined to ensure his country did not return to lose another world battle. This man was Adolf Hitler.

Prior to the rise of Adolf Hitler, the government of Germany underwent a period of instability. Various types of government would be structured only to have their foundation wiped out by a new set of government officials who wanted to try a new doctrine. In the midst of trying out new forms of government came that fateful day in 1929—the day the stock market crashed in the United States. At first, it appeared the stock market would only cause a depression in the United States; however, that hope soon crumbled as the largest free-market country in the world began decreasing its exports and imports, thereby crippling a large portion of the worldwide economy. Germany fell under the wheel of an economic recession as jobs and food became scarce. Since this recession snuck up on Germany during a time of instability for the government, German citizens were eager to look to someone who promised a stable government. Going further, German citizens were elated by the promises of world domination as well. In suit, Adolf Hitler rose to power in Germany and was crowned the Chancellor of Germany. What would follow would easily be the most devastating period of time in Germanic history. Millions were killed as a result of this man's hatred of one ethnic group of people. In May 1945, the world war finally came to an end but at a steep cost: thousands of Germans had lost their lives and it appeared another 9 million were homeless. The pride and manipulation of one man had devastated a country.

After the war, Germany was devastated; however, it was far from destroyed. The spirit of the people was injured but not crushed and they would one day return to hosting a pride for their country. As a country with no government, Germany was split into multiple smaller countries and some countries, with which Germany had annexed, were once again independent. While the country was well on its way to gaining prestige once again, damages from the coming Cold War would further inhibit the country from a quick recovery. As many people continued to hold hostility towards the German people for the atrocities of the German government, many Germans were deported from their countries or sent to special internment camps for the time being. These days would pass but would not be fully over until the famous relationship between Ronald Reagan and Mikhail Gorbachev was constructed. It was within this relationship that President Reagan uttered that famous cry: "Mr. Gorbachev, tear down this wall." This would largely be seen as the moment of true recovery as families that had been separated were finally reunited and the economy of Germany was finally able to begin growing once again.

Today, Germany stands as an important member of the European Union and the Eurozone. The politics and economy of Germany consistently lead the area and many attribute the Euro's recovery in the early-2000s to Germany's efforts. Germany stands as a great reminder of the resilience of a people. While the German people would have been excused for giving up their freedoms to give control to the government, they persisted and underwent one of the most tumultuous times in the world's history. Even after this moment, the Germans still faced the bitterness of separation with the Berlin Wall but continued to fight back. Even though it took foreign relations to officially bring the two sections of Germany back together, the people of Germany were the fuel for this fire and today, the images of the citizens using sledge hammers, pick axes, and other rudimentary tools to break down the wall are seen as an inspiration to all. Though the history of Germany is riddled with terrible men who manipulated the people, the future of Germany has been forged by that resilience that pushed Germany out of an age of captivity and into an age of modernism. This is the history of Germany.

Humble Beginnings

While there are various unconfirmed rumors of prehistoric dwellings and beings, the first documented people groups within the area now known as Germany were farmers and hunters who were recorded as being from the Anatolia region. While these dwellers are documented based on the history of other countries, there remains no identification as to who these people actually were. The first remnants that historians found were from the Corded Ware culture, a group of individuals who were known to have inhabited an area of land within the southern portion of Central Europe before eventually moving into Northern and Eastern Europe. Between 1300 and 750 BC, various cultures grew strong before dying out and being replaced by other cultures. The strongest of these cultures would be the Hallstatt Culture, which had followed the Urnfield Culture. Today, many of the individuals comprising this culture are now regarded as the Celts; however, there is still disagreement over whether or not the Hallstatt Culture was actually from the Celts. Those familiar with history will remember the ages of metal, more commonly referred to as the Copper

Age, Bronze Age, and Iron Age. These cultures were alive and thriving during these ages of history and are thought to have been the cultures that were responsible for the creation of the multiple trade routes Germany would enjoy for thousands of years later.

With the lack of written history, there is much debate over when the tribes that actually settled Germany came to be. For some, the thought is that tribes generally trickled into the area of Germany until its settlement while others contend that there was a great migration that took place leading to its settlement. Whatever the case, the history between 750 BC and AD 768 is murky at best. Today, the greatest source of truth for the German tribes is the trade routes of the Roman empire. As mentioned previously, the writings of Julius Caesar were meticulously composed. Additionally, there is strong evidence to support rumors that Julius Caesar was actually the person responsible for naming the country. During this time, Julius Caesar had been dominating the settlements of many countries. With the government of Rome growing more powerful with each country it overtook, it seemed that the government would forever be the world leader. As Caesar continued to gather more land, he was having trouble distinguishing between land he had conquered and land he was still set on conquering. Thus, he named Germany "Germania" so that he would know that land was still not conquered. While the land was distinguished from those he had conquered for now, it would soon come under attack, at risk for being conquered on one of Caesar's destructive tours.

Roughly one hundred years before the beginning of the common era, Julius Caesar began another fateful tour, set on destroying country after country until his resources were too thin to go any further. This tour would focus on going across one land block that had previously stopped Caesar: the Rhine River. After building what many to consider the first bridges over the Rhine River, Caesar and his troops made their way into the land inhabited by Germanic tribes and immediately desecrated a few of the tribes. The Germanic troops that had been waiting for Caesar turned and fled further away from the river, leaving Caesar no one to fight. Without coming into contact with troops, Caesar had no indication that any other troops lived in the country and instead of going further, chose to return to Rome. Unfortunately, this would prove to be a costly error for Caesar. When the Roman army returned to their country, the Germanic tribes came out of hiding and filtered with overtaking small factions of the Roman army. Of the most successful tribes was the Suebi tribe. Following their courageous leader Ariovistus, the Suebi tribe crossed the Rhine River and defeated some of the tribes that were stationed there. While Caesar was not worried about the small troop of German soldiers, he was worried that the German soldiers would attempt to settle on the Western side of the Rhine River, leading to Caesar's confrontation with the Suebic Army. Rome was barely touched by the Suebic Army and Ariovistus was forced to return to his home on the Eastern side of the Rhine River. Siding with Julius Caesar, the Emperor of Rome, Emperor Augustus was quick to support the actions of Caesar as vital to ensuring that the Germanic tribes did not mount another uprising against the Roman army. To ensure the Germans encountered resistance much earlier, the Roman Empire led in the construction of several forts along the Rhine River.

Even after the uprisings against the Roman Empire quelled, the Roman Empire was still worried that the Germanic tribes were attempting to unite. Therefore, several Roman factions waded deep into the land East of the Rhine River, the land known as the Germania Magna. Unfortunately, these factions would mean the demise of several Germanic tribes. Originally, the Roman Empire had thought it prudent to simply overtake the German government and impose stringent taxation on the Germanic tribes. That plot was severely hampered by the fact that Germanic tribes operated almost solely independent of each other and almost none of the tribes had any semblance of government. As a result, the factions found no other means of subduing the tribes than the pure destruction of the tribes' homes and lives. Many of the Germanic tribesmen were killed and many were made homeless at the hands of the Roman empire. To date, this was the first time the Germanic tribes had been defeated so broadly on their own territory.

As the destruction of their tribes continued, the Germanic tribes began to realize that maintaining independence as tribes was the surest way to be defeated in separate battles. After some secretive meetings, a plan was made that involved the combining of several tribes. One of the Germanic tribesmen, Arminius, had been studying the Roman faction's movements ever since they entered Germany. With a good knowledge of what the Roman faction was capable of, while also knowing what some of their formations meant, Arminius trained his small group of united

Germans and soundly defeated the Roman faction at the Battle of the Teutoburg Forest. Today, the defeat is considered to be the single most powerful defeat that the German army laid against the Roman Empire. Without this defeat, Germany might have become a part of the Roman Empire and would have seen no chance of maintaining its independence or proceeding to where it is today.

After victory at the Battle of Teutoburg Forest, the German army was further elated to hear that the Roman Empire had decided to consider the Rhine River the boundary of their conquests. No more Roman factions would be coming into the German land. While not all Germanic tribes were free from the hand of the Roman Empire, the majority would not hear of the Roman Empire antagonizing them for a good while. In 200 AD, the German tribes began to seep beyond their land East of the Rhine River. While there had been a few tribes who had chosen to subject themselves to Roman rule just so they could live beyond the Rhine River, the turn of the 3rd century marked the first time that the Germanic tribes were willingly going beyond their borders to discover new land. Along with the rise of Christianity in opposition to the Roman Empire, the Germanic expansion West of the Rhine River would be a leading influence in the eventual destruction of the Roman Empire.

Almost four hundred years after the Germanic tribes were constantly antagonized by the Roman factions, the Western Roman Empire officially fell and the Frankish Empire assumed the position as leader of the Germanic tribes. During the power of the Frankish government, the territories of Gaul and Swabia were taken by Clovis I, a member of the famous Merovingian Dynasty. Clovis was a figure intoxicated by power. He had aligned the Frankish tribes under his influence and would eventually be officially crowned the King of the Franks. Clovis was a man of independence within his views on religion as well, opting to forego the German tradition of assuming Arianism instead to simply be baptized and proclaim his allegiance to the Roman Catholic Church. As a result, Clovis brought the Roman Catholic Church into his family and his family would ensure that the alliance with the Roman Catholic Church survived beyond Clovis's death. Clovis would only reign as King of the Franks for two years until he passed away in 511. After this, Clovis's legacy as king was somewhat damaged when his sons chose to divide the kingdom into multiple parts. One of the most shocking developments was his sons' choice to create Austrasia. This country would undergo a hostile political scene, with many people vying for power in the nation and therefore leaving the citizens in a lurch as to which government they were actually a part of.

While Clovis I was a tremendous king, his greatest contribution included giving his people the inspiration to continue the fight after his death. The Merovingian kings were among the most feared during the 400s and 500s, resulting in the defeat of the Saxons, the Danes, and the Visigoths. These tribes were among the most powerful of the day so their defeat by the Frankish army was astounding. Even with the southern portion of Germany controlled by the Germanic tribes, Saxon rule continued to dominate the northern portion of the country. As the Merovingian leaders continued to fashion government for the land, they set their sights on developing the leadership beyond simply a government that ruled over the entire land mass. Rather, the leaders opted to set up leaders that were considered dukes. These individuals were most often of Frankish descent but in the absence of Frankish leadership, the Merovingian leaders chose a local individual. While the Merovingian kings sought to allow these newly placed leaders as much autonomy as possible, they did seek to align all of the new governments under the Roman Catholic banner and as such, it was considered proper to reject the teachings of Arianism.

As the Saxon government continued to push into German tribes once again, one of the Frankish kings, Charles Martel sought to control the extent to which the Saxons would succeed in their bullying the Neustrians. After diplomatic attempts failed, Martel resorted to war and declared war on the Saxons in 718. Though the war would end without a true conclusion, Martel's son Carloman would continue the war his father started in the year 743. With the focus of the war still on the Saxon government, Carloman took his forces against the powers of Odilo of Bavaria. As the battle waged on with the Saxons, another battle, one that had begun years earlier, was renewed. The Lombards were a group of people occupying the land that is now known as Italy. During the time of the Merovingian kings, they had begun growing their armies, signaling to the Merovingian kings that they were capable of defeating the Merovingian tribes and potentially occupying the Central Germanic government. Charles Martel had previously fought against the Lombards but it would once again be his son who would fight the Lombards, only forcing them to a neutral position with the aid of Pepin the Short. To give perspective of the transitions within the government, Charles

Martel's son Pepin the Short took over as the Duke of the Franks following his death. While Pepin the Short handled the diplomacy of the Frankish kingdom, Charles Martel's other son Carloman acted as the Mayor of the Palace and was highly influential in winning wars for the growing and dominant Frankish army.

In 751, the Merovingian line of kings came to its end with the succession of Pepin the Short to Pippin III, the first of the mighty Carolingian kings to assume the throne. Previously, Pippin III had held position as Mayor of the Palace but was able to succeed to the throne and thus begin a new dynasty of leadership within Germany. During his reign, Pippin III would be a loyal friend of the Roman Catholic Church, ensuring that the land would retain its sovereign nature with the Donation of Pepin. In short, the Donation of Pepin would be the foundation for the coming Papal States, which placed the country under the leadership of the Pope. It seemed as if Germany were following the blueprint of the Roman Catholic Church at the time; however, times would change very quickly.

Around this time, one of the most loved Frankish kings, Charlemagne, began his famous war against the Saxons and the Avars. Following in the footsteps of previous battles against the Saxons, the Frankish army was more than ready to fight the bitter foes. Charlemagne would eventually be known as Charles the Great and would be rewarded for his military success with the leadership of the Frankish empire during the years 774 until 814, one of the longest rulings of the early Frankish kings. Ten years before the end of the reign of Charles the Great, the wars with the Saxon government would end with the defeat at the hands of the Frankish army. Charles the Great did anything but go easy on the bitter rivals of the Frankish Empire, taking over their lands and forcing the people of the land to disavow their previous faiths in exchange for Christianity. Such a drastic change from the paganism of the land greatly humiliated the Saxon people; however, there was little they could do given the fall of their government. In 768, a new leader came atop the Frankish throne. While this ending was a time of jubilation for the Frankish people as their beloved military leader now became the leader of their country, it also marked the end of the Middle Ages in Germany. Despite a rocky and nearly quelling start, the Frankish people had regrouped and were now among the leading powers of the land, a power so forceful people from other countries feared imminent attacks from the Frankish army. While the early period of Germany's history was filled with war and devastation, the Middle Ages would see a turn to the religious movement of the day, signaling a new era for Germany.

THE MIDDLE AGES OF GERMANY

With the death of Pepin the Short in 768, Charles the Great was named the leader of the Frankish government. Among his first actions as king was the continued war with other nations. Charles the Great was a military genius and one whom had the respect of his men. Only six years after taking the throne of the Frankish people, Charles the Great also took another throne: the kingdom of the Lombards. One would remember that earlier, Charles the Great had been the one who brought the Lombards to neutrality against the Germanic tribes. The Lombards did not take too kindly to this forced takeover and immediately staged an uprising. Though it would take two years, the Lombards would eventually win the throne back from the Frankish government and in doing so, would injure the pride of Charles the Great. When Charles was unable to regain control of the Lombards, he resorted to overtaking nearby kingdoms such as the Saxons and the Bavarians. Charles the Great's injured pride was given all the remedy it needed on Christmas Day in 800 when the Pope of the

Roman Catholic Church, Pope Leo III, officially named Charles the Great, Imperator Romanorum, which is translated to mean the Emperor of the Romans. Finally, Charles the Great was the most powerful man in the world.

For the next fourteen years, Charles the Great would rule as the Emperor of the Romans; however, his death in 814 marked the end of an era as those who would succeed him were caught dividing the freedom rather than sharing it. Charles the Great's grandsons had apparently all inherited his resilience against giving up and therefore, the kingdom of the Franks was divided into three different countries. This was all made official in 843 with the passing of the Treaty of Verdun. To divide the country, Charles the Great's son, Louis the Pious, was first given authority of the Carolingian empire. It had been Louis's desire to see the kingdom divided into the three smaller portions so that he could rule the country as a whole with the aid of his three sons. Eventually, this would lead to the three sons, Lothair I, Louis the German, and Charles the Bald receiving portions of the kingdom. Originally, Lothair I had been aligned to receive the most land and therefore the most authority; however, this dream was destroyed when he decided to claim the entire kingdom for himself and therefore led to a civil war where the brothers actually fought against each other. After ending the civil war at the Battle of Fontenay in 841, the Oaths of Strasbourg solidified the agreement the three brothers held to divide the country into three parts. Included in the agreement was a portion that ensured Lothair would never again rule the Frankish kingdom as a whole.

In dividing the land among the three brothers, Lothair I was given Middle Francia. In all, Lothair was the least powerful of the kings. Louis the German, Louis the Pious's second son, was given East Francia. Of the three kingdoms, East Francia would go on to be the most powerful. That left the remaining son to receive West Francia. The kingdom would remain divided until the leadership of Henry the Fowler who divided the kingdom as a federation. Also of importance was Henry the Fowler's status as the first king of the Carolingian Empire who was not a Frank. After Henry the Fowler, Otto I assumed the throne in 936. Otto I was crowned the emperor of Germany by the pope at that time, Pope John XII. While Otto I was crowned king in 936, he would not be crowned emperor until 962 after he had been crowned the King of Italy in 961. One of Otto's achievements as king was the creation of a national church. Otto became even more powerful than many of his previous followers, going so far as to begin the tradition of appointing the bishops and the abbots. In doing this, Otto effectively extended his power throughout the kingdom, all under the facade of the "autonomous" bishops. During Otto's reign, he would lead in a heroic defeat in the Battle of Lechfeld where the Hungarians would be defeated soundly.

Otto's reign ended in 973 and the next great king of Germany would be Henry III who reigned from 1039 until 1056. During his reign, the Roman Catholic Church underwent a great transformation as the focus shifted from creating ornate buildings to reaching out into the communities surrounding the kingdom. Specifically, a greater emphasis was placed on the poor of the country in addition to preserving some of the traditions of the religion through the sponsorship of artists. After the reformation of the church, known as the Cluniac Reform, took place, the Roman Catholic Church in Germany took its endeavors a step further and advocated for peace throughout the world with the Peace of God. This is largely regarded as the first time in history that a movement of peace across the world was created, much less by the religious leaders of the world. While the Peace of God was designed to give the people a peaceful country, it was also designed to give the Roman Catholic church more power, as demonstrated by the practice of simony which followed the Peace of God. Simony is the practice of selling specific clerical offices within the church. Previously, these positions had been appointed; however, with the rise in popularity of the Roman Catholic Church, the popes realized the monetary gain that was represented by such positions. The final element of the Roman Catholic Church during this time period was the continuation of an act that had begun years earlier within the Roman Catholic Church: celibacy. Henry III continued to advocate for the abstention from marriage by all popes.

Henry III's kingdom would mark the pinnacle of the power that the government would exercise over the Roman Catholic Church. One would remember that there had always been a battle between the Roman Catholic Church and the governing authority of the Franks, or Germany. This battle reached a new climax under the authority of Henry III when he proclaimed the greatest extent of authority over the Roman Catholic Church that had ever been attempted. In response to such actions, the Roman Catholic Church constructed the College of Cardinals, which was essentially a governing body of Catholic leaders known as the Cardinals. While the College of Cardinals established a papal authority the likes of which had never been seen before, this authority was further demonstrated in the ensuing Dictatus Papae, which sought to give the authority of the land solely to the papal state. The ensuing kingdom of Henry IV would see even more conflict between the governing parties as he refused to accept the document as valid. When the Roman Catholic church grew rebuffed at his refusal to admit their authority, they proceeded to excommunicate the king from the Catholic church. Such a move was likened to being sentenced to an eternity in Hell and so King Henry IV obviously obliged the papal authority. In 1077, Henry IV was reinstated into the Roman Catholic Church when he surrendered in the fight over authority with the church at Canossa. This ordeal would later be recalled under the title of the Investiture Controversy. Though the king had formally submitted to the authority of the Roman Catholic Church, the relationship between the church and Henry IV would never be reconciled beyond his reinstatement into the religious function.

In the subsequent kingdom of Henry V, the soured relationship continued to wreak havoc on the country as the power struggle was renewed once again. With the power struggle eating away at the reputation and influence of Henry V, the king chose to sign the terms of the Concordat of Worms, an agreement that solidified who was truly allowed to appoint the bishops around the kingdom. Additionally, the agreement laid out the grounds on which a Pope would be appointed upon the death of the preceding pope. Incidentally, this power did not involve the German government or king. Once again, a king had dared to challenge the supremacy of the papacy and once again, the papacy had won and gathered the greatest authority in the land.

Today, the commerce of North America is greatly influenced by the conditions of NATO. During the Middle Ages, the commerce of Germany was largely controlled by the Hanseatic League, an alliance that included the various guilds that were comprised of the merchants and seafarers from around the country. The region most affected by the Hanseatic League was the land within the Baltic Sea, North Sea, and adjoining rivers. While many think of the Hanseatic League as a sophisticated means of transporting goods from one merchant to another, it truly went much further than that, with many merchants entering into pricing agreements and taxation privileges that ultimately benefited the merchants more than it did the citizens. The league would gradually continue to grow in power until it had secured the support of the most populous cities in Germany, effectively joining the heart of the Germanic commerce system under the wings of the guild. While the guild began as a means of benefiting the merchants through support, it grew in power until it had sufficient military backing to enforce new policies with force if needed. For a while, the military support was not used unless the merchants deemed it absolutely necessary. As is true with most instances of excessive force, the power was quickly abused by some merchants, driving the country into a war with Denmark. The war would last until 1370 but would fall short of crippling the Hanseatic League. In fact, the league would continue until 1450 when the league was unable to maintain its velocity for a number of reasons. Though the league had reached failure, the Hanseatic League is considered to be among the leading forces of modernization within Germany as it helped to pave the trade routes between the countries of Europe.

Moving Forward

In 1111, the Germanic kingdom would get a glimpse into the future of its politics when Henry V decided that it was his time to occupy the throne and lead in the overthrow of his father from the throne. As mentioned earlier, Henry V shared his father's sentiment against the Roman Catholic Church and therefore took up the fight against the seeping power church. Coming off the heels of the Investiture Controversy, Henry V added his chapter to the controversy with the appointment of Adalbert of Saarbrucken for his newly created position of Archbishop of Mainz. However, Adalbert fueled the fight in opposition to King Henry V, possibly because he found the new powers of the Roman Catholic government intoxicating. The official chapter of the Investiture Controversy dedicated to Henry V would be known as the Crisis of 1111. Twenty-six years after the overthrow of Henry IV, those tasked with finding the next prince of the government chose Conrad III. When Conrad III made the rash decision to take the duchies of Bavaria and Saxony from Henry the Proud, he subsequently thrust Germany into another war. This misstep would actually result in the division of the government into two parts. Henry the Proud was supported by the Welfs or Guelphs while the House of Hohenstaufen, the family of Conrad III, was supported by the Wailblings or Ghibellines. With the two respective leaders now able to fashion their government as they saw best fit, the two governments would take almost polar opposite approaches. While the Welfs were concerned with maintaining independence from the church, the Wailblings welcomed the opportunity to control the church and established this controlling arm of the government on the foundation of an imperial government.

These two groups of people would go on living in separate governments until the reign of Frederick I. Frederick I was from the Hohenstaufen line of kings and manufactured peace between the two nations when he was able to orchestrate the return of the Duchy of Bavaria to Henry the Lion. Henry the Lion was the son of Henry the Proud and was the current Duke of Saxony. The other duchy that had been taken and therefore was at the heart of the matter was the Margraviate of Austria. Instead of returning this duchy, it would be allowed to become an independent duchy, known as the Duchy of Austria and formally agreed to in the Privilegium Minus the same year.

During a period of time between the 11th and 14th centuries, Germany entered a new period in which the country began migrating to the east. This migration is now referred to as the Ostsiedlung, which translated means the Eastern Settlement. While the migration was encouraged, it was not supported financially or with instruction, leading to a very unsystematic means of migration as people simply moved on when the current opportunities dried up. The land the Germans were traveling to was hardly unsettled, the Slavs and Balts having been inhabitants for years upon the arrival of the Germans. During the latter months of the great migration, the German government began migrations of their own, in search of paganism among the tribes that were being settled. Any tribes that were found to be practicing paganism were either captured by the Germans or run off the land. This land would be held by the German troops until the disorganization of the migration led to fewer troops than appropriate being left in guard of the territories and subsequently losing the land as neighboring tribes grew in strength and began opposing the German army's advancement. In 1106, Lothair II had been appointed the Duke of Saxony and in 1133, would be crowned the Emperor of Germany. Two years later, Lothair would overtake Poland, Bohemia, and Denmark where he would construct a form of sovereignty. Lothair was not supportive of the conquered country's form of government and subsequently led in the reconstruction of the government, following Germanic traditions in each of the governments.

In the late 1100s, Frederick I began imposing his feudal form of government on some of the conquered land in the northern portion of Italy. This infuriated the country and church alike, bringing the country together to form the Lombard League. In 1176, the people aligned together as the Lombards were able to soundly defeat Frederick I during the Battle of Legnano. After a brief respite, the two sides were able to come an agreement that would be formally signed by Frederick I and Pope Alexander III and named the Treaty of Venice. The true peace would not come until 1183 when the two sides would meet yet again and sign the Peace of Constance.

Frederick I would be remembered as one of the few emperors who truly paid attention to the culture of the country. In the five years of his reign, Frederick I made perhaps his greatest contribution to the German society with the construction of the Diet of Pentecost in 1186. This meeting was held between the numerous members of the Holy Roman Church and precluded the royal wedding in which his son, Henry, would be wed to the princess of Sicily, Constance. After the death of Frederick I, Frederick would establish his throne and rule from 1212 util 1250. The reign of Frederick II would be best remembered for his rule from Sicily where he had established the state. Following in his father's footsteps, Frederick II would continue to conquer small portions of Italy at a time. This obviously led to serious arguments with the popes and entire Roman Catholic community. While Frederick would be remembered for this ruse against the Catholic Church, he would also be remembered for his blunt disregard for the Catholic precepts. Whereas previous emperors had been heavily influenced by the threats or actions of excommunication, Frederick II was unimpressed by such measures and committed acts of treason against the Roman Catholics such that he was excommunicated on three occasions. While this may not have done anything to the esteem of Frederick II, it did fuel the Roman Catholic Church while driving away support from Frederick II, leading to the destruction of the Hohenstaufen line of kings. Following his death in 1250, the government would be unable to procure a king for an astounding 23 years. Even after an emperor, Rudolf of Habsburg, was found, there was little respect for this man and the government of Germany fell into ruin.

The Spark that Started the Fire

Moving past the period of time in which emperor after emperor tried to rectify the government from the destructive run of Frederick Barbarossa II, the days of 1347 through 1351 were even more trying than the destructive government. During this time, a pandemic gripped the hearts of the Germanic and European people as the people witnessed the death of nearly 60% of Europe's population. Whereas the government had been having trouble gathering traction under another dynasty such as the Merovingians or Hohenstaufens, the country was now gripped in an economic depression due to the inability of the people to work. The people of Germany grew desperate for change, leading various people groups to begin attacking each other. In stark alignment with future actions within the country, the Jews were seemingly the common target of the destruction, with some going as far as to assert the Jews were responsible for the pandemic. With their people being bullied and sometimes killed, the Jews were forced to run from Germany, choosing to settle in Eastern Europe while awaiting the end of the Black Plague.

Even after the Black Plague began to dissipate, it left destruction in its wake with the government unable to control the people. Resistance against the government became commonplace and crimes skyrocketed. This unrest was further fueled by the Great Schism in which the Catholic Church was divided between two men who claimed they were the pope at the same time. With no governmental authority, the people divided between obeying one of two churches, and the Jews being incriminated for their alleged involvement in the spread of the Black Plague, rifts were running rampant through Germany. Indeed, it seemed as though the Black Plague had ushered in a disease more deadly than the plague itself. While the government desperately tried to grasp the remaining strings of authority, the people aided in the ushering in of a new form of government. Whereas feudalism had previously fueled the country's social classes, the Black Plague uprooted this social order and replaced it with the burgher class. Now, feudalism stood by the wayside as cities began to be erected and financial gains began to return to the country. Capitalizing on this gain would be one family in particular: the Fuggers of Augsburg. With a good deal of financial support, the Fuggers became the leading political family in the country and would remain so until the mid 1500s. During this time, the disparity in wealth by the Germanic people began to lead some of the knights into a new profession called Robber Knights in which they essentially hired themselves out as mercenaries of the people. When some of these knights found that this was not as effective as they wanted, they proceeded to demand that the people hire them for simple protection or they would not help them. Later in the fifteenth century, a new family assumed the leading dynasty of Germany and were able to gather a great deal of power in the country. This family was the mighty Habsburg family, the famed dynasty that would rule Germany until the 1800s.

Even with a new dynasty atop the government, the people of Germany refused to comply and their cooperation was still forced. The result was more rifts within society but now these rifts had consequences. During the second kingship within the Habsburg dynasty, Maximilian I tried his hand at doing something that had not been accomplished since Frederic II years earlier: peace among the people. When the people refused his demands for peace, Maximilian I attempted to coerce them into peace with higher taxes. The result was the obvious growth of rebellion towards the king. Germany was failing and failing fast.

Almost one hundred years after the mighty Habsburg family came to rule Germany, the Catholic Church began to assume the authority from the family. While the family still ruled the country, they had reduced their reliance on the imperialism of the government while decreasing the ecclesiastical independence. With the people firmly united against the government, the Catholic Church swept in and began to feed off of this discontent, making a profit off of the people's willingness to trade compliance with the government for respect from the church. The height of this profit from the people occurred in the early 1500s when the church began selling certificates that supposedly retrieved a loved one from Purgatory. Rather than let one's loved one suffer in the Catholic eternal torment of Purgatory, the Popes began selling "indulgences," which allowed these people to transition from Purgatory to Heaven. In addition, the Roman Catholic Church once again began profiting from the sale of official church positions.

While much of Germany bought into this false sense of security, there was one man who dared to stand up to the Roman Catholic Church, a monk who had actually pledged his life in allegiance of the church. Using the Bible as his authority, this monk, Martin Luther, began penning various counterarguments to the Catholic Church's current practices. The result would be one of the most famous decrees of modern time: the Ninety-Five Thesis. Upon completion of the document, Martin Luther took the document to a church in Wittenberg and nailed the document to the door, taking time to hand out subsequent copies of the presumed thesis to various government officials. Among the counterarguments as presented by Luther were calculated attacks against the Catholic Church, something that could have ended with his death if the Catholic Church found his actions detrimental to their cause. Upon the publishing of his document, Martin Luther became somewhat of a celebrity within the community, that popularity waning quickly when showed to the Catholic Church. While the Catholic Church was incensed that he would write such an accusation, the people were excited that someone had finally created a cause that went against both the government and the church. Recalling that the people of this time were still set on disobeying the government, one can only imagine how much unity came as a result of the new war that Martin had waged against the Catholic Church.

The Ninety-Five Thesis was just one man's assertions of what was wrong with the Roman Catholic Church of the day; however, its popularity quickly spread beyond the borders of Germany, leading to the moment in history that is now known as the Protestant Reformation. The year was 1521 and Martin Luther had just become the sole focus of the Roman Catholic Church. In a bit of irony that both amused Martin and his followers while also showing how the Roman Catholic Church completely missed the point of the Ninety-Five Thesis (disavowing the edicts of the Catholic Church), the church's first response to Martin Luther's assertions was to excommunicate Martin Luther, an act that many would assert had already taken place when Luther proclaim the hypocrisy and fatality of the Roman Catholic Church as outlined in the Ninety-Five Thesis. Nonetheless, Martin was removed from the church, a move that only added to his popularity. Now, rather than paint Martin as a villain who was attacking something holy, the Roman Catholic Church had painted Martin into the very fuel that leads to small social movements creeping beyond the tipping point: martyrdom.

For Christians, Martin Luther's inspirational message could not have come at a better time. Sparking the Protestant Reformation led to a renewed desire to see the Bible translated into the language of everyone. Through this time, the Bible had not been translated from Latin, leaving the Popes as the only ones who could read the Bible. Without being able to read the Bible independently, the Germanic people had no way of challenging the teachings of the Popes, perhaps being the leading influencer in the ability of the popes to sell indulgences even though that practice is mentioned nowhere in the Bible. Right around the time

Martin was leading the cause against the Roman Catholic Church, the printing press was being perfected in another part of the world. However, soon, the fuel from the Ninety-Five Thesis and the printing press would unite, creating a result that would become the most published book of all time: the Bible.

As a result of the Diet of Worms, Martin Luther was sentenced to death; however, he would escape from death in a mysterious fashion, living out the remainder of his days within the Wartburg Castle under the name Knight George. During these days within the castle, Martin would continue to translate the Bible. Were the Protestant Reformation to maintain its feverish pitch, the people would need to have a copy of Martin's source in their hands soon. Martin's exile from society due to safety would lead to his completion of translating the Bible into German. Of particular interest, Martin Luther did not speak the most popular dialect of German. Rather, he spoke a dialect that was only found in specific parts of Germany; however, with his authorship of the translation of the Bible into German, the people began reading his dialect and thus, his dialect grew to become the most popular dialect of German—all because of the printing and distribution of the Bible. In 1529, Martin's name would forever be remembered with the creation of the Lutheran Augsburg Confession, leading to the creation of the Lutheran Church, which continues to this day.

While the people of Germany quickly jumped from Roman Catholicism to the edicts of the Protestant Reformation, the Catholic Church was deftly preparing an attack that would wage ware between the new Lutheran Christians and the Roman Catholic Christians. The rebuttal to the Protestant Reformation would take until 1545 to come to fruition but would eventually be known as the Council of Trent. Leading this effort was the Jesuits, a new brand of Christianity that had been developed in 1541 by Ignatius Loyola. While Martin Luther had accomplished his reformation of the Catholic Church with writing, the Roman Catholic church's rebuttal would eventually be known as the Catholic Counter-Reformation and would focus on both writings and political force if necessary. Very quickly, the war between the Protestants and the Roman Catholic Church went further than diplomacy or writings. Soon, the Protestants had formed their own league, the Schmalkaldic League. In 1547, Charles V would emerge victorious against this league but outrage from the public led to the Roman Catholic Church officially recognizing the Lutheran Church as a true religious sect that would be honored. In retrospect, the effects of the Protestant Reformation are so much greater when compared with the Catholic Counter-Reformation of the day. While Charles V may have defeated the leading Protestant military league, the two sides would never come to agreement and the Protestant Union would emerge as the leading influencer of the Lutheran Church while the Catholic League would help support the dwindling Roman Catholic church.

The Catholic and Protestant groups would come under their greatest conflict in 1618, just two years before the Pilgrims would arrive in the New World. From 1618 until 1648, the Catholic and Protestant factions would war in what would become known as the Thirty Years War. The root of the war was focused on religious freedom as the Catholic Emperor

Ferdinand II was attempting to quell any factions of religion that would divert the country from being unified solely on religion. Today, this war remains one of the leading blights on the German people. All Germans were harmed from the war and the result was almost worse than the effects during the war. After the war was over, the economy remained stagnant and the countryside remained a testament to the pillaging that was commonplace during the war. With the men fighting, women were left to maintain the home, many of these women being raped or terrorized by thieves during this time. In addition to the war, the people of Germany also experienced droughts during this time which led to famines and hunger throughout the entire country. Everyone within the country became suspicious of one another, especially after the people were subjected to random searches regardless of whether they were guilty of subverting the Roman Catholic Church or not. During the war, the rate at which women were having babies dropped dramatically, leading to an overall decrease in the population by almost 38%. In 1648, the country was united under the Peace of Westphalia, which gave the world what many consider to be the prime example of what treaties of international proportion should resemble.

The Lasting Effects of the Protestant Reformation

While the Peace of Westphalia ultimately gave more power to the states controlled by the Roman Catholic Church, the Protestant Reformation will forever be remembered as the most transformative movement of the country and one that is enjoyed to this day. One of the greatest implications of the Protestant Reformation was increased literacy among the Germanic people. With the Bible written in Latin, people had held no ability to read the Bible, leading many to give up on literacy all together. With the Bible now being translated into German, there was a renewed interest on literacy since the Germanic people wanted to read its words for themselves. Beginning with Martin Luther's inspiration in 1517, there would be an estimated 10,000 religious works written and distributed. In addition to being literate in German, many Germanic people also desired to be literate in different languages, causing many to increase their literacy and thereby grow smarter.

This new love of learning led to a new interest in the heavens and science as well. Today, the name Johannes Kepler is remembered as being one of the leading influencers on the current understanding of the solar system and atmosphere. Kepler would go on to give the scientific community the laws on planetary motion while the works of other German scientists would inspire other scientists from outside of Germany such as Nicolaus Copernicus. Copernicus is of course remembered for going on to asserting the heliocentric motion the earth's orbit. Also inspired by Johannes Kepler was Galileo Galilei, most remembered for being the Father of Observable Astronomy. Perhaps the most well-known scientist to emerge from this time period though is a man known as Isaac Newton who would go on to propose the theories that govern the modern understanding of the gravitational force on Earth.

Given the surge of patriotism due to the Protestant Reformation, it was only a matter of time before some of the government officials of Germany figured out how to use this patriotism to their favor. In 1640, the age of exploration was beginning to overtake countries as they set their eyes on countries not yet discovered. One state within Germany that had always shown signs of being among the most active states was Prussia. Little changed in 1640 when Frederick William, referred to as the Great Elector, assumed the kingdom of Prussia and began reuniting the stragglers from the fringes of the kingdom. Eight years after taking control, Frederick held a part of the Peace of Westphalia when he helped end the Thirty Years War; however, his aid did not come without a cost. Rather, Frederick was able to gather the territory of East Pomerania.

From this point forward, Prussia would grow in strength and would remain so until the country was separated following the world war.

One would recall that the Thirty Years War devastated Germany's population. What started out as a dispute over religious freedom quickly grew to be one of the deadliest wars in history. This plight of the population was foregone in 1700 when the population of Germany began to grow. In 1700, the population stood at 17 million before growing to 24 million only one hundred years later. The growing population was most likely fueled by the stability of the country's economy and sustainability. Suddenly, the country was able to succeed on its own, the farmland slowly growing back while the economy of the country grew healthier.

In the late 1600s, Germany was the focus of another war when France became determined to harvest some of the fringe land out from under the watchful eye of the German government. As a result, Germany and France would enter the War of the Grand Alliance. The war was fueled by the carelessness of Louis XIV. While also defeating the lands, Louis XIV took it upon himself to lend his own interpretation to some of the previous treaties. This collection of re-interpreted treaties included the Peace of Westphalia, which Louis XIV intentionally misinterpreted. As a result, Louis XIV continued to annex nearby countries mercilessly, stealing the citizens and land of the nearby countries with reckless abandon. This annexation would meet resistance in 1697 when the Grand Alliance began to fight against the suppression of the French government. This fight would go on for a few months but would eventually be deemed ineffective and simply a drain on the financial resources of both countries. As a result, no formal agreement was ever reached and neither side conceded the battle; rather, both sides simply returned to their country under the good faith that the opposing party would do their part. The land stolen by France would eventually be returned to Germany under the Treaty of Ryswick.

After the threat of the French army was abandoned, another threat rose against Europe, once again from within Europe. This time, it would be the mighty Ottoman Empire. The Ottoman Empire was known for being fierce and as a result, the European countries realized that coming together was likely their only assurance of defeating the empire. As a result, the Holy League would be established with its sights set on the Ottoman Empire. The Holy League would largely be successful in its defense of Europe from the Ottoman Empire and Hungary was restored.

In looking at Germany during this time, the two powerhouses of the states were Prussia and Austria. The next countries in regards to performance were not even close. The disparity became so great that people started moving away from these smaller states and moved to the either Prussia or Austria. As a result, the governments of these smaller countries became terribly inefficient, leading to a great disconnect between the governmental leaders and their constituents. Two of these countries were Bavaria and Saxony. Both of these countries suffered the brunt of the various wars that took place in the land during this time. During the years of 1760 until 1785, the famous Frederick II, self-proclaimed "The Great," ruled and followed in the footsteps of those who were far more concerned with the paycheck accompanying the duties than the actual completion of the duties themselves. While Frederick II is remembered for his mismanagement of the country, he is more remembered for his radical government mentality known as Enlightened Absolutism. Under this belief, the government authorities would grab the popular ideas of the Enlightenment and restructure them in a way that led to them having more power. The leadership style could be compared with that of Machiavellian but more focused on the actual influence and less coercion. Enlightened Absolutism worked for the government because it convinced the people that the religious teachings of the day were completely in line with giving more authority to the government. Perhaps the most egregious error of Frederick II's reign came when he was propositioned the financial gain of lending his soldiers to Great Britain for the purposes of fighting the colonists in the American Revolution. These lent soldiers were known as the Hessians and would become a staple of the British war policy and strategy.

Following the reign of Frederick II, changes began to come to the people of Prussia and even Germany. Previously, the social classes of Germany had been uprooted when feudalism was disbanded. Now, peasants had replaced the servants of the day—expected to maintain the community through caring for the aspects of the city that were more unpleasant. Eastern Germany had never fully done away with the feudalism and the practice of serfs continued to lead their society. Beginning in 1770, the people of Germany began to gather more freedom as the serfs were given their freedom from the government. Not all serfs were free at once but a good number were systematically freed from their previous obligations. This meant for the first time that the liberated serfs were able to own land, grow their own food, and begin a life for themselves. While the engine of this movement came from within, the fuel for freeing the serfs came from the writings of those abroad who fought for free market economics. Additionally, the works of Adam Smith had a profound influence on Baron Vom Stein who would go on to be the primary influencer of the event.

Now, with the serfs free to own land and other freedoms from which they had previously been withheld, more reform came to society than simply allowing freedoms. Banks had to make adjustments to their policies to accommodate the rush for land sales that occurred. Many of the peasants and serfs moved to the cities due to the lower price of living and higher job opportunities. It important to remember that this reform was taking place in Prussia—not the rest of Germany. It would not be until 1815 that the rest of Germany would follow suit. An additional reformation that came from this movement was the decline of the Ganzes Haus system. Previously, this system had held that families were to stay together on one farm and that the father and mother were the leader of the respective genders, regardless of their age. In moving away from this system, the families were beginning to separate and operate their farms to feed more than just their families. While this era of transformation led to a stronger economy for Germany, there was another era that was gripping Europe as a whole: the Age of Enlightenment.

The Age of Enlightenment in Germany

The official dates for the Age of Enlightenment were 1715 to 1789. One of the leading influencers of the movement was Christian Wolff, a philosopher from Germany who would live until the midpoint of the Age of Enlightenment but would lead German to becoming the primary language used for most of the works from this age. Ten years before Wolff's death, Johann Gottfried von Herder was born and would go on to create one of the leading influential movements of the Age of Enlightenment, a movement by the name of Sturm und Drang. As the Age of Enlightenment was nearing its conclusion, there came an effort to combine some of the leading thoughts of the Enlightenment movement with ideas from Classical and Romantic eras. This movement was spearheaded by the thoughts of Weimar Classicism. It was during this time that some of the leading German musicians would produce their classical works of art. These musicians included Johann Sebastian Bach, Wolfgang Amadeus Mozart, and Joseph Haydn. Even with all of these contributions as result of the eye-opening events of the

Age of Enlightenment, the greatest contribution from this era likely came from another philosopher: Immanuel Kant.

Not all of the Age of Enlightenment was simply philosophy. Indeed, some of this age was dedicated to political reform and such was the focus of the writings and teachings of Immanuel Kant. In his writings, Kant would describe the importance of religious freedom while also delving into why freedom of speech was important to a country. The writings of Immanuel Kant would go on to be used in the founding of the United States of America, as many of the Founding Fathers were heavily influenced by Kant's writings. Though the Age of Enlightenment brought about tremendous improvement to society in Germany and all of Europe, a storm was coming, one that would lead one country in precisely the opposite direction that Germany was heading.

In 1789, the Age of Enlightenment ended and the French Empire began one of its most strict responses to the needs of the people: the French Revolution. The French government had recently changed its government from being controlled by the ancient regime to being a constitutional monarchy. This led to a revolt from the French people and utter chaos erupted. The whole world watched as laws were passed that would make it illegal to express discontent with the of the government. While France was in chaos, much of the rest of Europe was in confusion as it was not readily apparent who was in the wrong. While the German people applauded the efforts of the French people to fight for their freedoms, the German government actively condemned any attempts to overthrow the empire of France. Rising to the aid of their fellow

Europeans, the armies from Austria and Prussia would attack France but were soundly defeated at the Battle of Valmy in 1792. Even though this effort ended in failure, the German people supported the attempts to overthrow the violence of the French government. Unfortunately, it was 1815 before the French government would cease its bloodbath against the citizenry of France.

Along the eastern border of Germany stands a small street of land known as the Rhineland. During the French Revolution, the French army defeated the people of the Rhineland and began destroying the existing government in exchange for the new government that was overtaking France. While the French government held the Rhineland hostage, the new government of the Rhineland promoted ideology that supported freedom of religion amongst other freedoms. This led to greater societal reformation as the people of the Rhineland supported the changes being implemented by the new government. Napoleon, the new emperor of France, led in the construction of the Kingdom of Westphalia, a government he sought to establish throughout all of his kingdom. The French government had imposed itself long enough when it attempted to change the official language from German to French. During this time, the French language had grown in popularity and was largely considered to be the language of international relations; however, the German people remained true to their country and refused to change languages. Uniting their troops, Britain, Austria, and Russia attempted to overthrow the French government. This attempt would fail.

With little resistance, Napoleon set out to conquer much of Europe. Not all of Germany would be so accommodating, however, and Austria and Prussia would remain out of the grasp of Napoleon, at least for the time being. Later, the Confederation of the Rhine would be created by Napoleon and would constitute most of Europe while still being unable to gather the resources of Austria and Prussia. As Germany was dealing with the siege by Napoleon, Prussia was attempting to right itself from a series of poor decisions that had led to economic hardships. Frederick William II, the supposed "great" leader, had grossly underwhelmed and the man who replaced him was set on refraining from entering another war. While Frederick III was initially successful and controlling Prussia in such a way that removed it from the ongoing war with France, the people of Prussia, led by the queen, voiced their discontent with Frederick and rather than be overthrown, Frederick III grudgingly joined the Fourth Coalition in the Fall of 1806. This move proved to be disastrous and the Battle of Jena saw the Prussian army fall at the hands of the French army and Napoleon. The fallout from this defeat would be worse than originally thought, as Napoleon sought to both make an example out of Prussia's belligerence while also enacting a sick means of revenge against the defeated country. In addition to placing a limiting embargo on Germany's exports, Prussia was also forced to decrease the size of its army to under a mere 42,000 men—hardly the number of men needed to overcome the growing French army. All of these demotivating actions were heightened by the forced payment of French taxes while also being forced to accommodate the entire French army that was stationed in Germany. French soldiers were free to do as they pleased and the

German citizens were expected to feed, house, and accommodate them to the extent that the French army demanded. Under the extreme pressure, Saxony chose to forego any further persecution and became an active supporter of Napoleon. As a result, they were forced to turn on their fellow countrymen, joining the Confederation of the Rhine "willingly." For his part in ensuring the compliance of Saxony, Saxony's leader, Frederick August I, received the empty albeit it honorable title of King of a small tract of land that used to belong to Prussia. While the German forces were disappointed to see Saxony desert the cause, they were confident that they would be able to grow the patriotism of their country and eventually team up with another country to defeat the French army and Napoleon.

The opportunity to battle Napoleon would not come again until 1812. Precluding the battle, Napoleon made a series of ill-timed advancements, notably attempting to enter and conquer Russia during the heart of the Russian winter. As his army slowly froze, Napoleon's power and influence began to be replaced by the grudges of his men as they rebuffed their living and fighting conditions. This weakness did not go unnoticed by the Prussian forces who had been waiting for a moment to pounce on the vulnerable Napoleon. Even as their army grew, the Prussians knew they needed more men and so a Sixth Coalition was formed, this time including the mighty and strategically positioned Russian army in the group. After witnessing the initial success of the combined forces of Prussia and Russia, the Austrians joined the battle cry and the force began equitable, if not greater than, Napoleon's forces. This was confirmed at the fateful Battle of Leipzig where the Sixth Coalition took advantage of Napoleon's ignorance and dealt him the last defeat of his career in conquering the German countries. As is well-known, Napoleon would be difficult for France to get rid of; however, as far as Germany and the world was concerned, he had been defeated and pushed from his pedestal atop the most powerful army in the world.

One year after the Battle of Leipzig, Napoleon's forces finally ran out of the meager fumes that had been fueling them since their dreadful loss. With no other choice, Napoleon surrendered to the Sixth Coalition in Paris and Prussia once again regained its liberty from the man who had taken everything from them for the past eight years.

This time period was known best for the Age of Enlightenment and the ill-effects Germany felt as a result of the French government's rebuttal to the movement. Additionally, extending beyond the Age of Enlightenment would be the prestige and influence of Napoleon who would only be defeated by his poor judgement, no force ever being strong enough to defeat his army at full strength. Nevertheless, the period was completed by the forces once again uniting in the Sixth Coalition and ridding the world of the most dangerous threat during the time. This would hardly be the last time that Germany went up against a man set on conquering the world; however, the next time this happened, that force would not come from outside of Germany but rather from within.

An Explosion of Prosperity

While Germany was exuberant that the world was finally rid of the leader who had attempted to conquer the world for his personal gain, the country was also dangerously close to the extent of its resources. Europe as a whole was fought with devastation from the wake of Napoleon. While Germany had been somewhat broken up by the devastation of the Confederation of the Rhine, many of these countries had returned to Germany and requested to once again be a part of the country. This led to the formulation of the German Confederation. At first, this confederation did little more than simply agree to unite for battle. There were staggered attempts at unifying over other elements such as fiscal policy and diplomatic relations; however, these efforts were constantly drowned out by the calls of people who desired to remain autonomous and independent of a national government. Little did they know that one day, countries in Europe would unite for the very purpose of increased trade and reduced financial burden with the creation of the European Union.

With the creation of the German Confederation in 1815, the economy of German states began to accelerate and the growth rate for the population would stand at just more than 60% during the next fifty years. This acceleration would be replaced by historically low rates of both death and birth; however, the next few days would be a collection of the most prosperous times in German history. The reason behind this acceleration of economic growth was due to a revolution that was overtaking the world; however, this war was not fought with weapons such as guns and cannons. Rather, this war was fought with machines and factories. The Industrial Revolution was taking over the world and showing its global participants the wealth found in the industrialization of all major commodities.

Even as the Industrial Revolution raged around the world, Germany was a surprising late-mover to the event; however, once it became involved in the revolution, it became a great contributor. Beginning with the dramatic increase of the railroad infrastructure in the 1830s, the private entrepreneurship of Germany began to explode. Though the industrial revolution of Germany would not officially begin until the late 1850s, the construction of Germany began to explode following the implementation of vast railroad tracks. This was largely due to the lack of regulation within the industry. Following the boom of the construction and railroad industries, textile factories in Germany began to reap the benefits of greater connectivity both within and outside of Germany. This was further fueled as people began to trade the freedom of their rural life for the benefits and riches of living close to the factories. This is best seen by the large numbers of people who moved from the countryside to the city. While more than 90% of the German population was considered rural in the early 1800s, this would change in 1815 with the rise of the railroad. Nearly 654,000 people would be added to the citizenship of Berlin between 1815 and 1870. Other cities saw their residency double and even triple during the same time frame.

When one looks at the most successful industries during this time, it is hard to see past the successes of the railroad industry. While the industry was important due to the free trade that was beginning across the continent, it was also important to the national security of Germany since the government now had a means of transporting weapons, food, and other supplies to troops regardless of their location in Germany or even in other countries. One area that is routinely overlooked when comparing the growth of the railroad industry is the value of people traveling. People were no longer people holed up in their corner of Germany. Now, people were free to move around the country and even Europe as they saw fit, leading to a revival of cultural appreciation while also ushering in new nationalities and cultures. The greatest addition to the country that was brought about by the addition to the railroad tracks came through the improved patriotism. People were proud of their country now, the shame of being overtaken by Napoleon grossly removed from the country's image. Even as Germany's entrance into the Industrial Revolution was far later than many other nations, Germany was joining the show and was in time for the final act, one in which everyone would contribute.

In addition to the prowess of the railroad during this time, Germany also saw a resurgence in the value placed on reading literature. As a result, Germany's newspaper and magazine industries followed the railroad industry into a bullish period of success. Part of the success of the magazines and newspapers during this time is attributed to the ability to send various literature long distances using the new railroads. Despite this ability, many of the newspapers remained constrained to the region in which they were printed. Sadly, the newspapers and magazines were enjoying the greatest amount of freedom they would see for a while, as the laws surrounding their printing and content would become stricter as the country grew closer to World War I.

Alive for the first few years of the Industrial Revolution, the famed author Immanuel Kant would live to contribute to the beginning of the Industrial Revolution before passing away in 1804. Nearly 14 years after Kant left the political scene in Germany, another political figure would take his place, although this figure would be completely opposed to the ideology and thoughts of free market capitalism as preached by Immanuel Kant. This figure would go on to achieve almost more notoriety than Kant had, producing an ideology that lives to this day. This man was none other than Karl Marx. Though Karl Marx's opinions did not become popular until the mid to late 1800s, his thought process accompanied much of the Industrial Revolution and was present at many of the heights of German innovation during this time period. Turning to the religion of the country during this time, Frederick William III, the vaunted King who led Prussia in the successful defeat of Napoleon, would attempt to lead Germany in the lofty goal of uniting the religious sects of Germany into one religion. The two leading religions of the day were Lutheranism and Protestantism. Of course, these two religions had stemmed from the same movement almost three hundred years earlier but were now opposing each other. There had been other calls for unification so it seemed that Frederick III was simply echoing these calls while attempting to assure everyone that he had thought of this plan before anyone else. While Frederick III ensured the people that his goal was the unite the religions, his ulterior motive was to unite the religions under one so that he could lead the religion in addition to the country. The result of this forced union would be the Church of the Prussian Union. With Frederick III at the helm, the Prussian government was once again in full control of the religion and Frederick III added a capstone to the affair by proclaiming himself the most powerful bishop within the church. While the Protestants and most Lutherans did not object to the mandatory union of their faiths, there were a select number of Lutherans, self-proclaimed as the "Old Lutherans" who objected heavily to the combining of their religious sects. When the government refused to hear their cries of objection, the Old Lutherans resorted to taking their church to undisclosed locations. This resulted in an underground church of sorts and led to persecution against the church when certain meetings were discovered. When the risk of being found became too great, the church resorted to leaving Prussia, emigrating to other parts of the world where they were free to worship as they pleased.

The Lutherans and Protestant faiths would not see reform until the death of Frederick III, after which Frederick IV assumed the throne and immediately listened to the cries for separating the two faiths and removing the government from being head of the church. Prior to Frederick IV's ascension, there were also great changes to German politics as well. Napoleon had crippled political and economic growth in Europe due to the countries being forced to conform to France's political structure. After he drew France to its demise, Prince Metternich from Austria led the country in reforming the political structure to an independent German style. There were choices to make regarding whether to return to previous political structure or to start fresh with the new desire for winning that now embodied most Germans. While the government would take years to fully reform itself, the greatest contribution from this meeting was Metternich's instillation of nationalism as a mindset yet again. Germans had become so suppressed by the devastation of Napoleon that it had been difficult to retain pride in Germany. With Prince Metternich's rhetoric on the pride of Germany, there was little discontent from the citizens anymore.

The most divisive and controversial moment in Prince Metternich's history would come during a period of civil unrest between the conservatives and the liberals of the day. For years, the liberals and the conservatives had battled over the politics of the day but nothing was quite as bad as in 1819 when August von Kotzebue, a conservative voice who was a playwright, was assassinated by a member of the liberal party. The move devastated many within Germany and soon calls for an all-out civil war began to emanate from the heart of Germany. Metternich, seeing his country moving away from the progress it had been working so long to achieve, issued the Carlsbad Decrees, a document that outlined the extent to which the government was going to begin censoring the radical ideas that had allegedly produced the assassination of Kotzebue. For many, the Carlsbad Decrees were directly aimed at the nationalist movement that had previously been propagated by Metternich. Nevertheless, Metternich proceeded with the quelling of the liberal voices, leading to a period of persecution for the individuals most open about their liberal beliefs. What had begun as a movement of uniting Germany had led to the separation of many individuals, as those willing to voice their discontent with the conservatives were immediately shushed or sent to jail. This fallout was somewhat diminished in 1834 when the Zollverein was established. The Zollverein was a union of the states of Germany, with one obvious and glaring exclusion: Austria. This union sought to reduce the taxes incurred between interstate travel and trade. This would eventually establish a common currency among the member states while also providing a legal foundation should there be any need for litigation between merchants of different states.

In 1848, another one of Prince Metternich's legacies came under fire: The Congress of Vienna. The Congress of Vienna had sought to be the governing structure behind restoring Germany from the woes of Napoleon. For many years, this group had spearheaded the necessary government intervention while also quelling the small radical voices that would like to have seen Germany and the rest of Europe fall back under the flawed politics of Napoleon. During these years, the Congress of Vienna had been mostly successful at restoring Germany; however, with the disparity growing between the liberal and conservative voices, the Congress of Vienna found itself at a crossroads where it could either flex its influential power and become involved in the situation or it could remain out of the situation and taint its thus far, stellar record. Neither were optimal solutions but the one they chose would be detrimental to the country's success. In 1848, the Congress of Vienna sought to establish a clearer social order and in doing so, sparked the civil war that so many Germans had been trying to avoid. The civil war became known as the March Revolution and would be the driving force behind further reconstruction within the German government. As it stands today, the March Revolution was somewhat of a heroic moment as the German National Assembly hurriedly composed a constitution that would serve as the country's first documented source of truth. At this time, King Frederick IV from Prussia was given the chance to retain the imperial crown and preside over the government and church, a move he would adamantly reject on the basis of religious freedom. When the constitution failed to quell the riots of the people, the German National Assembly was deemed ineffective and promptly dissolved, ushering in the lurking German Confederation once again in 1850. The German leaders who had attempted the overthrow were removed from Germany, immediately boarding ships and uniting in the United States of America where they formed political parties.

The political front hardly improved with the dismissal of thousands of political figures who opposed the changes within Germany. This would continue for the next couple years as various German leaders tried to unite the country but would ultimately fall short. Among these leaders was Frederick IV whose repeated calls for unity were met with more political violence. This caused Frederick IV to become sullen and the opposite of the powerful figure he had been when he first joined the throne years earlier. What had begun as a spirit of nationalism was quickly fading due to the silencing of opposition that was taking place. Out of all of the states within Germany, Prussia was the most prone to this violence and the territorial expansion of Prussia during this time did not help quell the violent uprisings. While these days were difficult to bear for those who loved Germany the most, the future still offered hope and thankfully, there was still at least one man who believed Germany could be rescued.

A New Man at the Helm

As the year turned from 1857, Frederick IV, the king of Prussia who had become miserable on his throne, succumbed to the political stress and had a stroke. This left him incapacitated and the throne was open for the next individual in line. With no children, Frederick IV had not left an obvious candidate for his replacement so in the interim, Frederick's younger brother William took over as king. Four years later, William would officially be recognized as the true king of Prussia. While William was a breath of fresh air for the conservative voices of the day, his most notable accomplishment would come immediately after his crowning when he named Otto von Bismarck the Prussian Prime Minister. Germany had been divided for years now and many of the most influential people had fled to other countries such as the United States where conservatives were lauded, not silenced. Of all of the political leaders of Germany during this time, Otto von Bismarck would emerge as the most respected and thus, the only leader who is truly remembered to this day. William deserves credit though because without his leadership in appointing Bismarck to Prime Minister, coordinating the leadership of Albrecht von Roon and Helmuth von Moltke, Germany likely would never have survived the threat it did in the 1850s.

In one of his first coordinated movements after being named the prime minster, Bismarck led his defense team in the attack of key countries that had imposed their borders and had slowly been antagonizing Germany in silence while the country was divided over the fight between liberals and conservatives. Beginning with Denmark and ending with France, Bismarck coordinated the movement of the troops in a series of successful battles that did more than simply reclaim land, it also led to an increased sense of nationalism. For years, the nationalism of Germany had been the silent victim of the destruction by the liberals and Bismarck recognized that if the country was to return to its former self, the citizens would have to be proud of the country they were a part of. In attacking Denmark, Prussia opened Germany to a new war, but one that would be supported by the citizens, not only the government. During 1863 and 1864, Denmark and Prussia would fight over a small duchy named Schleswig, a small portion of land but one that both countries recognized as being important to the nationalism of their countries. These battles would eventually be known as the Second War of Schleswig and would be deftly won by Prussia thanks to the last-minute combination of Prussian and Austrian forces. While the victory steeped all of Germany in pride among the other European countries, it led to yet more controversy as Austria sought to lay claim to part of the duchy's future due to Austria's key part in defeating Denmark. Austria had sought to add the duchy as another state to the German Confederation but Prussia thought it would be better if the duchy simply became a part of Prussia by means of annexation. Sadly, the two states would not be able to come to terms before war broke out, giving Bismarck his first opportunity to unite the states. His efforts would fail and Germany would watch as two of her states embroiled themselves in another civil war.

The war would not last long, a mere seven weeks that gave way to the name, The Seven Weeks War. Nevertheless, the cost was great for both countries. Initially, both sent nearly 500,000 men to war each. As the battles continued to mount against each nation, it became apparent that Prussia held a strong upper-hand against Austria. This was primarily due to the fact that Prussia had technology on its side with the contribution of long guns being pivotal in the effort to avoid direct hand-to-hand combat. Austria would be defeated after the seven weeks was over and Bismarck was expected to hand sanctions or penalties towards Austria for its mounted war against Prussia. Rather, Bismarck chose influence as his weapon of choice and did not impose any crimes on Austria. The true loss of the Seven Weeks War was not Austria's defeat: it was the destruction of the German Confederation. The government recognized that the German Confederation had proven to be powerless and simply a figurehead to mask the chaos that normally took place during the confederation's meetings. With this in mind, the governments of each state decided to let the German Confederation sink into oblivion and instead erect the North German Federation in its stead. No surprise, Prussia was the leading influencer of this decision and took the head position in creating the new confederation. After years of undermining the politics of Prussia, Austria paid the price and was not included in the

North German Federation. This government would be pivotal to the future of Germany as in only four years, Germany would cease to exist as simply a federation but would become an empire in 1871.

In 1871, Otto von Bismarck began taking the federation in a new direction with the founding of the North German Empire. In truth, there was little difference between the North German Federation and the German Empire besides uniting the states even further. The empire consisted of 25 states with Prussia comprising the majority in all categories such as citizenship and land. It is important to note that the German Empire, while inhabiting many of the states from the Northern German Federation, also included some states that had only recently been reclaimed from French rule. As former French states, the people of these states were well-acquainted with the horrors of the French Revolution and had a particularly revolutionary attitude to political differences. The people were cooperative with the new form of government, however, and readily embraced the ideology that Bismarck was putting forth. In the first election, an astounding 52% of the citizens showed up to cast their voice for their imperial leaders. The people were proud of this new union that they had created. After the elections, Bismarck was declared the Chancellor of Germany and Bismarck began to mold the country even more. The future of the Germany Empire would look very similar to the state that Prussia had been in since Bismarck had been at the state's helm. Bismarck listened to the conservative voices of the day who proclaimed that there should be a clear separation of church and state, drawing on the legislation of the United States that had led to a profound freedom of religion. Indeed, the bitter taste of the thousands of emigrants who had fled Germany for the religious freedoms of the United States of America still lasted in the mouths of the German Empire. Unfortunately, Bismarck would be unsuccessful in such attempts, as the Roman Catholic Church remained the most powerful force in Europe, even in the newly formed German Empire. During this time, the fuel of culture was the Kulturkampf, a series of battles between the conservative voices of the day and the liberals who yet again sought for the oversight of the religious leaders. Translated, Kulturkampf means "Culture Struggle." Eventually, the culture of Germany would set its sights on anyone who adhered to a religious sect, leaving those who chose to rise against the culture on their own, individualized, and destroyed. Eventually, Kulturkampf would be removed from society, but the religious minorities of Germany continued to be discriminated against.

Under the new German Empire, a new social class was put forth. Many would remember that the social classes had not been severely implemented since the days of foregoing feudalism. Under the new empire though, a formal means of dividing society came about, beginning with the aristocracy. The aristocracy was the ruling class of Germany and all members were some sort of nobility. If one was a part of the aristocracy, any government or religious body would listen to their voice above the voices of anyone else. It would be under this transition that the Reichstag would be introduced to Germany, the eventual engine with which Adolph Hitler would operate his demise of the Jews through. In all, there were 7,000 aristocrats and all were citizens of Berlin, the new capital of the German Empire, or Potsdam.

The second class of individuals under the German Empire was the Middle Class. Those in the Middle Class were above the working class but were not in a position of government authority such as those in the aristocracy. Those in the Middle Class held the opportunity to marry into the aristocratic legion of elites; however, the process could and often did accomplish the opposite of that, with many aristocrats trading their lives of rich elitism for the less-fruitful positions of the Middle Class. Activists were included in the Middle Class of the German Empire and the leading organizations of activism during this time were all focused on ensuring equality between the working men and women of the day. The final class of people in the German Empire was the commoners, or the Working Class. Officially, the people of this class belonged to the Socialist Workers' Party. Under socialism, the working class of individuals would provide the nation's goods at a price that everyone could afford, effectively ending any semblance of capitalism in the new empire. The leader of the transition to the German Empire did not approve of the infiltration of Socialism, with Bismarck going as far as to attempt outlawing the groups that practiced its traditions. Nevertheless, the working class of individuals in the German Empire saw the common good of the people, effective equality after the law, as being the most influential party of the day. The group responsible for this would become known as the Social Democrats and as his approval decreased, Bismarck attempted to come to terms with the working class by introducing legislation that approved the creation of a social welfare program to provide common goods for all of the citizenry.

As more of Bismarck's actions would come to light after he left office, it would be found that Bismarck had begun offering social welfare as early as 1840, adding elements to the program until the program's height in 1880. In 1880, Bismarck effectively capped the program with several new "common goods" for the people including free medical care, pensions that were activated after reaching a certain age, and insurance for those involved in accidents and those who were unemployed. This government model would be the basis for the Socialist Workers Party in future years. In one final act of socialist appeasement, Bismarck levied major tariffs against the import of goods from other countries, effectively crippling the goods being imported by Germany from the United States. The United States had a far more robust manufacturing infrastructure and until Bismarck's interference, it had been cheaper for the country to import U.S. goods than to manufacture their own. What had begun as a bastion of hope against the liberal voices of the German Confederation had let down its guard and was now being infiltrated as the tentacles of socialism began to wrap themselves about the country's economy and government.

As Otto von Bismarck continued to try to make the German Empire as autonomous as possible, he was forced to confront a glaring interference from a sensitive topic in Germany: the control of the Roman Catholic Church. As an arm of Rome, the Catholic Church had the opportunity to interfere with the growth and success of Bismarck's plan to maintain independence. Unfortunately, most of the culture and society also embraced the Catholic Church's control over the country. Even as the Protestant Reformation had given the Germanic people a Bible in their own language, they remained chained to the security offered by the control of the Catholic Church. With culture against his dreams of independence, Bismarck set out to change society through war against this culture. Referenced earlier, this attack would be known as the Kulturkampf and would be set on exposing the nefarious goals of the Roman Catholic Church and specifically, the deeds of the Pope. The movement took a strong hold in Prussia where in shocking fashion, the German liberals became the most ardent supporters of Bismarck's education. This was primarily due to the German Liberals' disdain of the Roman Catholic Church due to its infringement on their actions. This hostility was both ways, with the Roman Catholic Church publicly denouncing the German Liberals and creating a political party, the Center Party, with the sole purpose of opposing every view point that the German Liberals stood for. While the Kulturkampf started as a mission to expose the Catholic Church, it became a bloody interaction when the Catholics of Germany began to be discriminated against. Many Catholics were forced to flee Prussia or denounce their faith. While Bismarck held power against the Catholic Church early, he failed to see how far the Catholic Church's political auspice, the Center Party, would go. In the elections of 1878, the Center Party was victorious in nearly 25% of the seats up for election. While still a significant minority, it was odd to see a political party so successful in its first run. Soon, Bismarck's attention was futilely divided between defeating the Roman Catholic Church while also fighting the mounting Socialist movement of the country. After weighing both groups, Bismarck correctly determined that the Socialist movement was of greater threat to the country and the Kulturkampf was abandoned in its entirety. This move would prove to be in Bismarck's best benefit as the Catholic Church found common enemies in the German Liberals and their embrace of socialism. The Roman Catholic Church would actually become one of Bismarck's strongest advocates in Germany as he sought to defeat socialism.

In the late 1800s, Germany noticed the strengthening of Russia and France, two countries Germany had never gotten along with. Bismarck became worried that the countries could unite and easily defeat the forces of Germany so he sought to make a league with one of them while also including the estranged Austria, which was trying to reunite with Prussia in the German Empire. Although these efforts would be futile, Germany would unite the three countries in the League of Three Emperors in 1873. Under this alliance, Russia, Austria, and Germany united in the fight against socialism and any country that espoused this political ideology. While Germany and Russia had little in common, Bismarck strategically positioned Germany as the stronger country against France, now that Germany had a large army at its call. France would not be bothering Germany any time soon.

As Bismarck watched socialism sweep across the European countries, he became worried that Russia was moments away from embracing this political ideology despite the agreement the three countries held. This forced Germany to do something it had despised only months earlier: an alliance with the rebellious nation Austria. Now, Austria was no longer simply Austria, it had pooled its forces with Hungary and Austria-Hungary was the result. In seeking peace, Bismarck would establish the Dual Alliance that solely focused on combining the forces of the three countries should Russia rise in objection to Bismarck's fight against socialism. Eight years after signing the Dual Alliance, Germany signed a Reinsurance Treaty with Russia in which Russia and Germany agreed to solidarity should France attack Russia or should Austria attack Russia. By now, it seemed that Germany was making treaties with everyone, pitting countries against countries in return for the guaranteed security from additional forces should Germany be attacked by any of the nations. This ruse came with ill-effects though, given that at least one country was destined to attack an accomplishing nation that Bismarck had agreed to defend. Five years after the countries signed the Dual Alliance, the Germany and Russia agreed to let Italy join the Dual Alliance, taking it to the Triple Alliance and once again pledging the support of the two remaining countries should France attack any one of the countries in the pact.

While Otto von Bismarck was busy creating peace with neighboring nations and ostensibly setting Germany up for peace for a long time, there were changes on the political front in Prussia that would soon threaten Bismarck's job. Emperor William I, the son of Frederick IV had been ruling Prussia since 1861 and had been the Emperor of the German Empire since 1871. In 1888, Wilhelm I passed away and Frederick III, the son of Wilhelm I assumed the throne. In a rare and tragic misfortune, Frederick III was diagnosed with throat cancer shortly after becoming Emperor. After a short ninety days, Frederick III passed away and his son Wilhelm II became emperor and king of Prussia. Wilhelm was much different than that of the previous generations of leaders, being noted for his conservative views. Emperor Wilhelm II did not share the country's admiration for the different classes of Germans and thus, began removing those from politics who were simply there for their title of aristocracy, not based on any accomplishments in their life. Included in the wake of Wilhelm's forced retirements was Otto von Bismarck, despite Bismarck's conservative fight against socialism. New moments were on the horizon for Germany, but unfortunately, these moments would usher in one of the most horrific moments in German history.

Ushering in the Storm

Wilhelm II, also known as Kaiser Wilhelm, ushered in a new sense of imperialism for the country, something Germany had always tended towards. Perhaps the worst thing to happen to Germany pre-world war era, the departure of Bismarck removed a great conservative voice that had years of experience to support the defense against socialism that had been creeping into the country. Even as Wilhelm II seemed to be more conservative than his parents, his early decisions were marked by a careless nature that threw the country's government into a lurch. The reckless nature reached a new high when the country was removed from its treaty with Russia, the Reinsurance Treaty. For reasons unknown, Wilhelm II simply refused to renew the treaty, after which Russia reciprocated by forming a new alliance with France called the Dual Alliance of 1894. This removed Germany's greatest asset and threw the country out from the good graces of Russia. The only protection Germany had now from an exterior threat was found in the Triple Alliance between Austria-Hungary and Italy. The precipice that Germany was sitting on was partially masked by the fact that Germany's economy was booming at the time. Advancements in the creation of steel vaulted Germany to being the leading creator of steel in Europe. Also, during this time, women's rights activism began to gain greater steam throughout Germany. While the women would not be afforded any new rights during this time, they were not discouraged from fighting for their rights, leading to mass demonstrations across the country.

As the country watched the turn of the millennium from the 1800s into the 1900s, it seemed that Germany was poised to emerge from the Wilhelm II era of government with little damage. Then, in 1914, a new era replaced the shiny facade that Wilhelm II had created, the era of World War I.

Germany in World War I

Trouble had been brewing in Europe for quite some time once the first world war commenced. Wilhelm's ruse of refusing to sign the Reinsurance Treaty was finally showing its terror as Germany was staring down the guns and war efforts of a combined France, Russia, and Britain. One year later, the Triple Alliance that had protected Germany with Italy would be broken as Italy jumped from the sinking ship of German politics to join the Allied Powers. Germany's Central Powers were markedly smaller than the Allied Powers, the initial alliance only being among Germany, Austria-Hungary, Bulgaria, and the Ottoman Empire. In attempting to attack each country systematically, Wilhelm II chose to attack the nemesis of Germany, France, first. This led to Germany surrounding Paris but ultimately being unable to capture the French as the Italian forces found ways to muddle the effort. This effort would become known as the Western Front and would become legendary in the history of World War I. The fighting medium of choice would be trench warfare in which troops fought with primitive fashion against the opposition. On the other side of the country, the Eastern

Front was also shaping up as a great battleground. Germany would see most of its victories on the Eastern Front in battles against Russia. Russia would prove to be detrimental to France's efforts to win the war as Russia became embroiled in its own internal crisis. In removing itself from the war, Russia signed the Treaty of Brest-Litovsk and essentially allowed Germany great positioning for the rest of the war.

The resignation of Russia from the war could not have come at a better time for Germany. Now, Germany was able to funnel its troops to the Western Front, an area where the Allies were destroying the Central Powers. However, Wilhelm II lost control of his navy and in what is now known as the German Revolution of 1918-1919, the German Navy stood against its continued mission in the war. The German Navy was essentially crippled with most of its crew refusing to sail, a move that would effectively seal Germany's fate in World War I. The move was an embarrassment to Germany and when the country was forced to sign the Treaty of Versailles, nationalism in Germany plunged. World War I was over but not before one man could witness the destruction of his country. That man was none other than Adolph Hitler.

Shortly after the war was over, new politics began to seep out of the Treaty of Versailles. The German people were looking for a new leader and thus, the Communist Party of Germany found new footing. While the Communist Party of Germany was finding new success, it would be a new leader who truly sparked the new movement. In the past four years, Adolph Hitler had watched as his country was destroyed in a war that the country seemed to have the upper hand in. One party that was enjoying newfound success in Germany was the National Socialist German Workers' Party and it would be through this party that Adolph Hitler would find his fuel to success. First however, Germany would have to endure defeat with the rest of the world by means of a global crisis: the Great Depression.

The official timeline of Adolph Hitler's ascension to power would take years, not the seemingly short period of time that many people assume. However, Hitler would ride the coattails of destruction to offer new hope to the German people in a time when they had seemingly been dealt blow after blow. As the world endured the Great Depression, which had followed the Roaring Twenties, Germany was hit particularly hard since the Treaty of Versailles had dealt significant reparations for the government to repay. Three years after the stock market of the United States crashed, the elations of 1932 saw a new party emerging as the leading contender for political power: the Nazi Party. The Protestants comprised a large portion of the Nazi's support with the divide between religions growing deeper as the Catholics became adamantly opposed to the Nazi ideology. Less than one year after the election took place, the Nazis received the support of the government when President Hindenburg of Germany named Adolph Hitler as the Chancellor of Germany. The next world war was still six years away but the preparation for the mass desertion began to sow its seeds the day Adolph Hitler was named Chancellor.

Germany under Adolph Hitler

With the ushering in of the Nazi Party of Germany, political dissent became something suppressed by the roaring Gestapo, Germany's secret police that sought to remove all opposition to Adolph Hitler's devilish agenda. It was also during this time that Hitler began removing Jews from their homes, sending them to internment camps for re-education and work. To ensure that the people of Germany were convinced of the deft actions of Hitler, Joseph Goebbels was the author of propaganda that the government ensured every German saw. Capitalizing on the desire for nationalism and the subsequent fear of being overtaken, the Nazis told of the supremacy of the German people while also educating the citizens on the threats the Jews placed Germany under.

Following months of German propaganda being spread among the people, a fire broke out at the Reichstag building. With what many consider no proof, Hitler condemned those who opposed the

Communist movement as being the ones behind the famed Reichstag Fire. Capitalizing on the fear of the people of another civil war, Hitler authored the Reichstag Fire Decree and president Hindenburg signed the document, immediately and deftly destroying most freedoms that the German people had previously enjoyed. No longer were people able to write their own newspapers and any demonstrations against the government were swiftly removed. This would usher in the most horrific time period of Germanic history: the Holocaust.

Hitler had been slowly educating the Germanic people on why the Jews were subhumans and why the Germans should not stick up for them. In 1935, Hitler went as far as to push for the passage of the Nuremberg Laws of 1935, which forbade any German from having a sexual relationship with a Jew. The crux of this law was not festered in simply ensuring the Germans were not friends with the Jews; rather, Hitler did not want the German bloodline "polluted" by the Jews. As this all began to take place, the Jews currently in Germany realized their time within the country was only putting them at more jeopardy of being sent to a camp. With this in mind, nearly 250,000 Jews emigrated from the country. The move proved to be in their best favor as Hitler wasted no time in preparing the German people for war. One year before Germany was to host the Olympic Games, Hitler ensured the German Air Force, known as the Luftwaffe, was ready. This directly defied the reparations outlined in the Treaty of Versailles from World War I; however, with Germany's propaganda and many in the West turning a blind eye to what Hitler was doing at this time, no one held Hitler or Germany accountable. During the 1936 Olympic Games in Berlin, Hitler would be able to show the whole world his growing success. After America almost did not attend the games due to Hitler's blatant anti-Semitic approach, the games went off without any problems and most of the West walked away sure that Hitler was simply doing what was best for the country.

Three years after the Olympics, Hitler made his ulterior motives known to everyone when he invaded Poland. There was significance to Hitler's choice of Poland: there were many Jews in the land and Poland represented a strategic location should Hitler create war. War was inevitable and by September 3 of the same year, France, Britain, and Australia had declared war on Germany. New Zealand, South Africa and Canada would follow before the United States would eventually follow after the bombing of Pearl Harbor. Germany started the war quickly, utilizing blitzkrieg in which the German troops attacked quickly and worked like "lightening." One of the most devastating moments of the war happened in the bombings of London when 43,000 citizens of the city would be killed while over one million businesses would be completely destroyed. It is hard to believe that less than fifty years earlier, Germany had held treaties with most of the countries it was now actively seeking to destroy. The war would last until 1945 when the United States ended the war with the atomic bombs over Japan. Though Britain was on the victorious side, to view Europe was to view a vast land of destruction. Most of the countryside had been destroyed by bombs while most of the cities now lay in heaps of rubble. Following the war, Germany would be forced to pay for the atrocities of the Holocaust while also paying for the reconstruction of most of Europe. The country would never officially pay it all back.

A War Fought with No Weapons

The final trials of Germany for its war crimes would result in Germany being divided into four zones that would be occupied by various countries from the Allied forces. The German government, deeply ashamed of the past years, would undertake a massive operation in which they would destroy most of the data form the war, going so far as to remove newspaper headlines and other memoirs of the war. Germany did not want to remember this war.

In what is largely seen as a failure by the United States in its mission to destroy Communism, the United States handed the reigns of part of Germany over to the Soviet Union, which immediately began placing Communist governments as replacements for the governments that had previously occupied the territory. As a result of this, Germany remained staunchly divided. After reports surfaced that told of starvation that the Soviet Union was imparting on the German residences, the United States and other Allied forces would orchestrate a massive airlift of food to the residents, an event that would later be known as the Berlin Airlift. This proved to be one of the smaller problems though. In the early 1950s, the Soviets began controlling the movement of the citizens within their military occupation zone known as the Eastern Bloc of Germany. The Soviets were worried that the residents of the Western Bloc would influence the Germans from the Eastern Bloc, creating a reason for the Eastern Germans to emigrate from the bloc. After a while, the Soviet Union established a border and a pass system so that it could track the movements of the people going back and forth. This proved ineffective as most of the working class within East Germany began to leave. In only fifteen years, the residency of East Germany had shrunk by almost 45%. With no other means of trapping the people, the Soviet Union began construction on the Berlin Wall in 1961 and was finished by August of the same year.

The move was terrible considering the current events. With the Soviet Union occupying the East Bloc, the United States was cut off from most of the communication with the country. This was due largely to the fact that the Cold War was raging between the United States and the Soviet Union during this time. With little communication, the wall between Eastern and Western Germany would remain constructed until President Ronald Regan demanded that the wall be torn down. Finally, in November 1989, almost 28 years after the wall had initially been constructed, the wall was torn down and the people were allowed to reunite. To have witnessed the reunion of families who had been torn apart by the wall was something of an exuberant experience. The German people gleefully tore the wall down, reuniting the two side of the country for the first time since the end of the war. For the German people, the destruction of the wall marked the end of a terrible legacy that had been started by the rise of a man named Adolph Hitler and had commenced with the courage of a United States' president who dared to speak against the Soviet Union's atrocities when no one else would.

Germany, Today

In 1998, Germany had elections again, the first sign of returning to a semblance of normalcy following the horrific period of history that had devastated the country. In more recent days, Germany was led by a courageous lady named Angela Merkel. With Merkel at the helm of the country, Germany was among the few nations that was able to walk away from the global financial crisis of 2008 unscathed. This stability would be followed by a period of instability in 2010 when economic disasters in Greece and other nations caused a ripple effect throughout most of Europe. The current ruling party of Germany is the Christian Democratic Union (or CDU), which was also the first party to regain authority after the destruction of the Berlin Wall. In 2021, Angela Merkel will hand over the reins of the most powerful position in Germany, Chancellor. Merkel had previously held the position as Chancellor for nearly 20 years; however, the COVID-19 pandemic and deteriorating relationships within the European Union has led the famed Chancellor of Germany to announce that she will be leaving her helm in the fall of 2021. This has left the Christian Democrat Union with the task of finding a replacement for her. While the task is great, it is heightened by the failures of Germany during the COVID-19 pandemic. Only time will tell if another power struggle will emirate from this authority vacuum.

Conclusion

Germany's history is one of courage and the ability to get back up after being knocked down so many times. There are parts of Germany's history that are completely tragic. And then there are other parts of the country's history that showcase the citizens' inability to give in. From the moments of the Thirty Years War in which the Peace of Westphalia hardly seemed sufficient to account for the lost lives to the terms of the Treaty of Versailles that fully embarrassed the countrymen, Germany has been through quite a bit and sadly, most of it was spawned on by men who abused their influence to work out their ulterior motives. It is one thing for a nation to willfully enter into a period of destruction on account of their own recklessness; it is quite another thing when leaders drive their country into such a period of destruction. In looking at the history of Germany, it will forever be remembered that Kaiser Wilhelm II was the man who essentially turned the country away from its period of growth. Oh, how history might have been different if Kaiser Wilhelm II was not so reckless as to forgo signing the Resurgence Treaty. However, despite these men's failures, the German people never allowed their destiny to be determined by one man. Even as one man determined their current consequences, the German people remained resolute in their drive for independence. Today, Germany stands as a stalwart in the European Union, a country that has seen tremendous heartbreak but has chosen to mask that heartbreak with the scar tissue of rebuilding. While there are parts of Germany's history that are used as examples of what to avoid, may the determination of her citizens serve as an inspiration for everyone to always fight for what is right, even when the leadership of a nation is set on driving that nation away from its heritage and into oblivion.

REFERENCES

Elkins, T. H. *Germany*. Chatto and Windus, 1972.

Garrett, Dan, and Charlotte Drews-Bernstein. *Germany*. Steck-Vaughn, 1992.

"Germany." *History.com*, A&E Television Networks, 21 Aug. 2018, www.history.com/topics/germany.

Gervasi, Frank. *Adolph Hitler*. Hawthorn Books, 1974.

"History." *Encyclopædia Britannica*, Encyclopædia Britannica, Inc., www.britannica.com/place/Germany/History.

"Home." *German Culture*, germanculture.com.ua/history/.

Majonek, Helmut, and Elizabeth Cole. Clark. *Germany during World War II*. 1986.

Rose, Jonathan. *Otto Von Bismarck*. Chelsea House, 1987.

Sempell, Charlotte. *Otto Von Bismarck*. Twayne Publishers, 1972.

Turk, Eleanor L. *The History of Germany*. Greenwood Press, 1999.

The History of Hungary: A Fascinating Guide to this Central European Country

Introduction

Nestled in the rich, lowland farming country of the Carpathian Basin of Central Europe, Hungary is a landlocked country bordered clockwise by Slovakia to the north, then Ukraine, Romania, Serbia, Croatia, Slovenia, and Austria to the west. The Danube River flows north to south through the center of modern Hungary.

Like most of the Central European nations, the location of Hungary has figured primarily into its varied and often violent history. Here in the thick of things, particularly located next door for centuries to the volatile Habsburg and Ottoman Empires, Hungary has a long and complex history – one occasionally bordering on incomprehensible – of successive populations, kingdoms, partnerships, rulership, and influencing cultures. It has dominated and been dominated. The combination of cultures that have come together here, willingly, or begrudgingly, has turned it into a land of amazing ethnic diversity. In the 20th Century, Hungary's revolution became key in the collapse of the Eastern Bloc.

Today, finally enjoying a hard-earned peace and prosperity, the country survives as a democratic parliamentary republic with a high Human Development Index and an important role on the world stage.

Early Days

The Hungarian/Magyar tribe is considered to be descended of Huns (which is partially the reason for the country's name) and Scythians who lived as part of numerous hunter/gatherer cultures in the region of the Ural Mountains, which runs north to south in through the western portion of Russia, and which today forms a portion of the unofficial boundary between Europe and Asia. These populations were able to successfully spread out over the wide territories afforded there, and during this outward migration a separate language set formed, that of the Proto-Finno-Ugric tribes (subsequent languages descended from these would become Hungarian, Finnish, and Estonian). Climate change, including the spread of marshlands and regression of grasslands, drove tribes southward, and it is at this point (circa 800 BC) that the Hungarian language itself seemed to develop separately from its sibling languages.

Currently, the exact progression of the Magyars from the Ural Mountains to southern Russia is a matter of debate; most of the study of this migration is conducted through language links, such as shared words with Turkish languages, implying a close connection to Turkic tribes. But there is not a definitive answer to their precise point of linguistic origin, and for approximately 1000 years, the Magyars dwelled on the steppes of Central Europe, mostly unnoticed by history.

Meanwhile, the Carpathian Basin was a busy area of war, a sort of territory of "musical chairs," that changed hands of power over a number of conquerors through the centuries. The Roman Empire held the western Carpathian Basin as Pannonia for some 400 years until the 4th Century AD. Germanic tribes and invaders from Central Europe then began migrating into the area. This began with the arrival of the Hunnic Empire. The Huns ruled the area from about 370 to 469 AD. Attila the Hun remains a central figure in Hungarian mythology. When the Hunnic Empire fell apart, the Gepids, formerly vassals of the Huns, were on hand to establish a kingdom. Goths, Lombards, Slavs and Vandals also came through, until finally in about 560 AD the Avars founded the Avar Khaganate and held the region for two centuries until they were driven out of power by the Franks (under Charlemagne) in the 790s. The Franks remained in power west of the Danube, while the First Bulgarian Empire (a chief competitor of the Byzantine Empire) conquered the lands east of the Danube, taking control over what was left of the Avars and other Slavic tribes.

In 830 AD, Hungary's first recorded historical event occurred, though the records are those of the Byzantine Empire and not the Magyars/Hungarians themselves. The Magyar tribes, led individually, gained Byzantine notice when they aided the Khazar Khaganate. Khazar was a powerful trade empire with its access to the Caspian Sea serving as a trade route between Eastern Europe and Southwestern Asia. The Khazar broke free of their service to the Byzantine Empire; Byzantine records specifically mention that the Magyars allied themselves with the Khazar for about three years. Byzantine retribution for their aid to Khazar, however, eventually drove the Magyars out of the southern Russian regions.

Led by Arpad (a descendant of Atilla, or so it was believed), the Magyars moved across the Carpathian Mountains and as a people they settled in the Carpathian Basin; Hungary was established in AD 895, then the Principality of Hungary in 896 AD. At that time there were basically three powers in place in the Carpathian Basin: the First Bulgarian Empire, the Franks and Moravia, which were each vying with the other two for control. The intervening Magyars drove out the Bulgarians, then took over the struggling remains of Pannonia and Moravia. The Magyars defeated three Frankish imperial armies, and finally targeted the Byzantine Empire itself. They were, however, resoundingly defeated by Otto, King of the Germans, in the Battle of Lechfeld (955 AD). Perhaps coincidentally, or perhaps not, by this time the Hungarian rulers, descendants of Arpad, had decided to settle the Kingdom of Hungary into Christian Monarchy that fit in more peacefully with the rest of Eastern Europe.

The Arpad Dynasty and King Saint Stephen

Grand Prince Arpad had led the Hungarian tribal federation through its conquest over the Carpathian Basin. Precise records of the prince's descendants are unavailable and the Hungarians were prone to tribal division that flew in the face of their "federation," so the exact relationships between Arpad and his son, Zoltan, and the rulers Grand Prince Fajsz and Grand Prince Taksony, are unclear, but nevertheless they are all somehow descendants of the dynasty. By the time Grand Prince Géza, son of Grand Prince Taksony, expanded his rule over areas surrounding the Danube, the Christian faith was spreading through his kingdom as well as the tribes that lay beyond.

Géza's son, Grand Prince Stephen, who was a follower of Christianity, became the first Hungarian King and unified the entire Carpathian Basin under his rule. For this privilege he had to fight off his relative, Koppány (his uncle, who claimed the right to the throne), but was able to win rulership with the German reinforcements provided by his wife, Giselle of Bavaria. Stephen applied to Pope Sylvester II to make Hungary a recognized Catholic Apostolic Kingdom (thus making himself royalty) – basically a title that conveyed Stephen's promise to convert the heathens of the Carpathian Basin to Christianity. An Apostolic king is an "apostle" of Christ; the kings that followed Stephen would be considered thus by the church.

Toward his purpose of spreading Christianity, Stephen moved to consolidate his power by making Hungary into a feudal state of counties, with its official language being Latin. Formerly, Hungarian writings had been in a sort of runic alphabet; with his reign the Latin alphabet was adopted for writing. Under his rule Stephen established an ecclesiastical organization with two archbishoprics that controlled several bishoprics. Through outright battle, family ties and some severe punishments to those who ignored Christian customs, he overtook the local tribes. During Stephen's reign, the country of Hungary enjoyed peace sufficient to make it the preferred route for travelers moving between Western Europe, Constantinople, and the Holy Land.

Stephen would later be sainted (as King Saint Stephen) by the church as the holy savior of the Hungarians through a careful bit of revisionist history that emphasized his holy works and downplayed his severity. Decades after his death, a cult of believers in King Stephen's healing powers rose, thanks to a strong press by King Ladislaus of Hungary, in what was probably a bid for support after Ladislaus had defeated his cousin Solomon, another contender for the throne. A lengthy session of prayer and fasting at Stephen's tomb resulted in healing miracles (cured blindness, deafness, lameness, cleansed lepers, and so forth). The truth of his earning sainthood probably lies more in the fact that he used his powers of monarchy to spread religion.

The Vast and Varied Lines of Succession

The Hungarian succession was never one of clear straight lines. King Saint Stephen outlived all of his children including his heir, Emeric, and therefore left the succession of rule to his nephew Peter Orseolo, who became king upon Stephen's death in 1038. This succession was contested by the family of Duke Vazul, a cousin with three exiled sons (Levente, Andrew and Béla). Andrew returned with the assistance of pagan tribes to overtake the kingdom and restore peace, then invited his brother Béla back to assume rule over one third of the counties.

Through the next two centuries the lines of Arpad family succession became increasingly convoluted as more dukedoms were created, and often dukes were more interested in forming their own kingdoms as opposed to bowing to the Hungarian King. This was further complicated by a continuing confusion over whether Hungary's line of succession meant that a king's son assumed the throne as opposed to a king's younger brother. Further complicating the history is the fact that Hungarian rulers frequently shared names, so that a bevy of Gézas, Stephens, Bélas, Ladislauses and Andrews took various positions of power, knocking each other constantly aside, until finally it seemed the dynasty ran out of members willing to fight.

Amidst this national squabbling, Hungary dealt with history outside of itself. King Andrew II led the Fifth Crusade to the Holy Land with the largest royal army in the Crusade History (1217). Hungary also endured the decimation of almost half its population in a Mongolian invasion; meanwhile King Béla IV allowed Cumans and Jassics, also fleeing the Mongols, to take refuge in Hungary and these people became assimilated into the Hungarian population and culture. One devastating attack by the Mongolians was enough to convince King Béla to fortify Hungary with an intricate system of stone castles, fortresses, and well-trained knights, who were able to thwart any attempted Mongolian attacks in the future.

The confusing line of Hungarian provinces, rulers and disputes was finally ended when King Charles I took a strong position in the year 1310 AD and reconsolidated a great deal of the power under one rulership. It is noteworthy, however, that the Arpad dynasty had by this time spread its members and lineage into almost every line of European aristocracy.

The Elected King Matthias Corvinus

Matthias Corvinus represents the first instance of an elected Hungarian King, but also was the last truly strong Hungarian King; when his rule ended in 1490, the decline of Hungary as a European power began.

Matthias was the son of John Hunyadi, a powerful nobleman who had risen to the position of regent through outstanding military campaigns as both a mercenary commander and in the Crusades. Matthias was not only a strong military leader like his father, but much in the style of the Renaissance was a patron of arts and education, and the commoners among Hungarians saw him as a protector and a just king. His Biobliotecha Corviniana was a great collection of 15th Century books of history, science and philosophy and was second in size only to the Vatican's library.

Matthias controlled a large mercenary army, the Black Army of Hungary. This mercenary army of paid, well-trained soldiers (an idea that Matthias had picked up in his studies of Julius Caesar), rather than conscripted farmers and laborers made the Black Army a formidable foe and were one of the first armies to employ the use of firearms – the arquebus, limited in its usefulness only by the expense of gunpowder. With his army, Matthews conquered parts of Austria and Bohemia and defeated Ottoman and Wallachian troops at the Battle of Breadfield. The Battle of Breadfield was a triumphant victory for Hungarians; the soundly defeated Ottomans, suffering several thousand casualties, dared not to attack Hungary again for many years afterward.

Matthias died without an heir, so powerful Hungarian magnates secured the election of Vladislaus II precisely because of his weak influence, figuring they could continue to enjoy their own power. For the next 30 years (1490-1526) Hungary's stability declined. The peasantry that had enjoyed the rule of Matthias now found themselves again bullied by local magnates, their rebellions against unfair treatment crushed by the nobility even as Hungarian power faltered. The rise of Protestantism caused further dissention within the country and the Ottoman Turks seized this opportunity to resume their conquest of Hungary.

Hungarian Hussars

The Magyars were always strong horsemen, and Hungarian Hussars, who began their service under King Matthias Corvinus and were mostly composed of Serb warriors, gained a reputation throughout Europe as important additions to a military force. Indeed, Hussars became part of most European armies, various countries adopting their own uniform styles and recognizable skills.

Famous for their superb horsemanship, the heavy cavalry knights became legendary in the 18th and 19th Centuries. The Hussars could manage against better-outfitted forces with their speed and skill. The horsemen carried as their weapons a spear, sword, and a shield. They wore armor – when they could afford it. The Ludovica Military Academy was a major training ground for the Hussars. Due to their brigand roots, the Hussars were known for being excellent at reconnaissance missions.

A Divided Hungary and the Habsburg Empire

The Ottomans overcame the Hungarians once more at the Battle of Mohacs in 1526, during which Hungarian King Louis II died. Hungarian nobility was still strongly divided against itself and elected not one but two kings to replace Louis II, John Zápolya and Habsburg Ferdinand I (who was married to Hungarian royalty). Then, in 1541, the Turks took over the city of Buda, dividing Hungary into a third segment, and the country remained in three parts until the conclusion of the 1600s: the northwest was Royal Hungary, annexed to the Habsburgs; the eastern part became the independent Principality of Transylvania under Ottoman rule, and the central capital of Buda became the Pashalik of Buda.

By 1686, the Holy League's army (supported by the papacy, and thus heavily influenced by the Austrian's Holy Roman Emperor) retook Buda from the Turks; this led to a series of battles defeating the Ottomans and by 1718, the entire Kingdom of Hungary was out from beneath Ottoman control and was almost thoroughly controlled by the Austrian Habsburg Empire.

Hungary's population had been affected vastly by the prolonged war with the Ottomans, including stunted population growth and the disappearance of many smaller communities. The Habsburgs settled various peoples (Slavs, Germans, and Serbs) into the depopulated areas of Hungary but would not permit Hungarians themselves to resettle on the Great Plain. Meanwhile, Habsburg Counter-Reformation efforts returned the majority of the country to the practice of Catholicism. Hungarians rebelled against Habsburg rule between 1703 and 1711 but were ultimately defeated.

For a period during the mid-18th Century, Hungarian cavalry particularly followed Habsburg empress Maria Theresa, who had vowed to protect Hungary from all aggressors. The horsemanship and valor of Maria Theresa, the only female Hapsburg ruler, won the approval of the Hungarians to the extent that their military aid kept her enormous empire mostly intact during her early reign.

The 12 Demands of Hungary: 1848 Revolution

It was not until the Napoleonic Wars, an entire century later, that Hungarian statesmen began to recognize the need for Hungary address urgent problems in the country and push for modernization. Habsburg rule strongly pushed back, imprisoning those who would speak out for the civil and political rights of the Hungarians.

In 1848, Hungarians rose up in mass demonstrations in the cities of Pest and Buda. The reformists made "12 Demands." These demands included freedom of the press, the end of censorship, an independent Hungarian government, and the right to assemble annually, a national bank, equal representation in juries and taxation, the end of serfdom and bondservices, and a national army. The House of Habsburg was dethroned, technically, but struck against the movement by using its own influence on Croatian, Serbian and Romanian peasantry to ignite further rebellion inside the country. Hungarian Parliament in July 1849 enacted the world's first laws of ethnic and minority rights, and members of various nationalities began to gain high positions with the Hungarian Army.

In reaction to the Hungarian rebellions, the Habsburgs under Franz Joseph I reached out to Russian Tsar Nicholas I. Russian armies invaded Hungary and forced surrender in August of 1849. Austrian Army commander von Haynau became the governor and ordered the execution of the Hungarian army leaders and the Hungarian prime minister. These brutal retributions served only to make Hungary increasingly volatile under Austrian rule. Not too many years passed before it became clear that concessions must be made to Hungary in order to keep them from rebelling.

In 1866, Prussia declared war on Austria, and Hungary saw this as a possible opportunity to gain their own independence. Emperor Franz Joseph moved quickly to ensure peace between Austria and Hungary.

The Austro-Hungarian Empire

In 1867, the Austro-Hungarian Compromise came into existence when Emperor Franz Josef granted significant autonomy to Hungary, permitting a "dual monarchy." Franz Joseph and his wife, Elisabeth, who was popular in Hungary, became monarchs of the nation. This clever move would keep Hungary as a part of Austrian territories and ensure that Hungary's military would be part of Austria as well.

Hungary of that day was a vast melting pot of cultures, and difficult to rule at a time when nationalist movements were growing in popularity. The Austrian monarchy respected the variety of citizens, allowing national groups to use their native languages in official capacities and permitting schools of different ethnicities. Regardless, Hungary's middle and lower classes felt underrepresented by the emperor in Austria.

Hungary enjoyed significant development under the compromise, with improvements in its economy as the land industrialized, moving away from a largely rural community. The older cities of Buda, Óbuda and Pest were united to form Budapest, and here grew the administrative system of Hungary that is still in place today.

When Archduke Franz Ferdinand was assassinated in Sarajevo, Hungarian Prime Minister Istvan Tisza, along with his cabinet, tried unsuccessfully to avoid the outbreak of war. Austria-Hungary drafted more than 4 million soldiers from Hungary to fight on the side of Germany, Bulgaria, and Turkey; however, very seldom was this massive gathering of troops used to protect Hungary itself and Hungary suffered significant losses.

Hungary and Austria's union was dissolved in October of 1918. The union was simply unable to organize under the strain of its ethnic diversities and the damages wrought by war.

The Growth of the Right

Following World War I, United States President Woodrow Wilson demanded pacifism and the disarmament of the Hungarian Army, thereby leaving Hungary without a national defense. Suddenly Hungary was vulnerable, and the Little Entente (an alliance of Czechoslovakia, Romania and the Kingdom of Serbs, Croats, and Slovenes) invaded the country to retake the lands that had been lost during the rule of the Habsburgs. Romania invaded Transylvania, Czechoslovakia annexed northern Hungary (or, what is today Slovakia), and a coalition between Serbs and French annexed Vojvodina among other southern regions.

Within the Hungarian government, pacifist social-democratic leader Karoyi was overthrown by communist regime led by Béla Kun, who declared the country now to be the Hungarian Soviet Republic. What followed was the Hungarian arm of the Red Terror Campaign, which carried out mass killings for political repression that resulted in the death of 590 people accused of involvement in the counterrevolutionary coup against the Hungarian Soviet Republic.

By 1919, however, Romanian troops invaded Budapest and removed Kun from power. An exhausted population accepted rightist Austro-Hungarian admiral Milos Horthy as its leader, establishing him Regent of the reestablished Kingdom of Hungary. While this new government worked to repair foreign relations, the White Terror campaign (an equally violent retribution campaign against those who had led the Red Terror) now moved through the country, where both Communists and Jews were killed.

On June 4, 1920, the Treaty of Trianon, prepared at the Paris Peace conference, established peace between the Allies of World War I and Hungary. It also established new Hungarian borders, which reduced Hungary by 71% of its territory and many of its raw materials sources, and 66% percent of its population. Additionally, 3.3 million Hungarians were now minorities in other countries.

Horthy's regime was unwilling to take military action against the Treaty, and while Hungary was holding free elections, Horthy's personality kept him dominating the political scene. The Hungarian government continued to drift to the far right, gravitating politically toward Italy and Germany. The Great Depression made fascist policies that promised social and economic recovery ever more popular.

The Nazis rewarded Hungary's pro-Germany foreign policy by peacefully restoring to Hungary many areas lost after the Treaty of Trianon. Thus, by 1940, Hungary formally joined with the Axis powers of Germany and Italy and participated in the Invasion of Yugoslavia.

Hungary in World War II

Hungary entered World War II on June 26, 1941 as an Axis Power, declaring war on the Soviet Union. For two years, Hungarian troops served on the Eastern front, but after the Second Army suffered severe losses at the Russian River Don in January 1943, the Hungarian government began to secretly seek a peace pact with the Allies.

When Germany learned of these attempts, it sent troops to occupy Hungary and ensure compliance; they replaced Horthy with fascist ruler Szálasi who threw all of Hungary's capabilities behind the German war effort. Szálasi sanctioned the Arrow Cross Party, a strongly fascist organization that ruled for only seven months yet promoted horrific crimes against the Jewish population.

During the German occupation of May through June 1944, the Arrow Cross Party and the Hungarian police astonishingly deported more than 400,000 Jews primarily to Auschwitz where almost all were killed. Historically, Hungary had a significant Jewish Community, over

800,000 people prior to World War II, but during the war almost 600,000 Hungarian Jews were killed in total – only about 250,000 were thought to have survived the Holocaust as it swept through Hungary.

Some efforts were made to rescue Hungarian Jews – Raoul Wallenberg, a Swedish diplomat, gave many Hungarian Jews Swedish passwords, and the Hungarian Aid and Rescue Committee bribed high-ranking SS officers to allow some Jews to escape. Regardless, Hungary's participation in the Holocaust remains a fact of considerable pain and controversy. The war was devastating to the country, destroyed more than 60% of its economy and resulting in astonishing loss of life. In addition to well over half a million Jewish deaths, tens of thousands of Hungarians were murdered or deported as slave labor by Yugoslavs, Czechoslovaks, and Red Army troops.

The Soviets surrounded and sieged Budapest in December 1944. Budapest surrendered on February 13, 1945, and by April the German troops left the country to Soviet occupation. Through the Paris Peace Treaties, Hungary was reduced to its post-Trianon borders once more.

The Age of Communism

After the defeat of Nazi Germany, Hungary became a Soviet Union satellite state. Mátyás Rákosi was installed to implement Stalinization in the country, and to initiate militarization, industrialization, and collectivization.

In 1949, the Hungarian People's Working Party was in control of the government and all other parties were banned. The Constitution adopted by the Hungarian government was modeled on the Soviet Union's 1936 constitution. Hungary was desperately poor at the time, for not only was it paying reparations to other countries (at approximately 20% of its national income) but the abrupt industrialization push from the Soviet Union's control meant that most of the products produced were going to the Soviet Union for use, rather than staying within Hungary. The most intelligent Hungarian economic minds were either being imprisoned, or they were escaping the country. The standard of living steadily declined.

The AVH, a secret police society, formed to enforce the regime and from 1948 to 1956, and somewhere between 350,000 and 600,000 people were imprisoned or executed, including people prominent during the Horthy-era or simply democrats or freethinkers. Those arrested were interned in Gulags, and many were deported to Soviet labor camps, where roughly one-third of them died.

Following Stalin's death, Rákosi was deposed and Imre Nagy became premier, but his goals of market liberalization and political openness were unacceptable to the hardline; Nagy was replaced by Ernő Gerő, who was, if anything, more tough-minded than Rákosi.

Dissatisfaction continued to rise. In 1955, Hungary joined the Warsaw Pact, which was a political alliance established between the Soviet Union and many countries of Eastern Europe. Its purpose was to provide a counterbalance to NATO, and it was meant to unite Eastern European nations in defending each other, but in truth the Soviet Union used it to mete out control and influence of the region.

The Revolution of 1956

Hungary had a longstanding rebellious streak. After the death of Stalin, Hungary watched as Poland had some success in driving Soviet troops from its borders and forming a reformist government. Petofi Circles began to form (named after a rather revolutionary poet) and talk grew in the streets of freeing Hungary from Soviet Control.

On October 23, 1956, 20,000 people gathered in Budapest where former Minister of Defense Veres Péter read aloud the "16 Points" that the people of Hungary demanded for themselves, including aspects such as the dismissal of Soviet troops, free elections, and freedom of the press.

The demonstration remained peaceful until one portion of the group broke off and made its way to a Hungarian radio station, where they demanded that their 16 Points be read live on the air. The radio station refused to comply, and AVH guards opened fire on the angry crowd.

Meanwhile, the Soviet Union sent 6000 troops and hundreds of tanks into town to try to control the growing agitation. One significant problem was that the Hungarian army was pretty clearly divided, some troops trying to keep the peace, while others not only joining with the rebellion but sharing weapons, resulting in an armed mob. Tensions increased until a massacre of protestors occurred on October 25, driving the Hungarians to quick, decisive action.

Quickly a new government was formed; by October 27, the Hungarians demanded that all Soviet troops leave, that the AVH be dissolved, order restored, and political prisoners released. Hungary withdrew from the Warsaw Pact and declared itself neutral.

This actually might have worked and been the end of a Soviet-controlled Hungary altogether except that the protestors had been so significantly angered by the AVH's actions that when the AVH surrendered, many of them were publicly executed.

In response, the Soviet Union sent massive numbers of reinforcements – 150,000 troops and 2500 tanks, to retake control of both Budapest and the Country. By November 9, the Hungarian rebellion was crushed. Almost 20,000 Hungarians were killed. 21,600 were imprisoned for political reasons, and about half that number interned and 230 executed. Nagy himself was among those executed by hanging. During the revolution, the Hungarian borders were briefly opened and almost a quarter million people fled the country before the revolution was suppressed.

The Era of János Kádár

After the Soviet's second military occupation, János Kádár was selected (by the Soviets) to lead the country through the Socialist Workers' Party. He was the party leader from 1956 through 1988. Kádár's main goal was to settle the situation of Hungary and normalize the communist lifestyle, meaning that his party would not take a "hard line" toward dissent. People were permitted to disagree with the regime as long as they cooperated, and many political prisoners who had participated in the former uprising were released. Kádár emphasized economic repair and increasing the standards of living by focusing production on goods and food rather than military expenditures.

In 1968, Kádár's government introduced the NEM (New Economic Mechanism), which allowed free market elements to enter Hungary's socialist economy. This provided a huge boon to the Hungarian landscape, improving their standard of living and inviting far fewer restrictions than were imposed on most Soviet-controlled countries (such as increased freedom of the press). Hungary became an "in between" place where tourists from Eastern-bloc countries, who were allowed to travel to their visit their Soviet-controlled neighbors, could get a glimpse of what Western life could be like.

The Fall of Hungarian Communism

Economic stagnation, political pressure, and a change in relationships with other Warsaw Pact countries brought about the peaceful transition from communism to democracy in Hungary.

When Kádár died in 1989, much of the world was in deep economic recession, and the Soviet Union and its states were unable to respond to the needs of its population and the end of its control was in sight. 1989 would see the end of the Soviet Union as the Eastern bloc disintegrated.

In March 1989, revolutionary hero Imre Nagy was reburied in a huge ceremony in Budapest, attended by more than 100,000 people. During this event, which experienced almost no government interference, influential speakers called for the recall of Soviet troops. This ceremony is considered the symbolic conclusion of communism. Only two months later, free elections were held, and the conservative opposition group,

Hungarian Democratic Forum, was elected head of the government with József Antall elected as prime minister.

The Modern Face of Hungary

Hungary's constitutional document is the Fundamental Law of Hungary. Since the fall of communism, Hungary has held multi-party elections. Its political landscape is conservatively dominated by the "Fidesz" (a strong right-wing party) and two medium sized parties of the left-wing "Democratic Coalition" and the liberal party "Momentum."

199 Parliamentary members are elected every four years to the National Assembly. The National Assembly is overseen daily by the Speaker, a highly influential position. A President for the Republic is elected by this National Assembly every five years. The President's role includes representative responsibilities, the formal nomination of the prime minister (at the recommendation of the National Assembly) and acting as the Commander in Chief of the Armed Forces. The President also has veto powers. Finally, the Prime Minister serves as the head of government and exercises executive powers. Usually, the Prime Minister

will be the leader of the Parliament's largest party. The Prime Minister also selects Cabinet ministers (and can dismiss them) though these ministers must be approved by the President and voted in by Parliament.

Throughout the early 1990s, Hungary, like many countries worldwide, continued to suffer serious economic recession. Thus in 1994, the elections resulted in a win for the Socialist party (Communism's political heir). Yet in 1998, the tone shifted back to the Hungarian Democratic Forum, then once more in 2002, the Socialist party took control again. But even as the vastly different political parties change government hands, Hungary continued to pursue integration, joining NATO (1999) and the European Union (2004), as well as the OECD, the WTO, and the IMF among other organizations. Budapest serves as home to more than 100 political embassies and representative bodies of international relations.

In fact, since the fall of Communism, Hungary's leading foreign policy has been integration with western economics and a fair number of peace and relief programs. The country has consistently tried to maintain good relationships with its neighboring countries, though occasionally the rights of Hungarian minorities can cause tensions in nearby countries where those minorities are instead the major populations (such as Ukraine).

Since 2010, however, a conservative parliament has been in control after scandal and dishonesty was discovered in the left-wing party. The staunch conservatism of the government, though controversial, has continued to win the elections of 2014 and 2018, and in September 2018 the European parliament voted to act against Hungary under the terms of Article 7 of the Treaty on European Union, seeing the Hungarian government as a threat to democracy. It was felt that Hungarian policy and legislation had begun to restrict freedom of the press, actions of non-government organizations and undermining judiciary actions. Article 7 is an instrument used to ensure the respect of Article 2 of the European Union, which emphasizes democracy, the rule of law, and human rights. Undergoing Article 7 examination is a complex process with three stages, which start with determining whether breaches have been committed and then conclude with sanctions against the country. Poland has also undergone Article 7 examination. The vote passed with the required two-thirds majority.

Hungary is no longer considered a democracy; it is now a transition, "hybrid regime" that many believe is being undermined from the inside by strong right-wing forces, namely Prime Minister Viktor Orban's attacks on the country's democratic institutions, possibly under strong influences from Russia and China. This is believed to be the case with many of the countries in the eastern European region.

The Economy

After centuries of economic difficulty, post-Communist Hungary has emerged as a high-income mixed economy with a skilled labor force and a high human development index. Its economic success relative to its size is impressively well-organized, 80% privately owned, and 39.1 overall taxation contributing to its welfare economy. The Hungarian market focuses heavily on exports with the European Union. Its important industries include food processing, information technology (particularly in the last 20 years, where the focus has been on mobile technology and information security), chemicals, metallurgy, machinery, electrical goods, pharmaceuticals, and chemicals. Hungary has several companies on the Fortune Global 500 and its entrepreneurial business arena is also strong. The financial capital is Budapest, one of the fastest-growing urban economies in Europe.

Tourism

Tourism remains an important and popular industry as Budapest draws visitors from around the world. Budapest is a surprisingly vast and regal city compared to the relative size of the little country it represents, but it, like Austria's magnificent Vienna, was once under the Habsburgs a co-capital to one of the largest empires in Europe. In Budapest, a surprising number of cultures have come together to form an exciting mix of the modern and the traditional. Musical events frequently occur throughout the city. The ancient cities of Buda and Pest are joined by the Chain Bridge, guarded by great stone lions. Buda is dominated by Castle Hill, topped by Matthias Church for 800 years – but it is important to remember that a great deal of historic Budapest was destroyed in World War II and has since been rebuilt. Budapest is also home to the Dohany Street Synagogue, the largest synagogue in Europe that can seat 3000 people and houses the Hungarian Jewish Museum.

Since the fall of Communism, an amazing amount of additional building has occurred in the city and tourists will find an almost endless venue for music, entertainment, dining, and shopping. Budapest is also a primary location to enjoy the hot springs of Hungary, with over twelve enormous public baths where the people gather daily to enjoy these wonderful thermally heated pools (the most famous is the Szechenyi, virtually a paradise of mineral baths and socialization).

Budapest is home to several special buildings designed in the celebration of 1896, including Hero's Square, a vast public park centered around famous Hungarian heroes, flanked by two museums and the various elaborate decorative remnants of the 1896 celebration, including a zoo, a circus, and more baths. Tourists interested in the darker aspects of Hungarian history can visit the House of Terror – a museum that uncovers the considerably ugly side of the secret police of both Nazi Rule and Communist regime; for a more analytical approach, tourists can visit statue park, where the remaining Soviet statues of Stalin, Lenin and Hungarian communist heroes have been gathered for an Ozymandias-like display of some irony.

Technology and Science in Hungary

Twelve Hungarian scientists have received Nobel Prizes. In the past decade, Hungary has ramped up its science and technology industry with significant government funding and a special focus on research, innovation, and development. Hungary is known for its excellent mathematics education. It is the native country of famous mathematicians, some of whom are:

» Father and son, Farkas (1775-1856) and János Bolyai (1802-1860). János was a founder of non-Euclidian geometry.
» Prominent mathematician Paul Erdős (1913-1996) developed Erdős numbers, which are a scientific collaborative equivalent to the American game Six-Degrees-of-Kevin-Bacon, and which have been applied to several areas of scientific study. Basically, an Erdős number rates how close collaboration can be linked between researchers in a field of study.
» John von Neumann (1903-1957), considered the foremost mathematician of his time, who excelled in game theory, quantum mechanics, digital computing in its pioneering era and was one of the chief mathematicians on the Manhattan project.
» One of the most famous Hungarian scientific inventions worldwide was the best-selling puzzle-game, the Rubik's Cube, invented by inventor and architect Ernő Rubik.

Transportation

Throughout Hungary are well-developed transportation systems of roads, railways (the MAV), airways and water transports. Budapest is home to three major train hubs with other large Hungarian cities serving as support hubs and main stations in the network. Large cities also have tram networks, and in fact the Budapest Metro is the oldest underground system in the world, with its first line constructed in 1896. Though Hungary is landlocked, Budapest and other cities have important ports along the Danube River.

Judicial System

Hungary's operates a civil law system of criminal, civil and administrative courts, based largely on the German system of law. The courts have local, regional, and supreme levels and the highest courts in the land are located in Budapest. The Hungarian Police serve as the largest state law enforcement agency under the command of the National Police Commissioner who reports to the Minister of the Interior. The National Police have control over the National Bureau of Investigation (sort of a Hungarian FBI) and the more militarized "Készenléti Rendőrség," a sort of stand-by National Guard that backs up police departments in emergencies. With a homicide rate of 1.3 per 100,000 people, Hungary's is ranked as the 17th safest world country.

The military

Hungary's President (currently Janos Ader) is the commander-in-chief of the national armed forces, which include the Hungarian Ground Force and the Hungarian Air Force. Since 2001, Hungary has purchased a number of $800 million-dollar European jet planes to bolster its air defenses. Since 2016, the Hungarian military has attempted to further modernize by updating its National Cyber Security Center. Currently about 700 Hungarian troops are stationed in foreign countries as members of international peacekeeping efforts. Military service is voluntary with the possibility of conscription in wartime.

The Demographics of Hungary

Administrative Divisions

Hungary is divided into 19 counties and Budapest is considered the 20th territorial unit of the country. Counties are focused on administrative developments; within the countries are some 176 various municipalities that deal with daily services such as water, trash, and rescue services plus the running of schools and care facilities.

Population

In the 2011 census, Hungary's population was just shy of 10 million people, with one quarter of these people living in the metropolitan area of Budapest. There are two national minorities of considerable size: the German and Romani communities.

Like most of Europe, Hungary is experiencing slightly negative population growth, resulting in the average age of its citizenry to be one of the highest in the world. The government has attempted to increase the birth rate by implementing a three-year maternity leave period and by increasing number of part-time jobs available.

Health

The government national health insurance covers 100% of the Hungarian population with universal health care; thus, it has become a major destination for European medical tourism, with dental work and plastic surgery being major draws. Hungary, home of natural mineral hot springs, has a spa culture that has added to its number of medicinal spas, also major tourist draws.

Language

The official language is Hungarian, which is the 13th-most widely spoken first language in Europe and is one of the official and working languages of the European Union. English and German are the most widely spoken foreign languages. Hungary also recognizes the minority languages of Armenian, Bulgarian, Croatian, German, Greek, Romanian, Romani, Rusyn, Serbian, Slovak, Slovenian, and Ukrainian. "Standard" Hungarian as a language is based on the variety spoken in Budapest but it has a number of rural and urban dialects throughout the country and also in neighboring countries with high Hungarian populations.

Religion

With the ascension of King Sant Stephen in AD 1000, and the succession of Apostolic Kings who followed him, Hungary became a Christian country with Roman Catholicism as the state religion and remained such for centuries.

Contemporarily, though Hungary has no official state religion and recognizes religious freedom as a right, Christianity remains recognized as an important influence. The Hungarian constitution permits the state to cooperate with churches for goals that benefit the community. Currently the country's census declares more than 50% of the population Christian, either Catholic, Lutheran or Calvinist. The country's ethnic minorities (i.e., Armenians, Bulgarians, Greeks, Romanians, Rusyns, Serbs and Ukranians) for the most part practice Orthodox Christianity. There is a Jewish population estimated at somewhat more than 100,000 members.

Education

Hungarian children are required to attend preschool and kindergarten from the ages of three to six; following this school attendance remains compulsory until the age of 16. Primary education is eight years long, then secondary education divides the students by their academic level. Hungarian students are noted to be extremely well educated in maths and sciences. The Gymnasium enrolls the most gifted students and gives them college preparation; secondary levels of vocational schools are available for intermediate students and there are a number of opportunities for children to achieve flexible educational assistance. Most Hungarian schools (universities included) are free up to the doctoral level and also provide free health insurance for their students.

Hungary has some of the oldest universities in the world including the University of Pecs (founded 1367), the Óbuda University (1396) and the Universitas Istropolitana (1465). The world's first technology institute was founded here in 1735 (it is today the University of Miskilc), while the Budapest University of Technology and Economics is the oldest institute of technology in the world still in operation with university rank and structure; it was established in 1782 by Emperor Joseph II.

Hungarian Culture

Hungary's people have a longstanding tradition of writing scholarly journals and lengthy essays describing the land's bevy of important landmarks, structures, and artifacts. As early as the 1600s, authors wrote of legendary objects held by Hungarian royalty - such as The Royal Crown and The Horn of Lehel (an artifact that holds mythological importance). Alongside their descriptions of historic monuments, churches, and castles, works of architectural study contained analyses of artistically significant interiors and how indoor spaces were arranged. They wrote also about libraries, picture galleries and "pleasure gardens." Similar kinds of topographical work emerged in the form of specialized literary travel accounts which detailed everything from specific artworks to entire museums. Hungary's passion for their land and its stories have withstood time.

Hungary's artistic history is defined by an overwhelming timeline of world-changing major historical events, one barely ending before the next would begin. The landscape's geopolitical movements have shaped the nation's contributions to the arts, both for the better and for the worse. When the land was occupied by Turkish forces, Hungary's renaissance was badly stunted. But during King Stephen's reign of Catholicism, he brought Gothic and Romanesque art and architectural inspirations to the land's Habsburg-inspired Baroque construction. The arts were especially prevalent during the Dual Monarchy and even under fascism. Mostly, the arts have reigned through the land's hardships, up until modern times as their current economic conditions slash funding for creation.

Architecture

Hungary is filled with the ruins of what were Gothic and Romanesque structures. These sites were pillaged and destroyed by either the Turks, Mongols and/or Habsburgs. Some of these sites still remain preserved, like Sopron's Gothic churches. One interested in "Hungarian" architecture will find their civilization clad in an abundance of Baroque structures such as the Archbishop's Palace and the Minorite church.

Hungary hosts many exceptional structures such as one of the largest basilicas in Europe (Esztergom Basilica), the largest early Christian necropolis outside Italy (Pécs), the second largest territorial abbey in the world (Pannonhalma Archabbey), and the largest synagogue in Europe (aka The Great Synagogue).

Distinctively Hungarian architecture didn't arise until the 19th century as Mihály Pollack, József Hild and Miklós Ybl changed the face of Budapest. Ödön Lechner's Romantic Eclectic style (the Museum of Applied Arts in Budapest is an example) and Hungarian Secessionist (multiple different types of the Art Nouveau style, Reök Palace is an example) brought unique architecture to Hungary by the end of the 19th century.

Art Nouveau and its many types brings a specific uniqueness to Hungary's architectural variations. It is based on national characteristics. Taking the eastern origins of the Hungarians into account, Ödön Lechner (1845–1914) was inspired by Indian and Syrian architecture and later by traditional Hungarian decorative designs. In this way, he created an original synthesis of architectural styles.

A significantly large portion of Hungarian citizens live in valuable buildings, particularly in urban areas. In Budapest's downtown, almost all its buildings are about one hundred years old with thick walls, high ceilings, and motifs on the front wall.

In 1896, Budapest was the site for a magnificent six-month-long Millennial Exhibition, celebrating 1000 years of Hungarian history. Though not precisely a World's Fair, it was treated with the same grandeur within the city, as buildings were erected and massive parks and showcases staged for the hundreds of thousands of tourists expected.

Hungary's Post-WWII architecture is almost completely unremarkable. The most important task Post-War was the country's restoration, rebuilding was their highest priority so there was a pause on architectural flourish. Experimentation initially continued, but social architecture was prominently approved of by the Soviet Union. Therefore, utilitarian reformation became the desired model. The only remarkably unique exception that flourished post-WWII was from Imre Makovecz who developed an 'organic' style using unusual materials like tree trunks.

Music

A major part of Hungary's identity lies in its abundance of folk music. It has produced a fair share of classical music, but the land's heart and soul composed within its folk ensembles and orchestras. The Busójárás carnival in Mohács is a major Hungarian folk music event, formerly featuring the long-established and well-regarded Bogyiszló orchestra. Other prominent folk ensembles include the Hungaria Folk Orchestra, the Danube Folk Ensemble, and the Hungarian State Folk Ensemble, all of which are popular attractions for visitors.

Hungarian folk musicians play violins, zithers, hurdy-gurdies, bagpipes, and lutes on a five-tone diatonic scale. Their songs often have a strong dactylic rhythm as the language stressed and emphasized the first syllable of each word. Roma – as opposed to Gypsy – music is different altogether, and traditionally sung *a cappella*. Some modern Roma music groups – Kalyi Jag (Black Fire) from northeastern Hungary and the newer Ando Drom (On the Road) and Romanyi Rota (Gypsy Wheels) – have added guitars, percussion and even electronics to create a whole new sound.

In terms of composers, one man is regarded to be far more accredited and influential than the rest: Franz (or, in Hungarian, Ferenc) Liszt (1811–86). He established the Liszt Music Academy in Budapest. He was a widely accomplished musician: a virtuoso pianist, conductor, music teacher, arranger, and organist of the Romantic era. He is regarded as one of the greatest pianists of all time.

The communist regime tried to censor Hungarian music but oppression, more often than not, fuels musical passion.

Dance

According to prominent folklore expert Gyorgy Martin, Hungarian dances can be divided into two categories: the middle ages, and 18th to the 19th century. In either case, Hungarians have a notably attuned sense of rhythm and its people can keep time with music more reliably than any other country.

Its most notably important dance is Csárdás, which features the country's recognizable embroidered outfits and lively music. The men hop in tune to intricate boot slapping, and the women dance in beautiful circles. This joyful style of dance is still celebrated throughout the country and is loved by tourists who associate the style exclusively with Hungarian tradition. The whirling dance is a complex mix of couples, few of whom are performing exactly the same movements at the same time. While one couple faces away from one another, another may be in between them performing the next section of the dance.

Other notable folk dances are:
- » Verbunkos. A one-man dance evolved from Austro-Hungary recruitment performances.

- » Ugrós (jumping dances). Performed in the middle ages for solo or for couples, these are marching dances and the remnants of medieval weapon dances.
- » The Legényes. A young man's solo dance. Women participate too but do so in lines surrounding the solo male, the women shout and sing versus toward the lead!
- » Karikázó. Women-only circle dances accompanied by folksongs.

Literature

Hungarian people have always loved its folktales and legends. Their early script was rune-like but their ancient dialect shifted when their language adopted the Latin alphabet. Most Romanian scripts were written in Latin until the Ottoman empire stepped in. Literature flourished under King Matthias (1458-1490) where poems and ballads were heard across its plains.

Sándor Petőfi (1823–49), Hungary's most celebrated and widely read poet, was akin to America's Francis Scott Key in that his work became a rallying cry for independence. In the late 1840s he penned a chanty titled *National Song* to implore his fellow men and women to rise up. It's opening line ("Up, Hungarian, your country is calling! Here is the time, now or never!") became the rallying cry for the 1848–49 War of Independence, a war Hungary unfortunately lost.

After Hungary's crushing loss in 1849, the land's poets and authors turned to Romanticism. People wanted to hear of fantasy, chivalry, and triumph, of heroes and knights in shining armor. People wanted to gather round the bar and hear epic ballads. Prolific novelist and playwright Mór Jókai (1825–1904), wrote of heroism and honesty in accessible works such as *The Man with the Golden Touch* and *Black Diamonds*. A perennial favorite, Kálmán Mikszáth (1847–1910), wrote satirical tales such as *The Good Palóc People* and *St Peter's Umbrella,* in which he parodied the gentry in decline.

A prominent figure of Hungarian language reform was Ferenc Kazinczy, who helped make the Hungarian language understandable and a touch streamlined especially when it came to scientific explanations.

As for modern literature, Hungarian literature has recently gained some renown outside the borders of Hungary (mostly through translations into German, French and English). Globalization of literature should continue to aid in the spread of Hungarian works throughout the world.

Folk Art

The eighteenth century brought prosperity to Hungarian's peasantry. The common person wanted to make their world beautiful. They decorated their clothing, they painted, and they crafted heirlooms. The people of Hungary are known for making and decorating their own furniture. Like it's music, Hungary is known for the art made by the people.

Nearly all varieties of folk art practiced in Europe also flourished among the Magyar peasantry at one time or another, with their ceramics and textile being the most highly developed in artistic technique.

Herders on the great plain made waterproof woolen coats called *szűr*, and these were masterfully embroidered. Actually, there were many groups known for Hungarian embroidery, such as the Palóc of the Northern Uplands, especially around the village of Hollókő; the Matyó from Mezőkövesd near the city of Miskolc; and the women of Kalocsa on the Great Plain. Their textile arts vary from region to region. Those of Kalotaszeg in Transylvania are products of Oriental design, sewn chiefly in a single color like red, blue, or black. Soft in line, the embroideries are applied on altar cloths, pillowcases, and sheets.

No Hungarian kitchen is complete without matching plates and bowls hung up on the walls from its world-class folk pottery. There are jugs, pitchers, plates, bowls, and cups, but the rarest and most attractive are the *írókázás fazékok* (inscribed pots), usually celebrating a wedding day, or produced in the form of animals or people, such as the *Miskai kancsó* (Miska jugs).

Porcelain

Herend Porcelain was founded in 1826 by Vince Stingl, who learned his porcelain craftsmanship in Vienna. The hand-painted, high-quality gilded porcelain received acclaim in 1842 when it won a bronze medal at the First Hungarian Industrial Art Exhibition. Herend crafted porcelain for the Habsburg Dynasty. Following the World Exhibition in London (a whimsical set of butterfly-and -floral decorated porcelain ordered by Queen Victoria now bears her name) and the World Fair in Paris, Herend became an internationally known luxury brand. Today Herend is one of the world's largest ceramic factories, and exports its tableware, figurines and ornaments to 60 countries around the world. New stores open each year, most recently in Dubai and Kazakhstan.

Sports

Football (American soccer) holds a special place in the heart of Hungarians. They've won three Olympic titles and have at least ranked in most competitive football matchups. People considered Hungary to have revolutionized the sport in the 1950s, employing tactical fundamentals of the sport while dominating the international scene with the *Aranycsapat* ("Golden Team"). This team included Ferenc Puskás who was the top goal scorer of the 20th century.

The post-golden age decades saw a gradually weakening Hungarian football team, though recently there is renewal in all aspects.

Historically they excel at most any sport they set their minds to. Hungarian athletes have been successful contenders in the Olympic Games, especially when it comes to water sports. In terms of medal quantity, nobody beats Hungarians in water polo. In terms of swimming, Hungarian men are fourth-most successful while women are eighth-most successful. Hungary ranks eleventh in terms of Olympic medal count. They have nearly five hundred. Hungary has the third-highest number medals per capita and second-highest number of gold medals per capita in the world.

Chess is hugely popular in Hungary. The game is an honored pastime. Hungarian players are the 10th in the power ranking of the World Chess Federation. If one should stop at Budapest's thermal baths, he or she will probably find floating chessboards and others playing chess poolside.

Baths

It is said that if one digs deep enough into Hungarian land, one will find thermal water. Most of the country has reservoirs of hot springs. Its people sought the water's spiritual and healing properties; thus, they've had a passion for spa culture since the very beginning. Quality heated water can be found over 80% of Hungary's territory.

The Romans heralded the first age of spas in Hungary. The remains of their bath complexes are still to be seen in Óbuda. Spa culture was revived during the Turkish Invasion and the thermal springs of Buda were used for the construction of a number of bathhouses, some of which such as the Király Baths and the Rudas Baths are still functioning.

Cuisine

A *csárda,* a distinctive type of old-style taverns, a sort of Hungarian Inn, and within them can be found the country's finest beverage and cuisine offerings. You won't get far into Hungarian food without hearing about their world-famous goulash of meats and vegetables. Hungarians spice their goulashes, along with a lot of their other foods, with paprika (ground red peppers). Their spices are so abundant they offer a heavy Hungarian sour cream, called *tejföl,* to diffuse the fierce amount of spice a Hungarian dish can pack. They also serve a famous Fisherman's soup (*halászlé*) that is a mixture of many kinds of poached fish.

Other dishes include the chicken paprikash, foie gras made of goose liver, *pörkölt* stew, *vadas,* (game stew with vegetable gravy and dumplings), trout with almonds and salty and sweet dumplings, like *túrós csusza,* which are dumplings with fresh quark cheese and thick sour cream. Deserts include the iconic Dobos Cake, strudels (*rétes*), filled with apple, cherry, poppy seed or cheese, Gundel pancake, plum dumplings (*szilvás gombóc*), *somlói* dumplings, even dessert soups like chilled sour cherry soup and sweet chestnut puree, *gesztenyepüré* (these are cooked chestnuts mashed with sugar and rum and split into crumbs, topped with whipped cream), and pastries like *perec* and *kifli.* A *bisztró* is a cheap dine-in of self-service. For the cheapest grub, go to a *büfé,* where customers eat standing at the counter. Confectioneries called *cukrászda* will have pastries for the sweet tooth.

For spirits, visitors should look for a *Borozó*, a type of cozy old-fashioned wine tavern, a *pince*, which is a beer or wine cellar, and a *söröző*, a pub that serves beer. Hungarians traditionally don't clink their mugs when drinking. Why not? Urban legend tells of Austrian generals in 1849 who clinked their mugs as the thirteen Martyrs of Arad were executed, thus Hungarians vowed to avoid touching glasses. Younger people often ignore this urban legend and claim that the vow was only meant to last a hundred and fifty years.

Cinema

The country's film scene was established in the early 20th century. Two hundred and seventy theatres were open and operating by 1910. Some of these places were large capacity film palaces, such as the Royal Apollo. By the end of the 1910s, film distribution had been thoroughly organized. Projectograph was founded by Mór Ungerleider in 1908, it made the first steps for the country's film industry. It was the first major company to produce film and equipment. They also shot documentaries and newsreels.

Hungary's artistic scene was very enthusiastic about cinema as an exciting new method of storytelling. Early Hungarian filmmakers were quick to demonstrate film's educational virtues even if their early works were on the more on the entertainment spectrum. A hybrid form of theatre and film emerged called Cinema sketch. Short projections were incorporated with, or interrupted by, live stage actors who might even be acting as their own characters on the screen. The genre inspired many prominent writers and comedians of the time.

The First World War stunted the budding Hungarian film industry. Film auteurs Michael Curtiz and Alexander Korda left the country. Hungarian filmmakers went not only to Hollywood but anywhere that supported a cinema landscape that wasn't tarnished by the great war. In the 1920s, international (mostly American) companies took advantage of Hungary's economic turmoil by acquiring nearly all of the country's theatres. French, American, and Italian movies, which were banned during the war, were then shown on Hungarian screens and their domination of Hungarian theatres left little room for Hungary's own productions. What few Hungarian film companies remained headed towards bankruptcy.

Government support kept the Hungarian film industry from complete collapse. In 1925, the Hungarian Movie Industry Fund was created. A law was passed that forced all film distributors to finance one Hungarian film for every thirty imported films. Theatres had to air newsreels made by the Office of Hungarian Film. The cinema scene slowly emerged again, and it was marked by the start of journal *Filmkultúra* with editor Andor Lajtha in 1928.

Then came communist nationalization. Once the communists took hold of Hungary, the only company allowed to create film was the Hungarian National Filmmaking Company. Newsreels and documentary production were managed by the News and Documentary

Film Company. Distribution was all handled through MOKÉP. All control over cinema was overseen by authorities who thoroughly censored story, themes, and setting. Scripts were often rewritten (multiple times) to incorporate ideological messages.

Hungary's cinemas were completely controlled by the government by 1950. New films had to be authorized and follow themes such as "socialist conversion" and "enemy sabotage." This chokehold on the Hungarian film industry wasn't all bad. Nationalization actually provided a lot of funding, the government's resources actually allowed for complex, technologically demanding, big-budget films.

Thankfully, by the 1960s, the Hungarian movie industry had been rejuvenated. After the harsher years following the events of 1956, the newly elected socialist government, headed by János Kádár, softened the cinema's harsh censorship regulations. As technology became inexpensive and widely available, the nation became close friends with the world of cinema.

Conclusion: Centuries of Conflict

The Carpathian Basin was inhabited for centuries by Celts, Romans, Huns, Goths, Gepids, Avars, and Franks. Until Arpad led the Magyars into the basin, it seemed no culture could hold permanency there. Rulers Géza and then King Stephen allowed Christianity to spread through the culture. Centuries of battling royal claims did not stop the country itself from forming a rich and vibrant cultures of its many mixed ethnicities. After a devastating Mongolian invasion, Hungary fortified itself and afterward enjoyed a period of some considerable prosperity as its territory was expanded by its conquering kings.

The arrival of the Ottoman Empire put new pressure on Hungary to fight to maintain its boundaries. The Renaissance came to Hungary under King Matthias, but the rulers who followed were unable to maintain Matthias's standards for learning and fairness. For many long and miserable years, the Carpathian Basin served as a battlefield between the Ottoman Empire and the Austrians, with little concern for the Hungarians living in the middle. When the Austrians at last managed to drive the Ottoman Empire away, Hungary still rankled under Austrian rule and made attempts to gain independence, resulting eventually in the Austro-Hungarian Empire as a compromise between the nations in 1867.

World War I divided Austro-Hungary and the Treaty of Trianon took most of its acquired lands away; an attempt to regain the same in World War II led to an alliance with Germany, which resulted not only in defeat but in the horrific decimation of the Holocaust. Afterward Hungary was under the thumb of the U.S.S.R. until its revolution of 1956 brought it some measure of independence, though at a high price.

After the fall of Communism in 1989, Hungary rebounded itself into a modern nation of considerable wealth and power, but even now it faces criticism as once more strong conservative forces press against its development. The rich culture and strong people of the country have always withstood political forces, managing to overcome the seemingly endless array of problems that have plagued the land. The COVID-19 pandemic of 2020 did little to help the conservatism of a country that focuses heavily now on the mistrust of immigration and cooperation with the European Union. Time will tell if these wounds can be healed or if Hungary will continue on the path of continuing conflict.

Sources

"A Super Quick History of Hungary." Mr. History. December 7, 2020. Via YouTube.

https://arthistoriography.files.wordpress.com/2013/06/marosi.pdf

Brittanica.com: The Arrow Cross Party; Holy League; Hungary

"Budapest: The Best of Hungary." July 2004. *Rick Steves' Europe.* Via YouTube.

"Central Europe: Article 7: The Cases of Hungary and Poland." October 24, 2018. Carnegie Europe. Via YouTube.

https://festival.si.edu/2013/hungarian-heritage/folk-arts-and-crafts-hungary/smithsonian

https://www.greatsynagogue.hu/gallery_syn.html

www.herend.com

https://history.state.gov/milestones/1953-1960/warsaw-treaty

"Hungarian Revolution of 1956." *The Cold War; Kings and Generals.* August 1, 2020 via YouTube.

"Hungary Before the Revolution of 1946." *The Cold War; Kings and Generals.* July 25, 2020 via YouTube.

https://www.lonelyplanet.com/hungary/background/other-features/b4113c72-6f8a-42a7-802c-4e1355153b17/a/nar/b4113c72-6f8a-42a7-802c-4e1355153b17/359519

https://www.mfab.hu/exhibitions/art-in-hungary-1600-1800/

https://www.oxfordbibliographies.com/view/document/obo-9780199920105/obo-9780199920105-0136.xml

Patterson, Arthur. (1969). *The Magyars: Their Country and Institutions.* University of Michigan Library.

https://www.politico.eu/article/hungary-no-longer-a-democracy-report/

www.wikipedia.org: 12 points of the Hungarian Revolutionaries of 1848; Arpad Dynasty; Battle of Breadfield; Black Army of Hungary; Erdos Number; Erno Rubik; Finno-Ugric Languages; Hungarian Art; Hungarian Prehistory; Hungary; Hussar; Little Entente; Millennial Celebration; Red Terror; Saint Stephen; Ural Mountains.

In the 1869 book *The Magyars: Their Country and Institutions*, Arthur Patterson described the dance: "they whirl swiftly round, two or three times, and then, breaking away, recommence the pantomime as before...One seldom sees two couples performing exactly the same figure at the same time. While two separated partners are doing their step with their backs turned on one another, another couple between them are spinning round in the ecstasies of reunion."

The History of Poland: A Fascinating Guide to this European Country

Introduction

When comparing the histories of countries, there are time periods in every country that can exist as a blight on the country's historical record. These blights can vary in size and can exist for a myriad of reasons; however, as is true with most types of leadership, the source of these blights can often be traced to the radical or unethical beliefs of a singular individual. Every country has its own blight, and it is the responsibility of the citizens to rise above that blight, showing the world that the actions of one man in one point of history do not dictate the ethics or success of the country. One such country that has endured a particularly terrible blight is Poland. While Poland is a beautiful country nestled in the heart of Europe, there is hardly an individual who can think of Poland without thinking of the atrocities carried out at the Nazi concentration camp, Auschwitz. While the atrocities of Auschwitz are worthy of a lifetime of grief, the history of Poland, both current and medieval, is far too robust to be constrained to a point in history where the ethics of common man were turned upside down. Through simple research, one can find that the beauty of Poland is found in the entity that was most affected by the horrors of World War II: its people.

Poland boasts a robust history spanning back to the first recorded event in Polish history in the year 966 BC. Adding to the mystery of the country, the history before this time is largely founded on the legends and folklore that have emanated from the numerous groups of people whose family names survive to this day. A small country, Poland only occupies 120,733 square miles, all of which are divided into administrative subdivisions. The climate of Poland is usually temperate, adding to the beauty of the countryside. Despite its status as a small country with regards to land mass, Poland has populated its small land mass with nearly 39 million people, making it the fifth-largest population in the European Union. The center of Polish government is found in the capital city of Warsaw while the commerce of Poland is supported by other cities such as Kraków, Szczecin, Gdańsk, Poznań, and Lódż. Most Polish commerce is supported by the close proximity of the Baltic Sea while other commerce is supported by the neighboring European nations.

Polish history is a bit of a mystery to the Polish people with the recorded establishment of Poland dating back to 966 BC. The legend surrounding this date involves a king who was once a pagan but converted to Christianity and adopted the emblems of Christianity. While Poland as a country was established in 966, it would not be until AD 1025 that the Kingdom of Poland was founded. The most successful and famous union in Polish history is its unity with Lithuania, which would come over five hundred years later in 1569. The result of this union was the Polish-Lithuanian Commonwealth, a union that effectively quadrupled the size of Poland overnight. The union fashioned a superpower of Europe, the result being a combined population that began immediately pressing for a constitution. It would be another two hundred years before the first constitution in Europe would be written on May 3, 1791.

Poland's supremacy as a nation was tested during the 18th century when the country was divided from Lithuania, crippling the economy and growth of both countries. This separation would last almost one hundred years until the eventual Treaty of Versailles would position Poland once again as an independent country. The season of independence allowed Poland to be a driving force within the commerce, economy, and politics of Europe. This season did not last long though as Poland was among the first European nations to be invaded during the march of World War II. After Poland endured the invasion of its borders by Germany in late 1939, the Soviet Union would subsequently invade Poland, following through on their regulations as outlined in the Molotov-Ribbentrop Pact. The devastation of World War II on Poland as a nation would cripple the country with an estimated six million Polish individuals dying during the war. Of these six million citizens, three million were Jews that fell prey to the march towards a "perfect race" as outlined by Adolph Hitler. Poland would eventually regain its independent status but not before virtually every citizen of Poland paid the price for both Poland's strategic location and Jewish occupancy.

The two largest blights in the history of Poland are found in the horrors of World War II: the Warsaw ghetto and the Auschwitz concentration camp. While the horrors of these camps will be further investigated in the chapter titled "The Modern History of Poland," the horrors cannot be adequately described in such a short manner. The Warsaw ghetto would go down in history as the largest ghetto that the Nazis established, housing 460,000 Jews during the height of its existence. The Warsaw ghetto acted as a holding location for Jews when the prison camps became inundated with the Jews that were being brought in by train from around Europe. When the housing in the ghetto reached its capacity, the Germans proceeded to overfill the rooms, eventually adding up to nine people per room until the end of the war. The highest expedition of ghetto residents took place in 1942, when almost 254,000 residents were sent to their deaths at the Treblinka extermination camp. The Germans were able to accomplish much of this under the very nose of the other European countries by labeling the transportation of Jews by train car as "resettlement in the East." At the bidding of some of its residents, the exporting of residents from the ghetto would be stopped before the war was over when a period of resistance known as the Warsaw Ghetto Uprisings threatened the lives of the German soldiers. Eventually, the Warsaw ghetto was destroyed at the hands of the Germans following the war. In total, over 300,000 people died while being held at the Warsaw ghetto. At the time of its closing, 92,000 people survived within the ghetto, all of which were dismissed to remake their lives in the broken country.

Perhaps the more tragic of the two World War II locations within Poland, the Auschwitz concentration camp would claim over 1.1 million individuals during the war. While Jews were the highest concentration of the individuals being held at these camps, there were also numerous people being held simply because they aided the Jewish people in some manner. Auschwitz was comprised of forty camps that operated as both concentration camps and extermination camps. The camps were mostly outfitted with gas chambers and laboratories to conduct experiments on the Jewish people. Auschwitz would become known to many as the Final Solution to the Jewish Question as outlined by the Nazis. Ironically, the roots of the Auschwitz prison camp were not found in the holding of Jews but rather German criminals. In 1940, the first load of prisoners would come into the camp while the first planned extermination of Polish and Soviet individuals took place in August 1941. While the occurrences at this camp may have been unnoticed by the other European countries, it was well-known to the Polish people what was happening at this camp. Prisoners were often beaten, seldom fed, and occasionally killed simply because the prison had run out of room for all of its occupants. There was no care and no compassion for any of the occupants of this prison. Perhaps the most excruciating detail of this camp were the numerous individuals who were unfortunate enough to become test specimens for the medical experiment labs of the German doctors. The German doctors were not against testing their own people, but towards the end of the war, the test subjects pool was completely comprised of Jewish individuals. There would be numerous uprisings during the history of Auschwitz, but sadly, none would be as successful as the Ghetto Uprisings. To this day, the largest blight on Poland remains its shared responsibility for not destroying the concentration camp. While the Allies would eventually be made aware of the atrocities of this camp, there would be no actions taken against the concentration camp until near the end of the war.

While the Warsaw ghetto and the Auschwitz concentration camp remain demoralizing margins of Polish history, the years following the war would focus on rebuilding the country. The strength of the Polish people grew in correlation with the amount of restoration needed, vaulting Poland to the status as a developed market and the most powerful country in its region of Europe. Today, the Polish economy has transitioned into being the sixth-largest within the European Union and has become an economy embraced by its residents, as denoted by Poland's impressive Human Development Index rating. As a country, Poland has dedicated a large amount of its resources to the education, prosperity, and living conditions of its residents. Poland is one of the few countries to offer free education that ranges from elementary school through university education while also offering free health care for its residents. Poland has taken special care to preserve the numerous national monuments that spot its geography, achieving UNSECO protection on sixteen World Heritage sites.

Politically, Poland exists as a representative democracy led by a president who acts as head of state. The true power of the country, however, would lie with the prime minister, who is considered the head of the Council of Ministers. Poland has joined the United Nations, the

European Union, and NATO, all segments which boost the country's economics and trading platforms. The official language of Poland is Polish, and as a country, Poland's primary ethnicity is comprised of Polish individuals. With only 3% of its land mass represented by water, Poland is able to offer adequate housing and land to its 39 million residents. In 2019, Poland's GDP per capita was $17,369, sliding the country into 54th place globally.

As a country, Poland has endured the heartbreak, tragedy, and loss that few other countries have felt; however, it has also been able to promote growth that few countries can achieve. As a nation, Poland has a close-knit residency that is primarily comprised of families. Through the history of Poland, one can learn that while the choices leading to a blight, such as World War II, brought on Poland were one man's actions, the response and growth from that blight will always be the choice of the people. Poland chose to respond to its tragedy with a tremendous rebuilding effort and one that has resulted in the powerful nation Poland is today.

THE FIRST DAYS OF POLAND

The earliest known inhabitants of Poland were found during the Bronze and Iron Age. These people were known as the Biskupin and occupied a fortified settlement, the ground of which is now one of Poland's sixteen UNESCO sites. Polish history from 400 BC until AD 500 was dominated by various ethnic groups that primarily stayed in their own region of the land mass now known as Poland. Various ethnicities included Germanic, Baltic, Scythian, Celtic, and Sarmatian groups. In addition to these groups, there is strong proof that various Roman Legions also made the land of Poland a common place to stage strategic attacks or rest from attacks. It is believed that during this time, the Roman government sent out various groups to explore land mass as far as they could. Many of these Roman groups made it to Poland but failed to ever claim the land for the Roman government. While there is no Roman record of such occurrences, the journals and historical records from numerous Slavic groups explains gatherings of such people. Within the 6th century in the common era, the Slavic people were the primary ethnic group of Poland, occupying the land under a pagan religion that did not tolerate any function of Christianity. In the few years prior to the Middle Ages, Poland's shape began to form.

In the middle of the 10th century, the religion of the Slavic people inhabiting what is now Poland had been paganism. That would change shortly after with an event now known as the Baptism of Poland. During this moment, the leaders of the small government in Poland transitioned from paganism to a full embrace of Western Christianity. Specifically, the leaders began supporting the religious thoughts of the Roman Church, causing quite a stir among the people. The individuals who had so long practiced paganism under the protection of their leaders were now being requested to transition to a new and completely adverse religion: Christianity. While the leaders of the country would transition to a new religion seemingly overnight, it would still be over a hundred years before the rest of the citizenry fully accepted the religious transition. Although the full acceptance of the new religion might have been years away, something much bigger was beginning to take place in the country: the formation of formal government.

Poland's first "true" government was established under the watchful eye of the Piast dynasty. With keen attention to the growing faction of citizens in the country, the Piast dynasty began laying the foundation for the creation of a territorial augment of government within the mid-900s. The man responsible for this transition to a more formalized government was the same man who had led Poland in its transition from paganism to Christianity: King Mieszko I. After the official Baptism of Poland in 966 in which the Catholic fathers formally recognized Poland as a Christian nation, the religious transition began to slowly seep into the population. After King Mieszko passed away, his son Boleslaw the Brave saw to it that his father's dream of a Christian nation was carried out. To facilitate this acceptance, Boleslaw attempted to hold a meeting, the Congress of Gniezno, where the metropolis of Gniezno was formulated. With the metropolis created, Boleslaw met his father's expectations with the creation of dioceses in Kraków, Wroclaw, and Kolobrzeg. Boleslaw would die before this creation was complete, leaving the legacy of his father to be carried out by his successor, Casimir I the Restorer. Whereas the people of Poland had simply been resistant towards accepting the new factions of their new religion under both Mieszko and Boleslaw, the people actually mounted a resistance against Casimir I the Restorer, resulting in the subsequent transfer of the capital city from Gniezno to Krakow. This uprising from those still adhering to paganism in Poland would act effectively as a large roadblock to the future of Christianity in the nation, and for the time being, no more talk of religious transition was made by the kingdom.

The successor to Casimir I, Prince Boleslaw III Wrymouth, held perhaps the most important battle of this time period when he led a conquest against King Henry V of Germany, meeting the German army at the Battle of Hundsfield, where Prince Boleslaw was victorious. This defeat of the German army was key as the German army had been attempting an advance into the Polish countryside. The details of the battle were so great that their full stories are measured in the 1118 Chronicle by Gallus Anonymus. Shortly before Prince Boleslaw died, he dissected his land among his sons, creating numerous duchies that would be ruled by each son.

Over one hundred years after the countryside of Poland was split into numerous factions by Boleslaw, the reigning Duke of the Piast dynasty, Konrad I of Masovia, mounted a campaign to fight against the Baltic Prussian pagans who were seeking to disrupt the Christian transition of the Polish people. By now, most of the Polish population had transitioned to Christianity; however, the Polish government was still worried that the dissenters within the fringe of paganism that still existed might act as an impediment to the future growth of Christianity. With this in mind, Konrad I of Masovia reached out to the Teutonic Knights for aid in the fight against the Baltic Prussian Pagans. While the Baltic Prussian Pagans would eventually be defeated, it would not be for an additional three centuries, leaving the Polish and the Teutonic Knights in constant warfare for almost three centuries.

Perhaps the most afflicted people group within Poland is the Jews, most notably afflicted during the World War; however, their affliction goes back centuries. In 1264, the General Charter of Jewish Liberties was not pleased that its people were being treated so ill in Poland. Thus, a resulting document from this time period granted a list of rights that Jewish people were given. While the Jewish people were now protected by the rights afforded in this new document, the document served as the largest barrier between the people groups of Poland, effectively shunning the Jewish people from the other ethnic groups within Poland.

To this point in the history of Poland, the majority of Poland was comprised of numerous people groups. While this allowed for autonomy among the different people groups, there was a looming lack of unity among the people. The 13th century brought new kings into the kingdom, all of which tried to unite these different Polish groups. Under the mantra of strength through unity, king after king futilely attempted to unite these different groups. The greatest attempt at unity came from the Silesian branch within the Piast dynasty. This branch was ruled by Henry I the Bearded and Henry II the Pious, and the unity of these nations was almost reached; however, the Mongols noticed the distracted people and decided to attack the Eastern portion of Poland. The kings had no choice but to retreat from the construction of a unified people group in order to defeat the advancing Mongols. As it would turn out, the Mongols had timed their advance against the Polish people perfectly, defeating the Polish Army at the Battle of Legnica. While the loss was a severe defeat within itself, the greater defeat was the loss of Duke Henry II the Pious. For the next one hundred years, the Polish kingdom would slowly split apart, each king futilely attempting to unite the kingdom. With each king, it seemed the desire to unite was shared by fewer people. However, in the year 1320, King Wladyslaw, a highly influential noble, used the full force of his power to overtake the throne and become king. Today, he is remembered as the first king that sat upon the throne of a unified kingdom within Poland. Additionally, this is considered the Golden Age within Polish history, as the country became unified for the first time. When Wladyslaw passed from the throne, his son, Casimir III, reigned in his stead. Casimir III is remembered as being the greatest

Polish king, primarily for his attention focused on creating an infrastructure that was supposed to withstand many of the attacks that the neighboring countries might place on Poland. Casimir III was a strong proponent of protections for the Jewish people, going as far as to encourage their continual immigration to Poland. With Casimir III increasing the rights of every Jewish person to the same standard as most Polish citizens, Jews began coming to Poland in droves. With a keen eye on the future growth of Poland, Casimir III began laying the foundation for a group of highly skilled educators to create a school for higher learning, the modern-day equivalent of a university. Casimir's primary purpose in creating this institution of learning was to educate future lawyers and politicians who could write laws for the country. The result of Cssimir's desire was the University of Krakow, the first formal learning center hosted by the government and approved by Pope Urban V. To this point in Polish history, the governing body of Poland had always been the Piast dynasty. To spread the governing bodies slightly, Casimir helped create the Golden Liberty given to the nobles of his day. The Golden Liberty entailed the protections offered to nobles who offered their military service to the kingdom. At the conclusion of their military term, these nobles were granted the status of superior nobleman, a status that placed them far above the status of the common man. The plan worked, for Casimir always had a strong supply of nobles to fight in his army. In 1370, the most beloved king in the history of Poland died when Casimir passed away. The succession for kingdom was complicated by the fact that Casimir did not have a male heir who could take his place as king. As such, the Piast dynasty, the first major ruling body of Poland, came to an end. Thus would end the early history of Poland.

When one looks at the early history of Poland, it is easy to see the infrastructure taking shape as the Middle Ages were beginning to take full effect. When the Piast dynasty came to its end, Poland was growing in unity and becoming the primary destination for Jews in search of equal rights. The coming days of the Polish kingdom would hold more battles but a greater sense of unity than the country had ever known.

The End of
the Middle Ages in Poland

With Casimir III creating a common path for all immigrants to follow into Poland, the ethnic groups of the Jews and even German, Flemish, Scottish, Danish, and Walloon immigrants flooded into the land. While the years from 1347-1351 created a large loss of life for most of Europe with the Black Death harvesting death after death, Poland was able to avoid the disaster for the most part, some historians pointing to the royal decree to quarantine the borders of the country as being the largest influential factor in Poland's avoidance of the plague. While the true cause of this avoidance will never be known, this time did help usher in the next dynasty of Poland: the Jagiellon dynasty. The first leader of this dynasty would be the Grand Duke of Lithuania, Wladyslaw II Jagiello. This king would unite the two kingdoms of Poland and Lithuania, giving both countries access to some of the best resources that the respective nation was able to create as a core commodity. Additionally, the union gave both countries a greater array of weaponry and defense should any of the other

European countries create hostility between the nations. This union between the two nations would continue for four centuries following the beginning of the Jagiellon dynasty.

Recalling the days when the Mongol army invaded Poland, one would remember that Poland reached out to the Teutonic Knights for their support and defenses. While this prevented the Mongols from advancing further into the country, it did create a problem when the Teutonic Knights continued fighting, this time setting their sights on the Polish Army. The constant struggle between these nations had continued for almost three centuries until a fateful day in 1410 when the newly combined forces of the Polish-Lithuanian army handed the Teutonic Knights one final loss. Almost fifty years later, another decisive victory took place in 1466 when the Thirteen Years' War ended with the subsequent Duchy of Prussia. During this time, the Polish force of power was at its peak, helping check the advances of numerous nations surrounding the country. Among the nations affected by Poland's large army were Bohemia, the Ottoman Empire, and Hungary. The battles between the Ottoman Empire and the Polish Army were by far the most extensive, a recorded seventy-five battles taking place between 1474 and 1569. While the Polish Army was quick to check the advances of most of its enemies, a serious problem developed when the Crimean army began making slave runs against the people along the shore of Poland and Lithuania. In all, it is speculated that over 1 million citizens of Poland were lost in the numerous slave attacks that terrorized the coastline. While the attacks on slaves would eventually end, the Polish people suffered a great deal under the inability of the Polish Army to curb these attacks.

Under the watchful eye and guidance of the Jagiellon dynasty, the government of Poland began to develop into a successful feudal system. The growing agricultural scene of the country provided it with one of the fastest growing economies of the day. Under the rule of Casimir III, the period of Golden Liberty had begun. This focus on nobility took new importance in the 1500s when a new act from Parliament titled the Nihil Novi Act shifted the power from the kingdom to the existing parliament of Poland. This parliament was comprised of the nobles who had previously served in the military and were not eligible to receive their status as men better than the common man. At its peak, the motto of the Sejm was "Free and Equal," denoting that the individuals below the Sejm were all equal. Those who know their history will also recognize this time as it corresponds with the Protestant Reformation, a time of revival in Christianity as sparked by Martin Luther in Germany. Until this point, Christianity had been the state religion of Poland, having replaced paganism centuries earlier. With the new focus on religious liberty, Poland followed the lead of numerous other nations in allowing its citizens the ability for religious freedom and religious tolerance. Once again, Poland observed the strife taking place in other European countries where the people's voices were not heard and made political decisions based on such research. It was through this that Poland was able to mitigate the dissension within its country.

In the late 1540s, the European Renaissance began to seep into Poland, resulting in new thoughts on science and education. With the new focus on education and learning, Poland began opening new trade routes, resulting in a surge within the Polish economy. As the economy of Poland began to swell, the cultural benefits of Poland also began to increase to the point that Poland was seen as a very inviting culture and the increase in immigration showed such sentiment. Perhaps the greatest contribution of Poland during the European Renaissance was through science when Polish astronomer Nicolaus Copernicus levied his assertion of a heliocentric world in his book On the Revolutions of the Celestial Spheres. The period of the renaissance within Poland would reach its climax in 1569 when the country passed the Union of Lublin, which effectively established the Polish-Lithuanian Commonwealth. While the two countries had been brought together under previous monarchies, this new agreement was a more formal means of identifying the union between the countries and also allowed the officials to be regularly elected within an elective monarchy. The primary goal of the establishment of the commonwealth was the creation of a central parliament to govern both countries. After the union was created, there would be subsequent political meetings where further legal establishment would be outlined, such as the Warsaw Confederation in 1573 where the religious freedoms of the Polish people were agreed upon. In total, the Union of Lublin created a joined entity responsible for over one million square miles of countryside.

When the union between Poland and Lithuania was first formally recognized, the stability within the two governments was almost surprising. One would expect some growing pains; however, the two countries were able to coexist with their formal separations but one joined government. The period of stability would stutter to a halt in the latter months of the 1500s when the formal dynasty rulers of Poland became known for their corruption. Such corruption subsequently led to conflicts with Russia, the Ottoman Empire, and Sweden. Poland would emerge victorious after the various battles with Russia, achieving victory in 1610 when Commander Hetman Stanislaw Zolkiewski was victorious at the Battle of Klushino. One year later, the czar of Russia formally announced his homage, decreeing his succession of the war.

As the union with Lithuania continued to grow older, the formal governing body, once touted by the Golden Liberties espoused upon those who gave of themselves to fighting in the army, began to deteriorate. Largely due to a general sense of greed for more power, the nobles began to trample upon one another, scrambling for even the slightest amount of power. The result was the gradual disintegration of the Commonwealth that had previously been described as the strongest governing body yet. When the Cossack Khmelnytsky Uprising disrupted the lives of the Polish people, the nobles were forced to allow the division of Ukraine, effectively giving the eastern portion of the Ukraine to the Russian government. The rest of the 1600s were entrenched in what is now known as the Deluge, a time when the Swedish army found a vulnerable portion of Poland's population and proceeded to invade the country. As the Swedish army moved forward, they proceeded to ruin farmland and agricultural opportunities, effectively stifling the Polish economy. With the diminished economic strength, the standard of living in Poland plunged, leaving many Polish people sick. Accompanying diseases and starvation would lead to nearly 4 million deaths, a stark number when compared with the usual population of 11 million individuals. In retrospect, the 17th century was the most tumultuous time for Poland yet. With her country now divided and dying, it seemed that the country had perhaps grown beyond what it was able to control. Fortunately for the country, there was a capable individual who was up to the task of reunifying the country.

John III Sobieski would be remembered as the man who was perfect for the job at hand: reunifying a country that was suffering from a loss of morale. The first moment of victory in a while would take place in 1683 when John III Sobieski would lead his forces against the Ottoman Army at the Battle of Vienna. In this army, the victorious courage of the Polish Army was re-established and the citizens of the country finally had something to be proud of. For the time being, Poland was once again the growing power it had been before the Deluge.

Even with the return to power, the power vacancy within Poland was evident to anyone watching from the outside. Historians consider this time period as being the end of the golden age that had vaulted Poland to one of the superpowers of the day in Europe. Perhaps the most significant contributing issue was the feeling that Poland was constantly at war with someone. As these battles continued to wage on, internal strife began to emanate from the kingdom, many people unsure that fighting battles was the best way to restore the kingdom to its former glory. This fall from the golden age would be marked by the terrible rulership of the kings during this time. With the country falling apart, the kings resorted to shady business dealings and an even more inconspicuous legislative process that passed a number of laws that directly hindered the citizens of Poland. On a number of occasions, the people of Poland rose up in anger against the Polish government, staging various uprisings such as the Lubomirski Rebellion. Before long, the highest governing body in Poland would be operated by numerous magnates instead of kings. While this may have seemed like a trivial disagreement or even growing pains, it was sadly laying the foundation for a glorious division of the country. As Poland continued its spiral from glory, Russia began harvesting the victories of this fall, gathering key victories at locations such as the Great Northern War. On the heels of this destruction, the Polish people pushed for reform in their society, a measure granted by Parliament with the ushering in of the Age of Polish Enlightenment. The beginning of the 1700s marked a time period in which the Parliament attempted various measures of societal reform; nonetheless, the people were not satisfied with merely an attempt at reform. As the multiple attempts at social reform fell on deaf ears, other transitions within the country began to take place, the most notable being the moving of the capital from Gdansk to Warsaw. While the country may have been drifting away from its prestigious and prosperous roots, there was no doubt that the divide was truly coming between the nobles and the common citizens of the day. Many nobles were able to maintain strong incomes during this time, often harvesting the lower-priced goods of their befallen countrymen. Sadly, this divide would lead to an even further division of the country. It has been said that great countries are not divided from the outside but rather from within. If only the Polish people could have seen the injurious future that was laying before them; however, none had the foresight to see such a moment and the terrible days that lay ahead rushed into the country with no warning, setting the country into a time now known as the Partition of Poland.

The Early Modern History of Poland

In 1764, Poland held a royal election in which the country gave the monarchy to a young man named Stanislaw II August. The primary influence resulting in his election was his connection to the groups of magnates that had been operating the country for the past hundred years. Perhaps of more concern was this man's allegiance to Russia, a factor that he held would not influence his decisions as king but an allegiance that he was nonetheless unwilling to break. In 1768, the Bar Confederation was formed and fueled the rebellion in protest of the Polish government, specifically the surmised traitor Stanislaw II. The goal of the rebellion was to remove the king and maintain the independence of Poland as had been outlined in the previous government. As a precursor to the division that would eventually rob Poland of its union with Lithuania, a dissolution of the union was begun as early as 1772 when an activity known as the First Partition of Poland took place. In this time, King Stanislaw II was attempting to bid Austrian aid that would have helped Poland loose itself from its Russian shackles.

Unfortunately, the bid for war was rejected when the partition was passed by Frederick the Great as his response to the Austrian's rumor of war. With Frederick the Great being king of Prussia, fear sank into the hearts of the Polish people as they wondered if their country would be taken over. With the partition official, only time would tell if the Polish people were able to rescue their country.

As the news of the partition set in throughout the countryside, the government of Poland refused to pay attention to the partition, instead using this time to create the Commission of National Education. This commission led to increased standards of living throughout the country, namely barring anyone from subjecting a child to the same corporal punishment of their adult peers. Parliament reconvened in 1788 under the title of the Great Sejm, and work was set out to completely overhaul the current government infrastructure. Under the leadership of the Great Sejm, a constitution was written, aptly titled the May 3 Constitution. This constitution would go down in history as being the first laws that governed a nation supremely in Europe. While the new laws within the constitution seemed to settle the political landscape of Poland, civil unrest soon sprang up, the citizens concerned that there were laws within the constitution that were intended to aid those in favor of a revolution and the dissolution of the union between the Lithuanian government and Poland. With the country rising in strong unrest, the Russian government saw this as an opportunity to attack the country while vulnerable and promptly invaded Poland. This would begin the Polish-Russian War.

At first, the Polish people, incensed by Russia's bravery in invading the country, were sure they would win the war, and fighting against the Russians was considered an honor; however, this courage soon turned to further disgust and anger when King Stanislaw II abdicated from his position as king and joined the very forces that were destroying his country. With no king on the throne, the Bar Confederation assumed the throne and sought to orchestrate a war. The transition to power by the confederation was actually a strong move on the part of the Polish people. Immediately, the Russian forces were concerned that they would no longer be able to defeat the newly inspired Polish Army, thus prompting the Russians and Prussians to come together to execute a second partition, officially known as the Second Partition of the Commonwealth. While the first partition sought to remove the union between Lithuania and Poland, this partition sought to cramp Poland's living spaces to the point that the people were unable of living without the aid of the Russian government. Two years of horror would follow for the Polish people, who, in their gasp for freedom, were unable to quell the forces of Russia. After the two years had passed, the Russian government passed one final partition, and with one final blow, dissolved the commonwealth between Lithuania and Poland. Poland had effectively been surrounded by its neighbors, at which point it was forced to give up its supremacy as a kingdom and return to its original land mass size.

Immediately following the third partition, the Polish people mounted a small resistance against those seeking to partition the country. One such uprising was known as the Kościuszco Uprising, a particularly valiant effort from a man who had previously served within the ranks of George Washington during the Revolutionary War in the United States of War. While this uprising had victories, the end would be a miserable defeat for Poland and one final defeat: Poland was no longer a free country. With the government in shambles, neighboring countries moved in to overtake the throne or set up various governments within the country. One such government was France, governed by the courage of Napoleon I who created the Duchy of Warsaw. This occupancy by France would last only until the end of the Napoleonic Wars, after which the country would once again fall and return to its divided state. Within the eastern portion of the divided country, Poland had fallen into the hands of the Russians who ruled the Congress Poland. The western portion of Poland, once controlled by the Prussians, would eventually fall into the hands of the Germans. The divide between the two portions of the country became quite different. While Polish people were granted their freedoms in the western portion of the country, the eastern portion of the state began to adopt more and more Russian government until the country was barely noticeable as a former Polish country.

Even as they watched their country become more and more like their governing nations, the citizens of Poland refused to go without a fight. Thus, it was not uncommon for the Russian, Prussian, and Germanic troops to be met with fierce resistance. While this resistance did little to stamp out the fire of the occupying countries, it was a good reminder to the people of Poland that their voices were still being heard. In 1830, the Polish forces combined in Warsaw where they were commanded by Lieutenant Piotr Wysocki. The location of Warsaw was strategic due to the Officer Cadet School being formed there. After a series of meetings in which the cadets were rallied to courage against the Russian troops occurring their city, a faction of Polish citizens joined these cadets in revolting against the Russians. The battle, for now, was successful with the Russian troops chased out of the city and to the north. While the cadets knew that the Russians would be back with more troops, it was an encouragement to know that they still were capable of standing for what they believed in. This particular uprising would become known as the November Uprising. The Russians would fail to secure Warsaw again for the next seven months, during which the Polish forces were able to defend the city heroically. With the Polish people mounting an offensive against the overarching powers of the Russian government, the Polish government attempted to secure the additional protection and troops that the neighboring countries had; however, the neighboring countries were none too eager to give troops to Poland. With no power, the Polish drive for victory disappeared into the night. The following day, Warsaw would be surrendered to the Russians, and days later, almost the entire Polish Army ran east where they crossed into the lands occupied by the Prussian troops and surrendered. With no defense, Poland was once again aligned with the Russian government, never before appearing to be so closely related. At the time, it seemed that Poland was destined to become a part of Russia, never to return to its independence.

For over fifteen years, the Polish people remained in subjection to the Russian government. There seemed to be very little hope that the Polish people could ever reinvent themselves as a country and inspire their people to fight again. However, as the Polish people grew angrier with their current state, various voices began calling for a new revolution. The result would be a new time of revolts named the Spring of Nations. The Polish people began scraping together whatever weapons they could find, joining in what would eventually be known as the Greater Poland Uprising of 1848. While the uprising began as a small group of Polish farmers who were attempting to create a skirmish with troops, the Prussian army exacerbated the party when it came crashing into the affair, killing several of the Polish troops. The result would be a renewed battle against the Prussian army but would sadly not last long. The Polish people were able to keep the Prussian army on the move for several days, but once again, without the access to resources such as the Prussian army had, there was no possible way the Polish Army could maintain the resistance. After surroundering yet again, the Polish Army returned home in humility, the new Grand Duchy promising to be harsher than the previous king had been.

The next eleven years would see the Polish people attempt to live on their meager rations and in terrible living conditions. In 1863, however, the Polish people had a new voice that once again called for reform and a renewed battle against the Russian troops. With a new sense of courage, the Polish people began gathering weapons, and the January Uprising took root. The early days of the January Uprising saw it emerge as a group of Polish people merely trying to antagonize the Russian troops that maintained their presence in Poland. As more people joined the daily antagonizing of the troops, however, the two groups began sparring more frequently, and soon, a new war had erupted on the Polish front. When the Russian army began gathering young Polish men to fight in the

Russian army, the battle broke out in a new rage. While the Polish troops were no match for the thousands of Russian troops, the Polish Army tried to fight with more than troops, often sitting ambushes for the Russian troops or resorting to assassinations. The Russians would best the Polish troops in every battle of this uprising, the Polish troops' lack of organized fighting coming back to destroy the attempted attacks. At the conclusion of this uprising, it was decided that no future uprisings should be held since the past few uprisings had failed to gather any momentum. Rather than destroy the Russian troops, the Polish people set out to improve their standard of living as best they could. Poland would be able to add factories to the country, and the people of Poland watched as their country's economy suddenly blossomed amidst the tragedy of the Russian occupancy. The Polish people set their mind to the task at hand, industrializing their nation, and by the end of the 19th century, the country was a fellow competitor for goods.

As the world turned one century older, Poland retained its status as an occupied country and failed to operate its government as its own. The beginning of the 20th century was calm, but the rising political unrest in the late 1920s seemed to signal that something much larger was coming. While the Polish radicals had attempted to curb any future uprisings given the grim outlook of overthrowing the Russian government, there were still voices that called for resistance. As the political unrest in Europe continued to grow, the rest of the world suddenly became involved, most major countries issuing statements on their stance regarding Poland's independence. None of these voices were stronger than the voice of Woodrow Wilson, who proclaimed that Poland should once again be granted its own constitution. This proclamation was made in the middle of President Wilson's famous fourteen points speech and caused ripples around the world. In a subsequent uprising in 1918, the Polish troops were able to gather some semblance of organization, going as far as to prompt Germany to agree to their armistice the same year. With the armistice signed, Poland made preparations to once again become independent. Finally, after years of fighting and numerous uprisings, Poland was able to proclaim its independence, officially recognized as the Second Polish Republic.

The fight for independence was not over yet, as Vladimir Lenin still attempted to bring his power of Communism throughout Europe. When Russia began antagonizing the Polish troops, the impending war was called the Polish-Soviet War. This war would last from 1919 until 1921 when the Polish Army had its second great win in three years, defeating the daunting Red Army at the Battle of Warsaw. To this day, the heroic efforts of the Polish Army are remembered as the Miracle at the Vistula. While the battle engrained victory in the hearts of the Polish people, it also served to cease the spread of Communism throughout Europe, acting as a key blocker against Russia's goal of global domination.

With the country back in formation, the government of Poland set out to regain all of the land that it had been stripped of during the various partitions. During this time, Poland also paid special attention to the formation of transit within the country, laying rail lines that ran directly into the capital cities so that the commerce of Poland could flourish. To further charge the emerging economy, Poland also established a port on the Baltic Sea that allowed ships to bring their goods to Poland while also allowing the export of Polish goods. As the country was reopening from the horrors of its partitions, the voices of Poland were strengthened by the emergence of several key individuals who had held prominent positions prior to the dissolution of the Polish-Lithuanian union. In 1922, the growth of the country was momentarily halted upon the tragic assassination of the current president of Poland, Gabriel Narutowicz. The politics of the country would continue to face several transformations over the next few years as constant attention had to be paid to the various radical groups that wanted to see Poland removed from its stable pedestal. As these radical groups continued to grow in number, the Polish government was forced to relax some of its lenient policies, following the example set by other nations in banning several radical organizations. In 1938, one year before the greatest tragedy to befall Poland would occur, Poland was gifted a small tract of land from Czechoslovakia, an act of good will and one that would bring the two countries together.

While the Polish people were proud to once again be a nation that was respected by the world, there was still a nagging feeling within many of them that the Russians were being far too quiet. Truly, the Polish people had no idea what horrors awaited them in the following year. In just one year, Poland would embark on a journey that would test the will of every citizen. Truly, the following time period would test the will of most of the world: that time period was none other than World War II.

The Modern History of Poland

While no nation desires to be at war, its existence is inevitable. Often, war is considered the last result in an expedition of attempted coercion or influence. Even as a nation at war desires to win the war, there is a stronger desire that hinges around not being invaded. There is somewhat of a crippling effect when a nation is invaded. Such was true for Poland on September 1, 1939. Poland had long been brewing in its hostility towards Germany. Poland had attempted to gain back some of the land that had been taken from it during the partitions; however, with a new man at the helm in Germany, it seemed that all hope was gone for Poland ever seeing that land again. This man, Adolf Hitler, spoke of wanting to unite the world; however, many were quick to see through his facade of unity into the core of a man who merely wanted to rid the world of any threat to the Aryan race. Poland would become the battlegrounds for the war as the Soviet Union followed Germany's lead into Poland, invading from the other side of the country less than one month later. Eleven days after Poland had been effectively surrounded by its enemies, the capital city of Warsaw became the latest victim in the march of Adolph Hitler. In a subsequent meeting which produced the Molotov-Ribbentrop Act, the country of Poland was once again divided, this time with the Germans and Soviets splitting the country equally. The Polish people would suffer tremendously under the leadership of their respective zones before eventually being deported from their own country. The Soviet army proved to be the worst of the two occupancies during this time, shooting and killing hundreds of Polish people while continuing to lead the charge towards removing Polish people from the country. By November of the same year, the German army was reading propaganda that called for the complete annihilation of the Polish people. While this would never happen, millions of Polish people would lose their life in the coming days.

The German and Soviet occupancy of Poland proved to be of utmost value to the Allies, who relied on the spies within the country who could tell of Soviet or German military advances. Eventually, in an act that would lead to the end of World War II, Polish physicists would be the primary influencers in a project that interpreted the codes from the Enigma, a sophisticated coding operative as given by the German army. For the time being however, the Polish influence within the country as mere spies was valuable enough. With the country effectively split in two, the Polish Army would hold different allegiances during this time. While some served as troops within the Polish government in the western portion of Poland, the rest actually served the Soviet government in the east. With the numerous battles that would take place during this war, the Polish troops proved to be invaluable to whatever side they were fighting on. One battle of importance is the Battle of Monte Cassino. Additionally, heroic battles such as the Normandy Invasion, the Italian Campaign, and the North African campaigns would likely have held different outcomes had the war not had the support of Polish troops. After all, when combined, the Polish troops constituted the fifth-largest army in Europe. While the Polish people disliked having the Soviets in their country, the Soviet army did provide troops for the Polish Army, leaving the Polish government content to focus on the German invasion and the subsequent attempts at removing these troops from their country.

Known as the Armia Krajowa, the Polish Army set out to develop a sophisticated world underneath the eyes of the German leadership. While the Polish people appeared to be in compliance with the numerous new laws that the Germans placed on them, the Polish people were actually involved in managing an underground world where all legal battles were settled and higher education took place. The German occupation of Poland took new significance later that year when Adolph Hitler began constructing various prison camps throughout the country. In shocking fashion, some of these prison camps were constructed as extermination camps, locations solely dedicated to the killing of prisoners. Additionally, Germany began establishing ghettos throughout Poland, cities that were dedicated to maintaining prisoners. Often, these ghettos were home to horrors and atrocities as the German soldiers did whatever they pleased with the Polish prisoners. The previous days of the resistance seemed to be over as any Polish individual seen as a threat to the German army or government was either exiled to a prison camp or executed on the spot. The current times were dark for all Polish people, but sadly, the darkest days ahead would be occupied by a select group of people: the Jews from Poland.

One would recall that in previous governments, the Polish kingdom had welcomed the immigration of Jews, leading to a large occupancy of Jews. When Adolph Hitler began his rampant run against the Jews of the world, the Polish Jews were anything by spared from his wrath. In regard to ethic composition of country populations compared before and after the war, it is hard to find a contingency of Jews more affected than the ones in Poland. Today, less than one percent of Poland's population is Jewish, an astounding 90% of the Jewish population falling to the brute of Adolph Hitler. The Jews were not the only people affected though: almost 3 million Polish people would be killed during the early portion of the war. While the loss of life is always a tragedy, it did not help the Polish people when they realized the majority of their doctors, nurses, pastors, and nobility were being killed by the German troops. The troops had been trained to create chaos by killing the leaders of various groups of people. Perhaps the bloodiest battle during this time for the Polish people took place at the Warsaw Uprising, a resistance that was destined for failure from the moment it started. At the conclusion of the massacre, over 150,000 Polish people would be killed. For the Polish people, there was little to no hope that the Germans would ever retreat from their position. With each battle, the Germans seemed to fortify their position in Poland to become even stronger, leading to a loss of morale for the Polish people. Fortunately, while it may have seemed that the Polish people were fighting alone, the truth is that the world was inspired by this small country who refused to be pushed around by the bigger countries. While the country was enduring tragic losses, its voice remained the same, growing stronger with the death of each Polish person.

The Soviet occupation of Poland would be markedly lighter on the Polish population, although 150,000 Polish people would meet their demise under the fists of the Soviet Union. The tragedy of the Soviet Union's occupancy of Poland was Joseph Stalin's decree that led to routine evictions of the Polish people. In all, over 2 million people would be forced to leave Poland, decimating the country's population and defenses while also dividing families. At the conclusion of the war, it would be revealed that of all of the countries involved in the war, Poland would suffer the largest loss per capita. Over 17% of the country's population being killed during the war, an estimated 90% of these deaths coming off the battlefield.

With the war nearing its end, the Soviet Union sought to gather some land before the war was over. As a result, the Oder-Neisse line was created, leading to Poland losing an additional 20% of its land mass. Whereas the country had once been the supreme authority of Central Europe with its union with Lithuania, Poland's population was dwindling as was its land mass. Towards the end of 1944, the Red Army from the Soviet Union began its march towards Auschwitz, resulting in the deportation of thousands of war criminals and prisoners. The deportation would be a death march though as most of these prisoners and criminals would be killed in concentration camps in Germany. In early 1945, the Soviet army reached the most horrific prison camp,

Auschwitz, where they were greeted with starving people and a myriad of German soldiers. Eventually, American troops would also enter the camp, giving America its first glimpse of the horrors that Communism had brought to the country. To this day, Poland religiously celebrates January 27 as International Holocaust Remembrance Day.

Prior to the end of the war, the Allies held a meeting at the Yalta Conference during which the leader of the Soviet Union, Joseph Stalin, announced his intention to create a new government in Moscow that would allow the practice of Communism. Such a move was infuriating to the Polish people who were currently seeing their country occupied by two countries, both in the name of Communism. Stalin further infuriated the Polish people by claiming that he had allowed the Polish government complete autonomy during the Soviet occupation of the country. Polish people would soon find that while Stalin did allowed elections, these elections were rigged and handed the power directly to the Soviet Union. With the rigged elections handing power to the Soviet Union, Stalin paid a special visit to Poland in which he outlined a new government that would adhere to Communist principles. Many Polish people refused to accept the terms, greeting the news with a militant response. Nonetheless, the Polish government, feeling trapped against the German army from the rear and the Soviet government from the front, agreed that the Soviet Union would annex the land that had previously belonged to Poland. Additionally, the Polish government accepted the Soviet Union occupancy of Poland with troops, a move that many Polish people considered traitorous. In 1947, the Communist government took over Poland's ruling body, and the Polish People's

Republic would eventually be formed. The days following the creation of this governing body were horrific for the Polish people. Anyone who spoke of resistance against the Communist government was imprisoned and likely never heard from again. It took until the end of the 1950s for the first resistance to take place, during which numerous people were freed from prison by the secret militia. These resistances would be small in number but would lead to short bursts of patriotism from those who remembered what Poland used to be like.

While the resistance was often unorganized, a growing movement in the 1980s was the "Solidarity" movement as championed by Lech Walesa. Lech Walesa would eventually win the election as president in 1990, becoming the first member of the Solidarity party to achieve a government position in Poland. The Solidarity movement would achieve fame throughout most of Europe, with many small governments retaking the reins of their leadership with such thoughts. The Solidarity movement would be responsible for destroying the prominence of the Polish United Workers' Party during the 1980s. As the Solidarity movement gained momentum, it would be able to remove many of the Communist bands that had crippled its growth for years. In the coming days, transformation was coming to Poland.

At the turn of the 1990s, the government of Poland began drifting away from its previous roots as a socialist economy into more of a market economy. Immediately after announcing such a change, the Polish economy endured a small recession that was common for countries moving away from the socialist economy. The legacy of Poland would not be cemented until it was able to restore the country to its economic prominence that it had experienced prior to being invaded. By 1995, the country was able to boast a GPD that resembled the country's GDP from before the war began. During this time, Poland also underwent what many consider the second-greatest social reform in the history of the country. Under the watchful eye of Leszek Balcerowicz, the country began passing legislation intended to give more freedom to citizens in the areas of speech, civil rights, political freedoms, and internet censorship. Under the previous government administrations and especially during the wars, Poland had lost much of its freedom and resembled some of the most Communist nations of the day. However, the Polish people had endured enough to not want to ever return to such days, allowing Balcerowicz unprecedented ease in adopting these new freedoms. Additionally, to aid against future attacks or invasions from foreign countries, Poland joined numerous organizations dedicated to world peace such as the United Nations and the European Union. To facilitate greater commerce and trade, Poland joined the Visegrad Group and also became a leading contributor within the North Atlantic Treaty Organization. While Poland would never unite with Lithuania following the partitions, the country did seek to build unity contracts with neighboring nations such as the Czech Republic and Hungary. By entering into contracts with these two nations, Poland was ensured of having two additional armies at its disposal if a situation such as World War II arose again. Though Poland began the process of joining the European Union in 2003, it would be over one year until it was granted full member status with that privilege coming in May of 2004.

Perhaps the most brilliant move for postwar commerce was the addition of the Schengen Area in 2007. The Schengen is a free-trade agreement that goes above the European Union. While only comprised of countries adhering to the European Union, the Schengen Area is a collection of twenty-six countries within Europe that have deemed passport and other primary forms of identification unnecessary for citizens traveling from country to country. Such a move has facilitated greater commerce as merchants from countries all over Europe are able to ship their goods to other countries without having to abide by normal border control legislation. The only requirement for citizens utilizing the law is a visa that is given out by the home country of that resident. Interestingly, there are four nations, Liechtenstein, Norway, Iceland, and Switzerland that have not joined the European Union yet but maintain active membership in the Schengen Area. In all, the Schengen Area occupies 1,664,911 square miles while also boasting a combined population of 420 million individuals. Such has allowed unprecedented growth in the economies of the member countries.

Though the war was over eighty years prior, the Polish government has made it clear that it intends to never repeat the atrocities that stemmed from the Soviet invasion of Poland in World War II. This has led Poland to focus most of its border patrol on the eastern border of the country, the border that Poland shares with Russia and Ukraine. Today, Poland is the proud creator of what many have referred to as Fortress Europe, a border that is reportedly impenetrable by any ground forces. In a subsequent effort to quell any ideas of invading either Poland or one of its neighboring countries, Poland has established an army combined with the resources of the Czech Republic, Hungary, and Slovakia. The combined army is called the Visegrad Battlegroup and consists of an army of 3,000 troops that are always prepared for a possible battle or hot spot that they could be deployed to. To guard against the eastern neighbors who might be tempted to invade, Poland has done more than construct the Fortress Europe: it has also joined in with Lithuania and Ukraine to form the LITPOLUKRBRIG, a combined army that shares more resources than the Visegrad Battlegroup. With these resources combined, it appears that Poland may be ready to weather any attack that a country foolish enough to attack it would levy.

The politics of Poland had been enjoying a new period of growth until 2010 when the ultimate tragedy struck the Polish government. Whenever a country loses an active member of government, it is a tragedy for both the family of the individual lost and the people of the country who now have to find a new person to sit within that person's former seat. However, when a country loses eighty-nine of its highest ranking government officials, a state of emergency develops within the citizens as the realization that almost one hundred leadership positions were just instantly vacated. Sadly, this is exactly what happened in 2010 when Leah Kaczynski was killed in a plane crash that also killed an additional eighty-nine government employees who were considered vital to the success of the government. The tragedy understandably shook the core of Poland as citizens were aware that their safety and security was now going to be found in an emergency election. Adding to the tragedy of the event, Kaczynski and his team were on their way to a service that was to remember the victims of the Katyn massacre. In all, ninety-six people were on board the plane that would perish when it crashed. While the cause of the wreck would always be disputed, what is known is that the pilots were forced to attempt a landing in dense fog, during which the pilots ventured too close to the neighboring trees and eventually struck one of the trees, demolishing the plane into a giant fireball. During subsequent investigations, the Polish officials would deem that the pilots tasked with flying the aircraft were not fit to be doing so, having neither been trained adequately on flying in regular conditions nor the conditions that were present when the aircraft crashed. As a result of the crash, the pilot program that had produced the pilots flying the president's aircraft was disbanded, and an additional group of military leaders responsible for the oversight of the flying program were forced into resignation by outrage from the Polish citizens. While there are numerous conspiracy theories revolving around an attempted assassination of the president, Polish officials have declared they have yet to find any evidence of this destruction being related to an assassination. Nonetheless, the event remains the most tragic event in the last fifty years of Poland's history and one that will remain a tragedy for the future of Poland.

One year following the tragedy of the plane crash, Poland held elections in which the Civic Platform emerged victorious. One year after these elections, Poland declared its dedication to science with a membership in the European Space Agency. To facilitate more commerce and tourism to the country, Poland joined arms with Ukraine in developing the UEFA European Football Championship in 2012. The event would be created in coordination with the Ukrainian government.

This subsequently led to Poland's entrance into the Development Assistance Committee, a group of countries that met to discuss the various ways that a country can help emerging economies in their quest for economic freedom. During this time, the politics of Poland fell under new light with many people impressed with how the country was being operated. Symbolizing this impressive record, the president of Poland in 2014 would be selected for the position of president of the European Council. In the subsequent elections held to occupy his vacant seat, the Law and Justice party of Poland would emerge victorious. The Law and Justice party of Poland has been the leading party advocating for greater investigation into the plane crash that killed the Polish president years earlier. Likewise, many have said the party best represents the middle class of Poland.

When looking at the history of Poland, it is hard to imagine a time period in which some tragedy did not take place. From being forced to partition the country to being invaded and named the central location for such atrocities as Auschwitz and the Warsaw ghetto, Poland has undergone tragedies that few countries will ever embrace. However, Poland has also made itself known as being one of the few countries that could grow from being in the depths of ashes to being near the top of the countries involved in the European Union. Poland is the perfect example of a people group who refused to be taken with the cares of sympathy or victimization. Rather than focus on the atrocities that the country has endured, Poland has always maintained a forward-looking mindset, focused on what the country is capable of creating, not focusing on what they have endured. The history of Poland is a beautiful representation of a people group united in their focus and stronger through the unity that tragedies can bring. In addition to making their country stronger, Poland has also been able to make the world stronger, adding to the equity of the European Union and giving the world an example to follow when looking at developing economies. Poland, a country of so much heartbreak, has emerged as a country of even greater courage, a courage that has developed opportunities few countries can boast of.

The Economy of Poland

In surprising fashion for a country of its size, Poland enjoys an economy whose gross domestic product is large enough to be ranked sixth among nations in the European Union. The country shows no signs of quelling this growth either, and the gross domestic product is set to overtake the fifth position within the European Union in the coming days. When the sectors of Poland are examined closely, it can be seen that the majority of Polish individuals are employed within the tertiary service industry, while an addition 30% are employed in some facet of the manufacturing industry. While Poland's economy was originally supported primarily by the agricultural industry, the percentage of Polish individuals in the agricultural industry has fallen to an all-time low of 10% and shows no promise of being able to maintain this level. Poland's economy is one that could be examined by other countries for practice, its historically low unemployment rate, low debt, healthy trade balance, and an excellent unified attitude among its companies all combining to aid Poland in doing more than surviving the recessions of 2008, an accolade no other country can claim. Indeed,

Poland did not merely survive the recession, but they were not even touched by the grasp of the economic downturn. Perhaps somewhat leading to this strong position is Poland's refusal to adopt the Euro as its primary currency, as is the practice with so many other members of the European Union.

Even with a strong economy, Poland is still in a state of transformation. With the country having been a Communist government less than one hundred years ago, there are still numerous plans in place to relieve tension within the economy through government policy. When compared with other countries, Poland once again rises above its small size in the pursuit of exporting. As noted in the high percentage of individuals working for the tertiary services industry, Poland is Central and Eastern Europe's leader in banking. Currently, Poland averages almost thirty-three banks for every 100,000 adults, which gives its citizens easy and varietal access to numerous banks that have been forced to compete on virtually every aspect of the customer journey. To encourage competition within the tertiary services industry, Poland led the way for numerous banks to become privately owned while also funneling necessary capital to banks that were in need of growth to remain afloat. The result has been an industry that remains the lifeblood of Poland today, supporting the business ventures that lead to the high percentage of export and ultimately, an excellent standard of living for the Polish nationals. In today's economy, not only do the Polish citizens benefit from their banking prowess; the rise of the banking sector in Poland has enticed almost forty foreign banks to open doors in Poland, eager to share the market of Polish people eager to invest their money.

While the agricultural industry of Poland was once far greater than it currently is, the industry is still considered one of the leading supporters of the food exports in Europe, with Poland set to lead Europe in the production of food if the growth is maintained. Even with fewer than 10% of its labor force employed in the agricultural industry, Poland's agricultural industry continues to grow and maintains low prices for food in the country. While Poland is known for its delicious chocolate, the country also maintains a name as one of the leading exporters of fish, meat, eggs, and milk.

While the country touts its low unemployment rate and the means by which it weathered the global recession of 2008, much of this strength is due to an export that the country would rather curb than grow: its workforce. With the country focusing on supporting free healthcare, education, and disability pensions, the tax burden on individuals and corporations has led to unprecedented emigration from Poland. As a member of the European Union, Polish residents are able to leave their country and work elsewhere as they desire, a move designed to facilitate better commerce but that has rather created a labor force deficiency in some countries. Poland is one of those countries, and economists now assert that the only reason Poland was able to leave 2008 unscathed by the economic recession is due to the alarming number of residents who had left the country, thus reducing the burden for the government. In all, nearly 2.5 million residents have left Poland for reasons strictly related to opportunity. For those who leave, better opportunities often exist outside of Poland in neighboring countries, and relocation costs are minimal when compared with the gains from the opportunity. For those who stay, the average pay per employee increases with every employee who leaves the country, leading to a nice trade-off for the vigilant employees. Nonetheless, the lack of workers in Poland, though nice for pay and benefits purposes, has left many companies in dire need of workers while also taxing the government with fewer taxpayers. Even with a strong economy and an unemployment rate that rivals most European countries, Poland has seen its unemployment rate rise to 5.7%, a number in stark comparison with other countries such as the United States where the unemployment rate averages around 4%. To encourage some residents to funnel more of their income back into the economy, Poland recently passed legislation that would allow workers who were younger than 26 years old to refrain from paying any income tax.

While supported primarily by its financial institutions, Poland is also one of the leading countries visited by tourists. With beautiful sites to see in Warsaw and other parts of the country, tourism has aided the economy of Poland tremendously. In 2019, the country enjoyed 21 million tourists who are helping the tourism industry challenge the tertiary services industry for the role of leading industry for the gross domestic product of Poland. Since joining the European Union in 2004, Poland has paid special attention to the tourist attractions the country offers, ensuring that natural heritage sites and other new sites are maintained so that the number of tourists only improves. While many tourists enjoy touring the various sites that were influential in World War II such as Auschwitz, the most popular tourist destination in Poland is the city of Krakow. With Krakow existing as the former capital of the country, the historical viability of the city is adorned in gold, high arches, and other elements key to the Renaissance period. For tourists desiring to see more culture than tourist destinations, they will find the people of Wroclaw very interesting. The city is known for its residents who are dwarfs, giving tourists the feeling they are reliving medieval history when they enter the city limits. In addition to the people of Wroclaw, tourists often flock to this city for its famous gardens and zoo.

As a country, Poland does not offer an overabundance of museums such as other countries facilitate history from. Rather, Poland has chosen to offer its tourists outside experiences such as mountain climbing, beautiful peaks for skiing, and green valleys full of various food crops. With the country bordered by the Baltic Sea, many tourists also flock to the northern portion of the country to relax on one of the beaches offered by the seaside. Even with the renaissance journey found in Wroclaw, the zoo, and the beaches of the Baltic Sea, many tourists are not content with their visit to Poland without a visit to at least one of the castles remaining in Poland. With over one hundred castles to choose from, the tourists maintain the economy of Poland nicely traveling from castle to castle.

With Poland's economic prowess taking on a national spotlight, many of Europe's largest companies have chosen Poland as their home due to the financial position the country's legislation almost immediately places them in. As a result of their passive legislation, Poland has become the home to almost half of the largest corporations that are from Europe. To facilitate global growth, Poland involves most of its stock trading on the Warsaw Stock Exchange. Today, the largest corporations in Poland are comprised of those within the oil and gas sector while the financial services companies are in close pursuit. With a focus on sustainability, Poland has placed priority on fossil fuel production. Today, Poland remains one of the largest exporters of coal, leading to strategic initiatives worldwide for companies able to obtain Poland's coal at a discount compared to other providers. With the energy market developed when it comes to fossil fuels and sustainability, Poland has recently begun new initiatives that will bring a new focus to renewable energy features. To date, the amount of energy produced by renewable sources is meager; however, the country has placed high projections on comprising 15% of its energy production with renewable energies. Already, construction has begun on numerous windmills and hydroelectric stations around the country.

The economy of Poland is a main component of the country's infrastructure, and likewise, the infrastructure of Poland has seen tremendous growth since it began its postwar phase of growth. The postal system of Poland is one of the earliest in history, remaining in operation since 1558. The postal service has obviously undergone tremendous transformation since this time and almost faced extinction in the early 1700s when the country was forced to remove the postal service due to a conflict with one of the neighboring countries; however, the postal service would emerge again in the 20th century with the resurrection of the country prior to World War I. Fortunately, the timing could not have been better as the military would overtook the rejuvenated postal service to conduct military communication while also scanning for intelligence. Today, Poland's postal service has transformed to meet the growing demand of the world, now including financial transfers and international delivery. In recent days, the postal service has also furnished a means by which to track the packages that are sent domestically. The postal service remains a government operation and is locally referred to as the Polish Post.

While Poland's primary support for the economy comes through its tremendous financial services industry, the country has also been a worthy proponent of science and technology, the most famous scientist in Poland considered to be Nicolaus Copernicus. Copernicus was, of course, the scientist whose revelations about the sun led to an acceptance of the heliocentric theory of planet orientation. Unknown to many, Copernicus was also an economist famous for his quantity theory of money. Another famous Polish scientist who changed the world was Marie Curie, the woman whose groundbreaking work in radiation changed the game for cancer treatments and other scientific efforts. Her research laid the foundations for the Radium Institute that she founded in Poland in 1925. Today, Poland's education has taken the reins of the scientific research industry in Poland. Its four thousand five hundred researchers and forty laboratories constitute Central Europe's largest research center. It is commonplace for every university to have its own research facilities, and coupled with generous government funding, Poland's research continues to cause ripples in the ocean of science around the world.

Poland's economy is also supported by the extensive demographics of the country. In regard to population, Poland's nearly 39 million residents rank eighth among European nations and fifth within the European

Union. The population is crammed into the small land mass, giving one hundred and twenty-two residents one square mile on the population density ratio. While the residency of Poland is dense, the country does not project strong growth in the future years, its current fertility rate only coming to 1.44 children per woman. This has been alarming to economists in Poland who have discovered that their median population age has increased steadily in the past decade, currently rising at 41.1 years. However, the death rate remains low with the aging population, and economists are hopeful that immigration will decrease the median age.

The Demographics of Poland

In regard to population location, the majority of Polish people are centered in urban areas; however, the differential between those living in urban locations has diminished to its current rate of 60% of people living in urban areas with 40% comprising the rural countryside. The ethnic background of Poland has changed considerably over the years, most strikingly during the horrors of World War II. Prior to World War II, the country encouraged and profited from a strong Jewish population. However, the atrocities of World War II all but completely wiped this race of people out of Poland's demographics while also costing a considerable portion of Polish people their lives. If one were to look at a line graph of the Polish population from the 1900s until now, there is a tragic and striking drop from 1938 to 1946. In just eight years, the population of Poland was diminished by almost 50%. Incredibly, Poland's population has grown back to even greater numbers since the war but has since flattened its growth. In most recent studies, a striking 97% of the residents in Poland are Polish with the remaining 3%

comprised of a myriad of other ethnicities including German, Silesian, and Kashubian, none of which comprise more than 1.3%.

To date, over 1.5 million people have immigrated into Poland, giving the country strong signals that the economy is attracting foreigners while it slowly regains the trust of its citizens. When looking at the variety of languages offered in Poland, one would be surprised to find that Poland only has one language accepted officially by the government: Polish. Other languages dot the land mass but these languages are usually tribal or restricted to a small people group. Some of these languages include Kashubian, of which only 366,000 people in Poland know how to speak. Poland's predominant religion is Catholicism, with 92.9% of the citizens identifying with the Catholic faith. With an astounding 94.2% of the country being religious, Poland is among the greatest religious nations in Europe. An additional 3% of Polish people identified as not religious or agnostic, giving credence to the long history of religious tradition that has driven much of Poland's innovation. While religion may be an important choice for many in Poland, the practice of religion has seen a tremendous decrease, falling to only 38% in 2019. The Polish people maintain that their country should remain free from an official religion, but the number of people who actively practice their religion has dwindled consistently since the early 1970s. Perhaps the most famous religious individual from Poland was the beloved Pope John Paul II who became the first person with Polish ethnicity to become a pope for the Roman Catholic church. Pope John Paul II would hold this position form 1978 until 2005, one of the longer papacies in history. Among the other religions that have small followings around the country are Protestants, Pentecostals, Christian

Orthodox, and Jehovah's Witnesses. While most of Poland hails as devoutly religious or holding some affinity with religion, the country has also shown a minority that is atheist as well. Poland produced men like Casimir Liszinksi, a man who showed his allegiance to proclaiming there was no God and being one of the leading influencers for the new atheistic movement in Europe. While atheism is spreading in other parts of Europe, Poland has seen very little growth in this movement. As a whole, Poland hails as a religious country, tolerant of all religions but primarily adhering to Catholic church doctrines.

Education has for the most part always been a government-regulated entity. In 1773, the government first took control of the education of Poland, establishing the Commission of National Education; however, education had long been the focus of the country dating back to as early as the 12th century. One of the signs of this dedication to education is found in the Jagiellonian University, a university old enough to rank as the 19th university founded that is still standing today. Its founder, King Casimir III, will forever be remembered as a king who held great affection for the needs of society, his government being responsible for encouraging the immigration of thousands of Jews.

The average Pole begins their educational career path when they turn five or six. The children then begin a road map that takes them from the earliest grade school, "0" all the way through middle and upper education. Of particular interest and different than most educational platforms around the world, Poland requires its schoolchildren to take standardized tests at the end of 6th and 9th grade years. While standardized testing is no new concept to the rest of the world, Poland uses this standardized testing to determine which school and even class these students will attend in the future. For students who fare well on the standardized test, great educational opportunities await them, and often, numerous schools accept the students leading to greater competition among these schools. For students who fail to pass the test in a fashion that distances themselves from the pool of students being recruited by secondary schools, there are still numerous options available for their use, including the lyceum, which is a school that students can attend for three years. During these years, the students will receive a more generic education while students who were selected by secondary school institutions will receive a specialized education that can grant them access to universities following their completion of the curriculum. While the conclusion of the secondary school platforms will differ based on the institution, the students enrolled in the Lyceum will participate in a mature exam that, if excelled by the student, could grant these students entrance into a university within Poland. Students from these organizations are typically chosen after those from the secondary schools. In 2010, Poland passed legislation that mirrored most of the free world when it banned corporal punishment within the schools. Previously, teachers had been instructed to not enact any form of corporal punishment against students, but this prohibition had few ramifications if broken. That would change in 2010 when it became illegal to participate in any form of corporal punishment within the school. Today, Poland has taken that legislation to a new form by also banning any corporal punishment at home, joining countries such as the United

States in their criminalization of parents using brute force with their children.

Students who fare well throughout their education will have the opportunity to attend one of Poland's five-hundred higher level education institutions. Within the selection of these universities, students are able to choose from attending an accredited institution or attending a university that is more specialized in their content delivery. The majority of universities in Poland focus on technology and its attributes while the lowest percentage of universities are centered on theology and its attributes. When compared with universities from around the world, the educational scene in Poland is well-respected with many of the higher education institutions offering advances in the medical and technical fields.

Within the framework of Poland's infrastructure is an impressive healthcare system that has recently become the center of a spotlight on government-provided healthcare. Citizens who have chosen to participate in the healthcare provided by the government are afforded the opportunity to receive complimentary healthcare services performed in hospitals that are operated by the government. Additionally, healthcare facilities are available across the country where anyone is able to go depending on their fiscal opportunity. It has become commonplace in Poland for every city to host its own hospital with most of these hospitals providing standard treatment for their patients. For patients seeking specialized medical attention, there are adequate facilities located in the major cities of Poland, the highest concentration of medical facilities being found within the capital city of Warsaw. Recalling that Poland's own Marie Curie was the discoverer of radium, Poland has one of the leading cancer research centers in the world: the Sklodowska-Curie Institute of Oncology. This center is solely dedicated to the research and mitigation of cancer, attracting scientists from around the world and largely considered to be in the top tier of cancer research centers. Poland's healthcare has done a remarkable job giving treatment to its citizens, largely being responsible for the average life expectancy of 78.5 years. Poland's healthcare continues to be a model that several countries around the world follow while also enticing other countries not yet offering government-provided medical assistance to consider this opportunity for their citizens.

Much of Poland's population is centered within the large cities of Poland. This aligns with the economics of Poland, which show a decreasing agricultural industry and an increasing technological or medical role. Warsaw, the nation's capital, has the largest population with over 1.8 million individuals living in the city. After Warsaw, the differential between the next largest city is stark, with Krakow holding 800,000 residents, over 1 million less than Warsaw. Economists point to the economic centrality of Warsaw as the primary influence in this disparity. While Poland's demographics show a country that is in need of immigration, its positions on education and healthcare reform with the economic surplus that the country enjoys offers unique insight for countries considering such a transition.

The Politics of Poland

The politics of Poland are dictated as a representative democracy. As a nation, Poland is governed by a head of state, referred to as the president. While the president retains authority as the head of state, the primary body of legislative power is found in the Council of Ministers, a parliamentary-style government whose governance is facilitated by a prime minister. The dichotomy of leadership between the president and the prime minister is a unique environment but certainly not a unique structure. Following the leadership of other countries such as the United States, Polish presidents are afforded the opportunity to construct a cabinet but does this with the guidance of the current prime minister. Following the democratic structure, the Polish president is elected every five years unless an emergency vacancy occurs at which time the parliament will decide whether or not to hold an emergency election or fill the position with a current position within the government. The body of legislative power, the parliament, reflects a democratic structure with four hundred sixty positions open in what they refer to as the Sejm, the lower house that reflects the House of Representatives from the United States. The upper house, or the Senate, is comprised of one hundred positions. To fill the seats within the Sejm, the country follows the proportional representation method, which focuses on the highest average for filling the seat. To fill the seats of the Senate, the country allows for one senator to represent the body of people comprising one of the one hundred constituencies of the country.

The government is united through the National Assembly, the joint efforts of the Sejm and the Senate. While this body forms a unified government, it is only through the occasion of three different times when the body is fully unified. These times are when the president is the subject of an indictment from the State Tribunal, when the president is elected to his position, or when the seat of president is occupied by someone who is no longer able to serve in the full capacity of his seat. Obviously, with requirements as such, the unification of the government under one roof is a rare experience, at minimum occurring only once every five years. While the legislative branch is considered the most powerful branch of the government, the day-to-day lives of the Polish citizens are governed by the judicial branch of the government. Within the judicial branch, offices such as the Supreme Court, the Constitutional Tribune, the State Tribune, and the Supreme Administrative Court aid the daily lives of the Polish citizens. As a mediator for the Polish people as their representative to the higher courts, the Commissioner for Civil Rights Protection is elected to a five-year term but is not elected via public vote. Rather, the Sejm submits the name of their candidate to the Senate, who then has to approve the figure before they are allowed to occupy that seat. The office of Commissioner for Civil Rights Protection is very important to the lives and freedoms of the Polish people since this position acts as the greatest oversight of new government legislation.

As a governing body, the judicial courts maintain the safety of the lives of the Polish people on a day-to-day basis. The standard by which they derive this safety comes from the Constitution of Poland, which is a collection of principles that are supported by Poland's Civil Law code. Poland was one of the first countries in Europe to demonstrate a constitution, of which multiple revisions took place until an entirely new constitution was adopted in April of 1997. The basic principles outlined in the constitution resembled most democracies, with the citizens of Poland entitled to the rights of free speech, choice of religion, choice of assembly and protest, protections from any medical experimentation, multiple political party affiliations, freedom to assemble a labor union, and freedom from corporal punishment. To ensure these laws are carried out to the fullest extent of the law and to every applicable party, the judiciary branch has implemented a four-tier government system that is comprised of multiple levels of courts, the jurisdiction and power of each court rising from the increasing levels. The most common position within the judiciary branch is the judges, which are given their position for the span of their life. These judges are elected similar to the process of the Commissioner for Civil Rights Protection except that the two parties in this case are the National Council of the Judiciary, the body tasked with submitting nominated judges, and the president, who receives the nominations and appoints the judges if approved. The most powerful positions within the state are occupied by the Constitutional and State

Tribunals, respectively. These positions are tasked solely with ensuring that the duties of the statutory law are carried out appropriately. With the statutory law stemming from the positions of the constitution, these two bodies of governance are extremely important to the protected freedoms of the Polish residents.

Within Poland's political structure is the free choice of governing bodies, the Polish residents holding the power to elect anyone to the office of president every five years. The right to vote is held by both men and women, with Poland joining the eleven existing countries in 1918 who allowed women to vote. The safety of Poland is one aspect that has also achieved global attention. Whereas abortion has become a highlighted topic in many countries, Poland has maintained the illegal nature of abortion in all circumstances unless the life of the mother is considered at risk. The only other time when an abortion is allowed is when the fetus is tremendously malformed. Even then, abortions are seen as a tragedy in Poland and are avoided at almost all costs. In additional topics that center on the ethical approach of Poland, the country has also taken a stand for marriage as defined as being between one man and one woman. While Poland may define marriage as such, it has not discriminated against those who defend or identify as a homosexual. Dating back to 1932, homosexuality has been legalized in the country and continues to be practiced by a small group of people in the country.

Within Poland, the country has been divided into smaller divisions known as provinces or "voivodeships" locally. The distribution of land among these various provinces is relatively equal; however, there are a couple of locations that are small as 3,900 square miles, while some can grow as big as 14,000 square miles. Following the example of other countries, the governance of all of these provinces falls on the governors of each province. Additionally, there is an accompanying legislative body within every province that helps spread the judicial branch of the government throughout each province. Just as states in the United States are further extrapolated to find counties, the Polish provinces have been divided further to smaller bodies of land known as powiats. From here, the typical structure of city exists although Poland refers to these bodies of land as gminas. It is not uncommon for some of the larger gminas to also be respected as powiats. In all, Poland has fourteen provinces that help facilitate the country's economy and political structure.

One element of Poland that has been decimated yet returned stronger is Poland's military. Poland's army was at its peak when Poland and Lithuania were united, creating a gigantic army that likely would have ruled Central Europe forever had the partitions never taken place. After the partitions, the Polish Army was grossly unprepared for the future invasion that would come during both world wars. After World War II, the country's military underwent tremendous restructuring until finally beginning to gather its former glory during the early 1980s. Today, Poland's army has subdivided into five distinct branches: the Navy, the Territorial Defense Force, the Land Forces, the Special Forces, and the Air Force. The division of the army as a whole was as recent as 2016 when the special Territorial Defense Force was created. The Territorial Defense Force is Poland's mobile war force, consisting of fifty-three thousand individuals ready to report for battle in less than one day should the country's current military resources be exhausted. The head of the military is the Minister for National Defense, and the President of Poland is tasked with heading up the military for wartime efforts. Prior to mobilizing the Territorial Defense Force, the military capacity of Poland stands at around one hundred thousand troops. These troops are spread evenly among the different branches of the armed forces, the Navy consisting of the smallest group of troops. This is primarily due to Poland's only need for naval resources centering on the Baltic Sea, a rather small portion of Poland's perimeter. In recent times, the Polish Navy primarily trains for search and rescue missions within the sea. In addition, the Polish Navy has also recently become more closely aligned with science, adding a division of the Navy that solely studies the weather and other metrics of hydrography. While the Polish Navy has had little conflict since World War II, it has aligned itself as a close ally of the United States Army, allowing the United States Navy to utilize the intelligence of its Navy while also giving use of measurement software and satellites that were vital in the United States' invasion of Iraq in 2003.

As a member of NATO, Poland's Army primarily maintains the borders of its country, facing very little resistance or attempts at invasion. For a brief period in the early 2000s, the Polish Army maintained a mandatory services in the armed forces for all eligible men in Poland; however, these practices have since been disbanded and the government now focuses on contracting much of its military efforts to agencies within the country. In addition to maintaining the border of Poland, the country routinely sends its resources on peacekeeping missions as outlined by NATO. The armed forces division of Poland's military was an active participant in 2003 when the United States invaded Iraq, aligning two-thousand five hundred soldiers and other resources with the seventeen countries that formed an alliance when invading Iraq. In 2010, Poland's military faced tragedy when the Chief of Army's General Staff was involved in a fatal plane crash. Among those killed was the Commanding General of the Polish Air Force. Poland would weather the tragedy and was able to maintain its strategic positioning despite the loss of leadership.

Poland's military services have long been antiquated, but current efforts are focused on rejuvenating these antiquated practices. In an effort that is set to spend over $35 billion, the Polish military is updating much of its infrastructure and equipment, further positioning it as a formidable force within Central Europe. The pinnacle of the updates includes a new selection of surface to air missiles and updated personnel carriers. With such additions, Poland appears to be well-fortified against the threat of invasion from any side.

While Poland's military protects the citizens from outside threats, the law enforcement of Poland is focused daily on keeping its citizens safe from the threats that pop up within the country. Poland's police force differs little from other countries, with a robust state police system centered on the full-time investigation of crimes while the local police focuses more on the daily protection and service of Polish citizens. Though not used as much, the Polish Border Guard actively protests against illegal immigration into the country. Just as the military of Poland is partially comprised of privately contracted agencies, the Polish police force is aided by the presence of private security firms that manage more mundane security work. To better serve the country's citizens, the country has also established the State Fire Service, which helps protect the citizens from various fire threats while also being on standby for essential emergency personnel. While the State Fire Service is operated by the government just as other countries, Poland has taken their emergency personnel a step further in a manner that distances themselves from other countries. Rather than allow the emergency medical service sector to be managed by private businesses or hospitals, the emergency medical services of Poland are directly operated by the government. This allows the Polish residents to receive complimentary medical services such as ambulance rides and emergency medical responses. As a whole, the country of Poland has taken the protection of its citizens beyond the common measures adopted by other countries.

While Poland has taken special care to maintain the health of its citizens, it has also established itself as a country always willing to help countries in need of services. To facilitate better trade with its neighboring countries, Poland is a full member of the European Union and is an active seat within the European Parliament. In all, an average of fifty seats are always occupied by the Polish government within this parliamentary body. With an aim for peace among all countries, Poland has been an active facilitator of meetings within its own country, absorbing the cost and allowing regional nations to hold peace-seeking talks within Polish government buildings. Poland has been recognized in being perhaps the most powerful country in Central Europe and one that is a key negotiator between countries. Poland's affinity with maintaining its numerous diplomatic relationships has led to its status as the greatest economy within the collection of the Three Seas Initiative. Due to its strategic location and the willingness of the Polish government to help, the United Nations has established the prominent border security office for Central Europe, Frontex, in Warsaw. In addition to maintaining its active membership within the United Nations and the European Union, Poland has also achieved status within NATO and the World Trade Organization, two alliances committed to reducing the barriers of free trade around the world. In a move that many economists attributed to the country's rise from political destruction, Poland has also joined the Organization for Economic Co-Operation and Development, also known as OECD. In an alliance that seeks to align all trade within Europe, Poland is also a member of the European Economic Area, an agreement that allows the member country's citizens the freedom to travel from country to country without the identification normally needed to leave the country. Additionally, this organization has also led to various tax breaks for the citizens as the people are permitted to sell and manufacture goods in various countries without paying excessive taxes.

Even as a country whose infrastructure is leading Central Europe, Poland remains committed to the scientific development within the world, achieving this global initiative by joining various scientific agencies such as the International Energy Agency and the International Atomic Energy Agency. Poland is also a voice of freedom atop the Council of Europe and the Organization for Security and Co-Operation in Europe. Due to the youth of Poland's economic prowess, the country has not been internationally recognized as an economic leader. Its economic success has led to the spotlight of Central Europe, but many international economic boards have long refrained from inviting Poland to occupy a formal seat. There are winds that signify this is changing, however. Recently, Poland was invited to occupy a guest seat at the G20 Summit where the country was highlighted as one of the developing economies in the world. Even though it has not achieved G20 status yet, many economic agencies and even countries have noted that Poland appears to be mature enough to sit on the Summit.

A conversation about Poland's politics is not complete without paying due homage to the country's deepening ties with the United States of America. Poland has always held great respect for the United States, and recent times have shown how far the country is willing to go to maintain this allegiance. The admiration of the Polish government was best seen in 2003 when the Polish government willingly gave access to key intelligence committees to the United States as the War Against Terror campaign kicked off. When the war reached the point of an actual invasion, Poland was among the first nations to give resources to the American government, going as far as to allocate nearly two-thousand five hundred troops to serve on the front lines of the campaign. After pledging the support of these troops to the United States, the Polish government inspired actions from the Australian government, who also sent troops to join the fight. Even as the war in Iraq reaches new phases that do not require the activity of the Polish government, the Polish government has turned its aim to negotiations and mediations. The most recent demonstrations of this came during the administration of President Donald Trump. During key negotiations, the dialogue between the Trump administration and key powers within the European nations has fallen apart. In many of these situations, Poland has rushed to the Trump administration's aid, helping to restart these negations, and in many cases, acting as an influence for the United States' favor. Today, Poland stands tall as one of the leading allies that the United States holds in Europe. Many have pointed to the war in Iraq as taking longer or even facing different outcomes without the aid of the Polish government. Even with the differences of the two countries on various healthcare and social reform measures, Poland's affinity with the United States remains a key relationship that will doubtless show its worth in the future of both countries.

The Geography of Poland

As a nation nestled among a vast array different climates, Poland's weather and geography changes incredibly across the various provinces of the country. From the balmy northwestern coastline of the Baltic Sea to the hot southeastern portion of the country, Poland's climate fits all types. Beginning at the top of the coastline, the country has an admirable coastline that facilitates a good deal of Poland's commerce. Beginning at the western border of the country, the Baltic Sea forms a natural border for much of the northern border, cutting an almost perfect straight line across the top before eventually retreating away from the shoreline.

While the northern border of the country is jutted with a coastline that would resemble that of a lake, it is not solely bordered by the Baltic Sea. There is a remaining portion of the border that is carved out by the Northern European plains. This beautiful country is home to some of Poland's most stunning mountains and basins. In all, there are four major mountain sets that give plenty of breathtaking views of the country. While these mountains take the place of the Baltic Sea for bordering the country, they also have valleys in which are a set of lakes. These lakes are famous for their crystal clear water that will often reflect the beautiful surrounding mountain systems at sunrise and sunset. Of all of these mountain regions, the most famous mountain system is formed by the Carpathian Mountains, whose Tara Mountain juts out above the rest. These mountains are found along the southern portion of the state. In all, there are seventy mountains that cut a beautiful natural skyline in Poland. The mountain system of Poland is one that has achieved significant notoriety in Poland. While the Tatras of the Carpathian Mountains are the highest, the second place position belongs to the Beskids, the highest peak of this mountain ranging nearly one mile. While these two mountain systems are known for their height, other mountain ranges in Poland are more suitable for climbing, the most famous of which are the Table Mountains. This mountain system has an impressive structure of rocks that seem to jut out of the hills at various peaks. Numerous national parks team together to give tourists and residents a beautiful set of trails to explore this mountain system. While Poland is not particularly known for its mountains and hills, these high peaks have given Poland a gorgeous backdrop while also providing shelter for some of Poland's earliest residents.

Surrounded by water and a mountain system, not all of Poland is mountainous. The Vistula Delta, Poland's lowest point, is home to the impressive waterways of Poland. Even with this water system, there is a desert region of Poland, known as the Bledow Desert. Within this desert, the ground lacks significant vegetation due to the terrible conditions brought about by the sand. This desert is 12 square miles and is not visited often. Of particular interest, this desert is different from other deserts in that scientists do not classify it as a desert. Whereas other deserts are natural formations due to climates, this desert was the result of the combination of the mismanagement of land and warfare from neighboring countries during the Middle Ages.

Depending on the scientific beliefs of each geologist, the age of the land mass Poland is centered on could date from 60 million years old to 10,000 years old. Regardless of the exact date, the beauty of this country is evident in the numerous layers of rock formations that contain numerous fossils. The ecosystem of Poland is supported by an extensive waterway system that snakes its way across the country. With rivers allowing the connection of cities, commerce is brought to Poland with the Baltic Sea but is distributed throughout the country in part by the numerous rivers. The longest of these rivers is the Vistula, which pushes water throughout the country for 651 miles. This river is supported heavily by a feed of water from the third-longest river in Poland, the Bug. At 531 miles long, the second-longest river in Poland is the Oder, which is found along the western border of the country and is fed by Poland's fourth-longest river, the Warta. The majority of the rivers in Poland snake their way throughout the country before finally emptying their load of water into the Baltic Sea. The rivers that do not feed the waters of the Baltic Sea are responsible for feeding into the Black Sea. Poland's impressive waterways have given beautiful tours of the country while also providing a means of commerce for the locals through both transportation and fishing.

With most of the rivers in Poland have been around for all of the country's existence, they are a primary means of historical record as their existence and use has given historians a common location to measure events in both time and location with other events. In early history, there are records of the Vikings tribes making their way up the river in their intimidating longboats, either on their way to battle or returning from battle. These travels were primarily the result of the former union that Poland held with Lithuania, a time when Poland controlled most of Central Europe's resources. Even as Poland's waterways have provided the country with fantastic trade and transportation opportunities, the country is also able to maintain opportunities for a clean water supply with many of the springs that bubble around the country. One of these springs is found in Tomaszow Mazowiecki, where a karst spring has been used for virtually thousands of years. The spring is fed by the Pilica River and is a featured part of the Sulejow Landscape Park. Adding to the fame of the spring, its location and rich mineral content combines to form a beautiful array of red and purple rays that reflect from the surface when touched directly by the sun's rays.

As a country with a relatively small land mass, the high concentration of lakes within Poland has distanced the country from other countries, giving it the rich history of having the second-highest number of lakes in Europe, Finland beating Poland with its network of lakes. In all, the country has nearly ten thousand lakes across the country, all of which are greater than 2.5 acres in size. The existence of these lakes has helped maintain what was once the country's leading industry, agriculture, for centuries. The presence of these lakes offers the farmers the opportunity to cut irrigation patterns around the countryside, making most of the country rich in nutrients and ripe for new vegetation. The largest lake in Poland is Lake Sniardwy, which is responsible for nearly 39 square miles of coverage. Its immense size is followed by Lake Drawsko, Lake Lebsko, and Lake Mamry. While the river system of Poland allows the naval transportation between the various provinces like a connected roadway of water, the fishing industry is almost entirely supported by the combined efforts of the Baltic Sea and the lakes of Poland. Not all of Poland's lakes are found on the plains of Poland, however; there is also an extensive array of mountain lakes that dot up in the thousands of miles that are covered by mountains in Poland. Most of these lakes are found in Masuria, also the home to Lake Mary and Lake Sniardwy. The deepest of these mountain lakes Lake Hancza, a member of the Wigry Lake District of the Podlaskie Voivodeship.

Poland's extensive array of lakes offered settlers in Poland the opportunity to live near their chief mode of transportation and food. The historical remains of these villages are still able to be seen in many of the UNESCO sites located around the country. One of these sites is found in the Greater Polish Lake District which is home to the Lusation people of Biskupin. It was here that the earliest residents built stilt houses to protect them from the annual flooding of the rivers and lakes. To protect from the threat of invading forces, numerous castles were also built along the shorelines of these lakes. Today, towers such as the Kruszwica Tower still stand tall along the Lake Goplo, telling the story of heroic Polish people from thousands of years ago.

Today, the Polish waterways are the prime location for the water sports that dominate the springs and summers of Poland; however, the greatest land in Poland is found atop the fertile fields of the agricultural plains in the country. It is difficult for many farmers to find adequate land to farm on due to the extensive forest system that dominates Poland's skyline. With a forest system claiming almost 30% of Poland's land mass, there is a great ecosystem for animals of the forest while also providing ample resources such as timber and firewood. Even with this large forest, the Polish government continues to seek more forestation within the country, attempting to increase the percentage of land covered by forest to 33% in the next 30 years. Despite the extensive forestation, Polish agriculture continues to dominate the country, with most of Central Europe leaning heavily on the agricultural growth of Poland. Today, Poland leads Central Europe in the exports of potatoes and rye. While the agricultural industry of Poland has fallen from its pedestal atop most successful industries, the country continues to provide ample resources for the farming industry to be attractive. As such, the country has nearly 2 million private farms that combine for the agricultural success of the country. In addition to the tremendous grains that are able to be grown on the fertile land of the country, Poland also grows several variants of meat, such as pork, beef, and chicken. Of these three meats, Poland's chief export is pork, further cementing its importance in export to the European Union.

Poland's climate settles on temperate for the majority of the country. While there is a range of difference in temperature from the northern tip of the country to the southern border, the country's average temperate of most of the cities settles around 78' in the summer and 29' in the winter. With the ocean bordering the northern border of the country, the country does not boast the high temperatures usually accompanying a coastline. The higher temperatures are found in the Lower Silesia portion of the country, the average temperate ranging as high as 90' in the summer. Winters in Poland can be brutally cold, dropping as low as 21' in northern portions of the country. However, with temperatures rarely going below freezing, this has created a great climate for the animals of the country, giving the forests a vast array of animals who make Poland their home year-round. Throughout the country, it is not uncommon to see animals such as beaver, moose, deer, wild boar, and even the lynx. With many animals able to be eaten, Poland's forests provide the country with an additional resource that is also favorable to the competitive hunting industry of Poland. Of particular interest to the country, Poland is known for its strategic location in bird season, giving birds a location to rest due to its temperate climate. The most prominent bird in Poland is the White Stork, which brings 40,000 breeding pairs to the country year-round. Poland's climate has given the country yet another beautiful site, the unencumbered daily lives of animals all available for observation from either the mountains, rivers, or plains of Poland.

Conclusion

When looking back on the extensive history of Poland, it is impossible to witness the greatest moments of Poland without also seeing the time periods of tremendous tragedy. When over 50% of a population is destroyed due to the hateful lust of one man, it seems nearly impossible for the country to return to its former glory. And truthfully, Poland did not return to its former glory: it exceeded it. The country went from being demoralized by one of the most tragic concentration camps in the world to being one of the leading economic powers of Central Europe, a country whose existence is seemingly required for Europe's success. The drive and determination of the people of Poland is one that can be mirrored by anyone and is a clear example of how to return from tragedy.

References

"Auschwitz Day Trip." Krakow by CIVITATIS, www.introducingkrakow.com/history-of-krakow.

Biskupski, Mieczysław B. The History of Poland. Greenwood, 2018.

A Brief History of Poland, www.localhistories.org/poland.html.

Dunham, S. A. The History of Poland. First Rate Publishers, 2015.

Gieysztor, Aleksander, and Stefan Kieniewicz. History of Poland. PWN, Polish Scientific Publishers, 1979.

Halecki, Oskar, et al. A History of Poland. Dorset Press, 1994.

HISTORY OF POLAND, www.historyworld.net/wrldhis/PlainTextHistories.asp?historyid=ab01

"History of Poland." Encyclopædia Britannica, Encyclopædia Britannica, Inc., www.britannica.com/topic/history-of-Poland.

"Poland History." Stay Poland, www.staypoland.com/poland/poland-history/.

"Poland Profile - Timeline." BBC News, BBC, 28 May 2018, www.bbc.com/news/world-

europe-17754512.

Poland. DK Eyewitness Travel, 2019.

"Poland." History.com, A&E Television Networks, 21 Aug. 2018, www.history.com/tag/poland.

Prazmowska, Anita. A History of Poland. Palgrave Macmillan, 2004.

The History of Slovakia: A Fascinating Guide to this Central European Country

Intro

Slovakia is a small country. It calls Central Europe home and is next to Poland, The Czech Republic, and Germany. The borders are made in part by beautiful rivers that stem from the mountains and contribute to the flourishing landscape that covers Slovakia.

The amazing history that this country holds is unlike any other. There is a great culture that shines through prehistoric times up to the present day. There were many advancements that came straight from Slovakia that have greatly influenced the world as we know it.

This roughly 19,000-square-mile country is the home of many famous museums, including the Slovak National Gallery, the Museum of History in the Bratislava Castle, the Červený Kameň Castle, and the Nedbalka Gallery.

There are also many historical castles located all over the beautiful country. They include Trenčín Castle, Orava Castle, Strečno Castle, Bojnice Castle, and many more along the hills of Slovakia.

If you are looking for a beautiful and amazing place to visit or maybe even move to, then Slovakia could be an amazing opportunity. There are many great educational options to travel through Slovakia, and they are all just as beautiful as the last. There is no reason not to look into a vacation in this area of the world.

If you are lucky enough to already live in or around Slovakia, then you already know and have seen the beautiful landscape and architecture. What you may not know is the rich history that goes along with this amazing country. This history has greatly influenced the culture that surrounds Slovakia today.

Hopefully, this book will give you insight into what Slovakia has gone through since the prehistoric era in which the country existed. Slovakia has made it through many other countries conquering it, communism, and quite a few revolutions. Let's get into the culture and history of Slovakia as a whole.

BASIS

Slovakia is a relatively small area that has a very rich and deep history. The history of this country is incomparable to any other. Although other countries have a vast and great history, it cannot be compared to Slovakia's past. Slovakia went through tortuous times more often than many other countries, and yet they still have their own identity and culture.

When driving through the countryside of Slovakian land, there are rolling hills and beautiful architecture. As you drive past castles and other homes as well as historical, natural landscapes, you are getting a view into the vast past that this country has. Many places are open for tours and historical learning opportunities.

Even more are viewable from the outside, but this doesn't mean you won't be learning about them. There are many online travel guides for the country that bring you on historical trails of conquests or architecture. There are also self-guided tours across the castles of the country so you can see how ancient Slovakians really lived.

Due to the vast history that Slovakia holds, there is no real date of when the country was established. This makes for some confusion when going through the history of this country, but it does not change any of it. Just like Slovakia as a country has held strong, so has its history. Let's begin.

In prehistoric times, Slovakia was on the map, although it did not have that name yet. It established itself in these early historic times of the world. Quite a bit of information from that time period centered around Central Europe, and with that, Slovakia. Without it, we may not have as great of a look into ancient life.

There were individuals living there and thriving off the land during this prehistoric time period. There were notable settlements in Smolenice, Nitriansky, and many other places throughout the countryside. Today, there are a lot of artifacts from this time period that are still viewable in museums or at least in pictures and other documents.

Slovakia is actually where the famous prehistoric Neanderthal skull cast came from. This is one of the only ideas of skulls that are available from that time period. It has given us great insight into what life was like back then and even more so what humans were like back then. It was a great piece informing the history of the world and Homo sapiens as a whole.

Since then many things have changed, obviously. However, many advancements may not have been possible if we did not harness the idea of what things were like before we individually roamed the earth. The present time is just an accumulation of history and research.

Slovakia was home to many Celtic settlements in the prehistoric time periods just as places around it were. Many Central European countries gave way to the Celtic way of life and the religions and history that came with it. The most recognizable one from this area was Havranok, which was near Liptovska Mara.

Slovakia was also a border of the Roman Empire, which gave it an even larger place in historical context. The Roman Empire is one of the most well-known periods in history no matter where you are from. Connecting anything to that mighty empire creates a much larger place in history for it.

Romans did not keep things very friendly with Slovakia during their empire years. They actually led many conquests into Slovakia to steal their land. As Slovakia was a much smaller settlement, Slovakian people attempted to fight back and save their land, but it was no use. The Roman Empire was not a force to go against, and if you did, you certainly did not win.

The most notable artifact from when the Romans came through the land is a carved inscription related to the victory goddess on an area of rocks. This area of rocks would later be where the Trencin Castle was built.

The Trencin Castle is still standing today. Although it goes back to the age of the Roman Empire, it now is part of a large exhibition of the area's museums. This is a castle that is unable to be missed as it sits on a hill towering over water and the city of Trencin.

Due to the location of Slovakia in Europe, it was present in many important parts of history, including many violent parts of history. Mostly wars and conquests came through the area, but it gave them a great historical spot. Besides the Roman Empire, the Turks also came through Slovakia with a military fit to destroy.

All through these conquests, Slovakia still stood strong. The people were not wiped out, and the culture was not diminished in the least.

Somehow, even with all of these military conquests coming through the area, Slovakia is still vastly different from every other European country. These conquests did not have a lasting effect on the history or culture of the area. These conquests most likely gave them even more of a rich culture that they still stand on today.

When the Middle Ages hit Slovakia, construction in the country hit an all-time high. Castles were thriving in this time period, and most of them are still standing today giving a great view of the landscape wherever you are. The insides of these castles give a view into what was important back then and what life was really like.

Along with these castles, some amazingly beautiful cathedrals were also built during this time period. These are cathedrals that could rival those built in Italy, the mecca for beautiful cathedrals.

As more modern times came around, Slovakia was lumped into a communist regime around the year 1948 with Czechoslovakia. Luckily, the communist regime fell off in 1989 when the Velvet Revolution took place in this area. Once again, this did not shake Slovakia's culture or history. It most likely gave them an even stronger culture to stand upon.

The country's identity is still one of the strongest in the world. And it looks like that will not be going away anytime soon.

Slovakia has a very deep and rich history that no book could completely cover. This book will try to relay its rich history up to modern times but will surely not even make a dent in the identity the country has established.

Prehistoric Through Iron Age of Slovakia

Slovakia, or the area now known as Slovakia, has been inhabited since the prehistoric period of the history of our world. The prehistoric era of the world is basically described as the time period before written records came about, which could be millions of years. This is a time when many advancements in human society occurred, and it is essential to understand exactly where we all came from.

Much of this time period is unknown because it is impossible to have clear records from it. However, that does not mean it is unimportant to learn about and look back upon. This is the time period that shaped many things in our world today and truly made us who we are as a society.

Carbon dating has put the oldest artifact that came from Slovakia around the year 270,000 BC. That puts it at over 272,020 years old as of today. This artifact was found near Nove Mesto nad Vahom in the very early years of the Paleolithic era.

The Paleolithic era is when humans started to group closer together to essentially form small societies. This is when hunting and gathering were commonplace so that people worked together to survive. There were some stone and woodworking done during this time but nothing compared to later years.

The artifacts found in Slovakia were actually tools made from stone and bones. This shows the mind working at a more survival-based yet intelligent form. This was one of the first signs of human-scale intelligent life in the area.

Other tools that were made out of stone were found from the years 200,000 BCE as well. This shows that even 70,000 years later, there was still human-scale intelligent life in this area which means it was seen as a great settlement area for these individuals at that time.

This was around the same time that a Neanderthal skull cast was found in the area of Northern Slovakia. As stated earlier, this was a huge find for archeologists. This helped form the history of humans that we now have.

In addition to this skull, other archeologists have found prehistoric human skeletons in the country. Since there is no written history of the area from this time period, the bones of the people who lived here give us the best insight we will ever get.

From these bones, archeologists are able to figure out what these people may have eaten, drank, what their bodies may have been like, and how they lived. These things are essential in mapping out human existence. Slovakia played a big part in that.

Near many of these skeletons were artifacts from the Gravettian culture. The Gravettian culture is a culture defined during the Upper Paleolithic era that started around 33,000 BCE. Those who were part of this culture were known as hunter-gatherers, and their lives were greatly influenced by the climate they lived in.

An amazing find while in the region where this culture was most prevalent was the first real sculpture made out of mammoth bone. This was the sculpture of a naked woman and has formed many opinions about the upper Paleolithic period. This artifact was not found until 1940, but when it was found, it made waves in the historical knowledge of the country.

After the Paleolithic era, the Neolithic era took place. This is the time period that started around 10,000 BC mostly in the fertile crescent of the world. The main part of this era was the practice of agriculture, as it was quite new to the world.

From this time period, many tools and pottery were discovered in the Slovakian region. The odd thing that many historians found was that places with a very high altitude held a lot of gravesites. This suggests that during the Neolithic period, many societies chose to live higher up where people today would not be as comfortable.

The pottery found in these areas has a great shape and very delicate art on the outside, proposing the use of many different tools and advanced knowledge of art. Within this is also the first attempt at using color in art. This shows a want to branch further into the artistic minds of humans at a very early time period.

Although pottery from this time period has been discovered in many other parts of the world, most of these pieces did not have the color or this kind of linework. Slovakia holds the first attempt at real, formidable artwork that we have discovered as of today.

In much of Europe, including Slovakia as a whole, agriculture came into play during this time period. As stated above, this was one defining part of the Neolithic time period. Clearing pastures was a large thing taking place in Slovakia. After the clearing took place, it was much easier to plant seeds and jump into agriculture at even this early stage in history.

Along with these great advancements in art and agriculture, society started to smelt metals. This helped to create stronger tools and more for the societies that existed.

All of this together formed a great trade area for the communities around Slovakia and Central Europe. They would trade things they made, such as pottery and other art or tools. They were now also able to trade crops due to their advancements in agriculture. This put Slovakia on the map for the European trade routes that were to come.

After the Neolithic era, the Bronze Age and the Iron Age took place. The Bronze Age was a historical period that was characterized by none other than the use of bronze. This helped to replace stone and bone tools with much stronger bronze tools.

The Iron Age was very similar, although it started after the Bronze Age in the 8th century BC. Generally, this age is split into the first part of the Iron Age and the second part of the Iron Age, although both show the discontinuation of the Bronze Age as they appear.

The Bronze Age in this area was not just one area of development; it actually went through three stages. The third stage was completed by 800 BCE. Although the Bronze Age may seem like just an enhancement in the making of tools, it actually had great political and economic effects in Slovakia as well.

Copper was becoming a very stable source that was profitable in both central and northwest Slovakia during this time. It was used primarily in the building of many large fortifications that the Lusatian culture built in this time period.

These large permanent buildings had many rooms and even administrative centers. They were far more organized and durable than any buildings created before them. This was a pivotal point in architecture for the Slovakian region.

Along with the great advancements in architecture, tombs were now much more intricate. There was now art in tombs and very beautiful carvings that created a wonderful place for those they loved to be buried.

There were many more things being manufactured during this time period as well. Things such as shields, dishes, and jewelry came more into play in society and trading circles. This can be linked to the arrival of many different Thracian tribes coming through at this point in history.

Although the arrival of these new tribes somewhat upset the cultures that were already thriving in Slovakia, it did have a large impact on the country's history and worked for the better. Without the interference of these tribes, Slovakia may not have advanced as far as it did in art or trading over the years.

During the end stages of the Iron Age is when Celtic cultures weaved their way into Slovakian history. They came from the south and used the rivers to guide them north, which eventually took them through the entire country of Slovakia. This was one of the biggest impacts on Slovakian culture as it is today.

Much of the Celtic culture that was weaved into Slovakia meshed well with the already established culture that was there. This made things much easier for the people of both cultures. Unlike other tribes that had come in, these two got along well. They helped to build large shrines in the area to promote the religion that they had brought with them.

They also brought silver coins along with the idea of money and an economic system as a whole. These coins that are still viewable today online and in Slovakia show the first known writing to ever come out of this country. This pushed them up to one of the leading intelligent countries in the world, although their military power was not one to rival others.

The Prehistoric to the Iron Age era of Slovakia was a large piece of their history. Many things changed over the years that formed who they are today and what their culture is today.

Without knowing these advancements, Slovakia would have seemed to come out of nowhere, and their culture would not be half as rich.

The Era of
the Roman Empire

Slovakia was birthed in Eastern Europe by several cultures. Over time, the region witnessed many changes in leadership and government, but nevertheless, the people have retained their national identity and history.

The earliest group dominating the region was the Celts, around 400 BC. Other groups who struggled for control over the territory include the Franks, the Tartars, and the Turks. By 1 AD, Germanic tribes pushed the Celts out of the territory. Despite the success of the Germanic people, the area was not entirely peaceful for long.

During the Marcomannic Wars, many battles and events troubled the area. The war left Rome's northern border weak as around half of Rome's legions were stationed along the Danube River. In response to an influx of Germanic settlers in these weakened regions, Rome also established two new provinces known as Marcomannia and Sarmatia. Today, these regions are recognized as Moravia and Western Slovakia.

During the Migration Period, a variety of Germanic and Slavic tribes traveled and settled throughout the region. In the 6th century AD, the Slavs began establishing themselves under the Tribal Union of Samo's Empire.

By the end of the 8th century, the Moravian Principality united the different tribes of the region. In 833 AD, the Principality of Nitra won in the conquest for Moravia, establishing the Great Moravian Empire. This state would be the first shared state of present-day Slovak and Czech ancestors. Great Moravia would reach its largest size in the 890s.

However, the empire was short-lived when Louis the German invaded the Great Moravian Empire and replaced King Mojmir I with his nephew Rastiz. There is no surprise that Louis the German, also known as Louis II, was the grandson of emperor Charlemagne.

He ruled Bavaria until 843 and obtained East Francia in that same year, making him its first king. Throughout his rule, Louis faced rebellions and consistent fighting in attempts to claim Italy. However, he did find success in obtaining Moravia, ending decades of conflict with the region.

Rastislav became St. Rastislav and attempted to emancipate Rome from Carolingian influence, and he sent envoys to Rome, who refused to hand over the missionaries. As a result, St. Rastislav sent missionary

Saints Cyril and Methodius to Rome who had translated religious texts into Slavonic. Saint Methodius became the first Moravian archbishop, however, after his death, German influence forced his disciples to flee the country.

In 890, the empire of Moravia stretched across modern-day Eastern Europe. However, after the death of leader Svatopluk, the Great Moravian state became overrun by Magyars in 907.

The state was divided. However, Hungarian tribes invaded the territory. The region would be known as the Kingdom of Hungary for thousands of years. This kingdom would rule from the Middle Ages until 1946. Hungary would become a Christian empire through the coronation of King Stephen I around 1000 AD.

During the Middle Ages, Hungary witnessed the construction and reconstruction of outstanding cathedrals and palaces.

The Kingdom of Hungary witnessed centuries of internal struggles between nobility, rulers, and economic growth that forced the state to consolidate. After the death of King Matthias Corvinus in 1490, few nobles wanted a strict ruler, so they obtained the accession of King Vladislaus, who ruled over the Kingdom of Hungary until 1516.

He preserved his popularity among his subjects and other nobility by donating most of the Hungarian Royal estates, causing a significant decline in royal power. However, consolidation and relieving the tax burden for the nobles came at the expense of the empire's defense.

Additionally, the mercenary army of Matthias Corvinus was dissolved by the aristocracy alongside the national security systems. Internal conflicts continued to riddle the country, and the nobles continuously ignored King Louis II's pleas for help from the invading Turks. Then, in 1514, a major peasant rebellion was crushed by nobles.

However, only twelve years later in 1526, the Turkish invasion was celebrated by the peasants. The Hungarians were no longer united people but were divided by social, political, and economic struggles. The occupation of Central and Southern Hungary divided the territory into three different municipalities.

King Louis II's marriage to Mary of Habsburg in 1522 was seen as a threat by the Ottomans to their power in the Balkans, forcing them to work to break the power. At least one offer of peace was made by Suleiman I, who came to power over the Ottoman Empire. However, Louis refused with the belief that war would bring a better outcome than peace.

A bloody war followed, but Hungarian nobles had not recognized the reality of the approaching danger of the Ottoman army. The House of Habsburg overcame the Hungarian throne after the Battle of Mohacs, in which the Habsburg Monarchy ruled the Hungary provinces until 1918.

However, the region would not remain peaceful and instead witnessed revolutions and battles based on the differing governing parties over the region. In particular, the Hungarian Revolution of 1848 was a turning point for Hungarian national identity.

The revolt began after King Ferdinand passed the "April Laws," which were consequently revoked by Franz Joseph I, creating conflict between the Hungarian parliament and Franz Joseph. As a result, the Batthyany Government fell, and Lajos Kossuth, the leader of the revolt, demanded full independence of Hungary.

In the end, Hungary was placed under martial law by the Austrian Empire after Franz Joseph I called upon Russia for help.

The 19th century was a turning point in Slovakian history when the Slovaks created their own form of political ideology for the first time. Joined by national identity and history, the Slovaks were hopeful that they would receive international recognition as an independent country. These hopes were dashed by the Austrian-Hungarian Compromise, which was signed in 1867.

The Austrian-Hungarian Compromise was a document that regulated relations between Hungary and Austria and established the Dual Monarchy between the two nations.

The compromise put an end to a military dictatorship over Hungary, which was started by Francis Joseph after the Hungarian Revolution of 1848. This document restored the territorial integrity of Hungary, and the Kingdom of Hungary was no longer subject to rule under the Austrian Hungary.

For the next several decades, Slovaks were subjected to Hungarianization or Magyarization. This is a process of assimilation by which non-Hungarian nationals voluntarily and involuntarily came to adopt Hungarian language and culture.

The concept of national culture and national identity was important to Hungarians, as intellectuals proposed concepts that featured "political nations" that enforced the linguistic and cultural assimilation of ethnic minorities. Additionally, the Hungarian Nationalities Law of 1868 reinforced the concept of a single, indivisible Hungarian nation.

However, minorities were granted equal rights and respect, regardless of their nationality, under Hungarian law.

However, the First World War activated anti-Austrian-Hungarian sentiment among Slovaks and other European states. At the end of World War I, Slovaks joined the Czech Republic and became the Czechoslovak Republic, also known as the First Republic.

The country was comprised of ethnic Czechs and Slovaks. Additionally, in the aftermath of the war and the division of the Austrian-Hungarian Empire, the newly formed First Republic gained former territories from the empire.

By 1933, Czechoslovakia remained the only functioning democracy in Central Europe operating as a parliamentary republic. However, the Munich Agreement caused a significant disruption in the political sphere of Czechoslovakia. The Munich Agreement, also known by Czechoslovakians as the "Munich Betrayal," was a document signed by the Fuhrer of Germany, Adolf Hitler, on September 30, 1938.

This "agreement" forced the secession of the "Sudeten German Territory" of Czechoslovakia to Germany, which provided Germany easier access to Central and Eastern Europe, especially Poland. Most world leaders celebrated the agreement because it postponed war with Germany, especially as Adolf Hitler had been a significant threat to most of the major powers in the prior years. However, for the Czechoslovakians, a nightmare was coming.

From the signing of the Munich Agreement until the fall of the Third Reich in 1945, Czechoslovakia was annexed under Nazi Germany. The German occupation of Czechoslovakia met resistance from a small, coordinated resistance network comprised of former military leaders, most notably Frantisek Moravec, who was head of Czechoslovak military intelligence.

Jews living in Czechoslovakia witnessed the same horrors that Jews living in Poland, Germany, and Austria experienced as well. Confined to ghettos, transported to concentration camps, then finally death camps, the Jewish population of Czechoslovakia witnessed a whopping 84.6% decrease in population from 1930 to 1946.

However, Czechoslovakia was not only used as a strategic location for Hitler's war. As a result of the occupation, the Czechoslovakians produced significant amounts of heavy weaponry for the Germans during the war. Additionally, the German economy, which had sunk into a deep depression in the aftermath of World War I, set up an extremely high exchange rate between Czechoslovakian currency and German currency.

This was a great time in the history of Slovakia. A lot of things changed extremely quickly. Although this seems like a difficult time in history for Slovakia, that is most likely because of the quick succession at which things were happening. When looking at history, this normally puts a smokescreen over what is actually happening and makes it seem like pure chaos.

In reality, these things were happening in a much slower succession. That means that in reality there was more time to develop things and create them within the Slovakian culture. This helped to create the Slovakian culture that we know today.

This also helped Slovakia maintain its own identity. While many other nations lost their own identity during this time or anytime another country conquered it, Slovakia just kept on going with its own cultural agenda.

The next period of time happened to be when Slovakia was overtaken by the Czechoslovakian communist agenda. This was another rough time in its history, as it seems that much of its history consisted of. You will see that yet again Slovakia made it through with a lot to show for it.

The Communist Era of Slovakia

In October 1918, Czechoslovakia became a country that contained both the Czech Republic and Slovakia together. Slovakia was not consulted when this happened, therefore, it had no choice.

The basis of Czechoslovakia on paper was extensive rights to minorities. These were very important after World War I ended and people were drawn to this promise.

By 1930, Czechoslovakia was under a lot of pressure from Germany, Poland, and Hungary due to its failure to adhere to the rights to minorities that it promised when founded. This revision of the borders led to the Munich Agreement of 1938.

The next year, Slovakia was already fighting to reverse the Munich Agreement of 1938. It did not appreciate the border requirements that were set in place. It wished to reverse them as quickly as possible.

In 1948, Czechoslovakia was declared a people's republic, which is a country's common step towards becoming socialist. Becoming socialist then led to Czechoslovakia becoming a communist country. The economy was dedicated to determining community plans and goals and ending private ownership.

The Soviet Union then made Czechoslovakia a founding member of the Council for Mutual Economic Assistance in 1949. This economic organization gave the Soviet Union leadership of countries of the Eastern Bloc. This leadership also let the Soviet Union lead other Socialist states everywhere in the world.

The National Assembly created a new constitution in May 1948 that contained many liberal and democratic laws. Stalin began sweeping political changes in his satellite countries. In Czechoslovakia, the Stalinists accused their opponents of going against the people's democratic order and accused them of treason in order to remove them from power.

There were many high-scale arrests of Communists with an "international" background, including Jews, veterans of the Spanish Civil War, and bourgeois nationalists. These arrests were then followed by trials.

The increased amount of metallurgy, heavy machinery, and the coal mining industry caused a large increase in supplies in Czechoslovakia. This helped keep things moving forward with the Industrial Revolution that was also going on in the rest of the world.

After the Yalta Conference, Czechoslovakia came under fire by the Soviet Union and the Warsaw Pact. This caused over eight thousand people to be put into forced labor camps from 1948 to 1953. Around this time during the liberalization, one-hundred and thirty-seven Czechoslovakians were killed, and five hundred were injured.

Although Czechoslovakia was still its own independent country, it was basically under the rule of the Soviet Union for some time. It was never absorbed into the union though, which helped it break free in the long run.

Lastly, between 1948 and 1989 on the border shared with Germany and Austria, six hundred men, women, and children were killed in Czechoslovakia. This was another large tragedy in Czechoslovakia but the Czech people made it through this stronger than ever.

It wasn't long after this that the Czech Republic and Slovakia decided to cut ties and become independent. This was a great move forward for Slovakia as a country and a large part of its history.

Slovakia 1990s Until Now

Starting around 1991, the Czech Republic's GDP was far higher than that in Slovakia. This helped in the past by budgeting more money to Slovakia, but these payments halted in January 1991. This caused some differences among political parties in the region and what the society overall wanted.

Many political parties wanted complete independence from the Czech Republic because they thought it would be far more beneficial to them in the long run. However, many people in Slovakian society believed that staying a part of Czechoslovakia was better for their economy and their military.

In 1992, Slovakia had many of its own political parties. There were really none showing up from Czechoslovakia, and that is based on the fact that many in Slovakia did not want them there. But it happened the same way in the Czech Republic as well. Therefore, it just made sense for the two to break at this time, although they did not.

In June 1992, however, it seemed as if a change was going to be made. The Slovakians and the Czechs started very intense negotiations about splitting. On July 17, 1992, parliament in Slovakia put into play the Declaration of Independence for the Slovak Nation.

This Declaration was said to be a resolution of the Slovak National Council. This was seen as a demand for independence by the Czech Republic. This was the starting point for the dissolution of the Czechoslovakian communist nation, which was probably the largest event in Slovakian history.

It was only six days after this declaration went into effect that the Czechoslovakian president at the time resigned and stated that the country agreed to dissolve the joined nation. This put into place a lot of voting from the people of Czechoslovakia and a lot of negotiating on the side of politicians. By December 31, 1992, acts passed, and the dissolution was agreed upon by all parties.

Many of those in society wondered why politicians would want the division. The main piece of the puzzle was them determining if separating was inevitable in the long run. If it was, it just made more sense to dissolve the union now so that each country could get started on building up their own political parties and economy.

The main reasons were not because of violence or keeping of goods but because of differing morals. Slovakia was not on the moral side of communism, whereas Czechoslovakia was much more agreeable with it.

Although that is how both were ruled for some time it did not mean it worked out for both countries.

Many also believe that non-unified media in Czechoslovakia created a divide in the countries rather than creating one as they were trying to do with the government. This seemed to push the people apart, which was the exact opposite of what was supposed to be happening at this period in time.

January 1, 1993, is one of the most important dates in Slovakian history. This was the date that the dissolution of Czechoslovakian communism happened. Interestingly enough, Czechoslovakia came about with the dissolution of Austria-Hungary at the end of WWI. This made the Czech Republic its own independent country as well as Slovakia becoming its own independent country.

In February 1993, Slovakia became democratic, as Michal Kovac became its president. This marked the end of Czechoslovakian communism. This was a reason for all of Slovakia to celebrate and all of the world due to one less communist country out there.

Because of this, the word 'socialist' was taken out of the two republics so that the parties no longer represented that idealism within the country. Before this time, the two republics were called the Czech Socialist Republic and the Slovak Socialist Republic.

Even though these two countries split during the dissolution of Czechoslovakia, it didn't provide any ill will. Both the Czech Republic and Slovakia maintain closeness today. They both cooperate with others in the Visegrad Group as well so that there is more peace in Central Europe.

Most recently in March 2004, Slovakia became a member of NATO and the European Union. This helped tie the country to larger powers in Europe and create better ties all around the world. In January 2009, it finally adopted the Euro as its national currency, creating even more ties in the area.

Although things have been quiet in Slovakia for quite some time, it did make waves with its first female president in 2019. Slovakia did something even the United States has yet to do, and it has proven wonderful. Since 2019, Zuzana Caputova has been president, making Slovakia a great place to live.

Important Artifacts

Artifacts are a great way to look into the history of a country. Slovakia is no different in this sense. With the deep history that Slovakia holds, it has much more in its artifact history than many other countries around the same area.

If you are trying to get a fast review of the history of Slovakia and the major points in its history from the Paleolithic era to modern history, then this is the chapter for you. Looking at the artifacts that have been recovered from Slovakia gives a great view of who the people were and what they stood for during any given time in history.

Some of the oldest artifacts discovered from the Paleolithic era include ancient flint tools. The creation of tools was very rudimentary in style. This was the very first instance in time where tools were being made. However, this presented a huge piece of the puzzle when looking at ancient history.

Discovered near Nové Mesto nad Váhom, radiocarbon dating proves that they were found in the early stages of the Paleolithic era at 270,000

BCE and were made using the Clactonian technique. This is a technique where the creator would strike thick, irregular flakes from a core of flint.

They would then use the smaller flakes as crude knives or scrapers. They would also use flint to make arrow and spearheads to hang larger Ice Age animals. These tools prove that there was ancient habitation in prehistoric Slovakia as early as 3 million years ago.

Other stone tools were discovered in Prepost cave (Prepoštká Jaskyňa), which is near a historical town called Bojince located in Central Slovakia at the upper Nitra River and from other nearby villages.

These tools originate from the middle of the Paleolithic age (200,00-80,000 BCE). However, one of the most monumental discoveries from this time period includes the Neanderthal skull that was discovered near a village in northern Slovakia called Gánovce.

The Neanderthal cranium was an important discovery because the Neanderthals are the closest relatives to modern-day humans. They lived throughout Europe and Asia and excelled at hunting large Ice Age animals like the woolly mammoth (Elephas primigenius).

Other prehistoric settlements were excavated by Smolenice, Čaka, and Ockov. After the discovery of the Neanderthal skull, archaeologists began uncovering a number of other prehistoric Homo sapiens bones in the surrounding region. They also discovered numerous objects and other remnants of the Gravettian culture.

The Gravettians were a group of hunter-gatherers that lived in a viciously cold period of European prehistory. Their lifestyle was heavily influenced by the harsh climates, and Pleniglacial environmental changes forced them to adapt. Their remains were primarily found by the Nitra River valleys, Hron, Ipel', Vál, and even as far as the settlement of Žilina.

They even found remains near the foot of the Vihorlat Mountains, which is a volcanic mountain range located in Eastern Slovakia and Western Ukraine, and the Tribec mountains, which is a crystalline range located in Western Slovakia. A section of the Vihorlat mountain range is also listed as a World Heritage Site.

There were two types of regional variants that archaeologists discovered. There is the western Gravettian, which is known mainly from cave sites located in France, Spain, and Britain. Then we have the eastern Gravettian, which were more likely to be found by Slovakia since they were located in Central Europe and Russia. The Gravettians adopted some of the Pavlovian culture.

Pavlovian is described as an upper Paleolithic culture. It also happens to be a variant of the Gravettian culture that we discussed earlier. These cultures were very prevalent in all of Slovakian history and were great influences on the artifacts and history of this country.

Instead of struggling, the people of this area were more sophisticated. They used great tools and knowledge to get through the rough tundra that they lived in for part of the year.

Their economy was based mostly on hunting. Hunting provided this group of people with fat fuel, tents made out of hides, and large bones for creating tools and building shelters. Since the Gravettians had adopted some of the Pavlovian techniques, they were able to hunt larger Ice Age animals which are how they created a well-known prehistoric female figurine that will be introduced in the next paragraph.

Some of the most known finds in this region include the oldest dated female statue created out of wooly mammoth bones (22,800 BCE), the famous Venus of Moravany. It's a small, prehistoric female figurine that was discovered in the early 20th century in Slovakia.

Discovered by Štefan Hulman-Petrech, a farmer in Podkovica near the village of Moravany nad Váhom. The doll originates from the Gravettian hunter-gatherers and was estimated to have been plowed up sometime before 1930. This doll is proof of the passing cultures and may be one of many discovered figurines.

The Gravettians also made needles out of mammoth bones, and it wasn't uncommon for these ancient humans to have made carvings of not just women but of animals, too. They also found textile impressions that had been pressed with wet clay. This gave the oldest proof that humans were weaving, which is an amazing feat in history.

Archeologists also discovered numerous necklaces made from the Cypraca thermophile (organisms that thrive at high temperatures) shells of gastropods like mollusks or snail shells, which originated from the Tertiary period.

These artifacts were also discovered in the Hubina village. These necklaces made out of shells provide evidence of ancient commercial exchanges and trades carried out between Central Europe and the Mediterranean.

There have also been discoveries of tools and pottery in several archaeological sites and burial grounds throughout Slovakia during the Neolithic era. What may surprise you is that these sites include the northern regions at relatively high altitudes for their species.

These pottery pieces are important to Slovakian history because they reveal the first attempts at the use of color in the pottery. Creators also used delicate linear decorations, and the deliberate adornment proves that they were developing an aesthetic sense for the Neolithic craftsmen. This pottery was found in Želiezovce and Gemer.

Other important archaeological discoveries have been revealed in a couple of formerly inhabited caves. One example includes the Domica Cave, which is estimated to be almost 6000 meters long and includes a depth of 700 meters. This cave is in the southwestern area of Slovakia near the border of Plesivec.

This is in the Rožňava District that is actually in southern Slovakia. The Domica Cave is paired with the Baradla Cave, which is another great cave in the history of Slovakia. This tends to take up a fairly big part of the Aggtelek Karst, which is also on a border.

This means that potentially these ancient human sub-species could have had access and passage to an entirely new region than where they were originally from. The tribes that inhabited these caves existed for more than eight hundred years continuously and created beautiful pottery with the first usage of color.

When the Neolithic era was coming to an end, these ancient humans were starting to clear pastures and develop more agriculturally. They also started smelting the first metals at a local level. They made a style of pottery called the "Retz" style of pottery. They also started experimenting more and creating fluted pottery.

People built quite a few fortified sites during the fluted pottery era, and some of these vestiges still remain today, more frequently in higher altitude areas. Most likely because they were less likely to be built over because of the difficulty to get there since our ancient ancestors had dug pits to surround some of these more well-known sites by Nitriansky Hrádok.

The geographic location of modern-day Slovakia means that it was a popular hub for a dense trade network for goods like shells, amber, which is a fossilized resin that's created from tree sap, jewels, and weapons. Since it's right in the middle of Euro-Asia it was popularly used and included in the European trade system, and quite a few trade routes ran through Slovakia.

With the beginning of the Bronze Age, Slovakia went through three stages of development that took place between 2000 to 800 BCE. It had major cultural, economic, and political development, and the usage of copper production increased exponentially, especially in central Slovakia.

A variety of shields, jewelry, statues, and dishes have been discovered in some of the diverse tombs located in Central Slovakia. The excavations of the Lustian hillforts have documented the substantial development of trade and agriculture during that period.

The Celts entering Slovakian territories marked the beginning of the late Iron Age in that region. They brought silver coins that had the names of their Celtic kings inscribed on them. The silver coins were called Biatecs, and they were the first documented known usage of writing in Slovakia.

When the Roman era began, they occupied only a thin land strip on the right bank of the Danube and an extremely small part of southwestern Slovakia that held a Roman military camp named Gerulata, a Roman castellum, and the popular Devin Castle. The Romans rarely ventured into the deeper parts of the river valley up until 174 CE. The emperor Marcus Aurelius penetrated deeper into the valleys of Váh, Nitra, and Hron.

There on Hron's banks, he wrote his philosophical work called Meditations, which was a series of personal writings that dated from 161 to 180 AD. They were private notes about himself and his ideologies on Stoic philosophy. Then, in 179 CE, the Roman legion carved onto a rock of the Trencin Castle the ancient name of Trencin (Laugaricio) which marked the furthest northern point of their presence in that part of Europe.

Geography of Slovakia

Slovakia has many different geographical types. It is not all mountains nor all valleys. There is a great number of different landscapes all across Slovakia. This was even notable back in the prehistoric era due to many artifacts and bodies being found very high up.

The climate of Slovakia is very normal to most of the world. Because it lies in between two climate zones, it is prone to warm summers that can get up to 100 degrees Fahrenheit. It is also prone to cold winters that can get to negative 40 degrees Fahrenheit. Southern Slovakia seems to be the warmest as are most southern areas of countries.

Just like the temperature range would suggest, there are four seasons that take place in Slovakia. Spring starts around March 21, summer starts around June 22, fall starts around September 23, and winter begins around December 21. Those are the official dates, but generally, temperatures can range anywhere.

The weather is the most unstable in the spring due to the ocean air bringing in a lot of rain during this season. It then dries up for summer, which is generally quite dry but not as dry as fall. And just as in many other places, winter is snowy due to the climate area it is in.

The Tatra mountains are categorized as the highest mountain range in Slovakia. They are a part of the largest mountain range in Slovakia as well, that mountain range is named the Carpathian Mountains. This mountain range goes through more countries than just Slovakia but the highest parts of the mountains are in Slovakia.

The Tatra Mountains have 29 peaks that are over eight thousand feet tall. Altogether this area of mountains is 290 square miles, and over three-fourths of this mountain range falls into the Slovakian borders, which gives way to the best view from any city in Slovakia.

This mountain range offers popular hiking and skiing mountains that are closer to the Slovakian border with Poland. This part of the mountains also has very scenic lakes and valleys that are wonderful for sightseeing and wildlife.

Slovakia is a smaller country, but that doesn't mean they don't have a great array of natural places to look at and sightsee. There are nine different national parks in Slovakia. They take up about seven percent of the surface area in Slovakia.

The earliest national park to open in Slovakia was the Tatra National Park in 1949. This is home to the Tatra Mountains that were previously talked about. Because this park is so old, it is home to a great history of what happened during the Czechoslovakian era.

The most recent national park to be established in Slovakia was the Velka Fatra National Park in 2002. This is home to the Greater Fatra Mountains, which is another great site to see. Most of the national parks in Slovakia have mountains in them that are historically important due to being there for hundreds of thousands of years.

Due to these mountains being so prevalent, caves are also very prevalent. Stalagmites and stalactites are very common in all of these caves because of the way the land created these caves and the climate they are most often in. Slovakia has five caves that fall under the UNESCO World Heritage Site status, and these are a must-see.

Another great addition that the mountains have put into the geography of Slovakia are the many rivers that stem from them. There are many rivers that have created natural country borders for Slovakia, such as the Dunajec and Danube Rivers that are to the north and south. Although these rivers do not completely form the border, they do fill in some of it.

Other rivers only partially go through Slovakia due to it being such a small country surrounded by many other countries.

The rivers in Slovakia range from 250 miles long to only 122 miles long, and these are the longest and shortest measurements as there are plenty in between these ranges. When the snow melts in Slovakia, these rivers produce a lot of water and floods that help vegetation grow in the spring months.

Due to this vast difference in geography all over Slovakia, animal and plant life thrives. There is a wide range of biodiversity in such a small country and it shows. With the beautiful landscapes to look out onto the wonderful foods that you are able to try, Slovakia has a great range of nature.

Recap

Slovakia has a great history and culture that has been around for hundreds of thousands of years. This is a country that may be small but has never lost its identity throughout the world's history. This is more than many countries can say, which is sad but has shaped the world into what it is today.

Even though there have been many places that have gone through exactly what Slovakia has gone through in its history, not many have come out with such a great country. This is both a testament to its culture and the people that live there.

Dating back to the Paleolithic era, there have been human bones, animal bones, art, and tools discovered. These tools show an emerging society right out of Slovakia. The bones that were found on the land also pushed historians to figure out the history of humanoid figures. Without these human bones and the famous skull cast, we may have known far less at this point in time.

This Paleolithic era skull produced many advancements in science that went over human genealogy and evolution. This is a great thing for everyone whether they are interested in the adaptation of science or not.

During the Neolithic era, Slovakia produced the first attempts at using color in art. This was a breakthrough for art history, and after it, many notable things happened in the art world. They have also shown great and decisive linework on pottery that may have advanced modern pottery to what it is now.

Art may not seem like the most important thing in a country's history but it really tells the story. Expression comes out through art, and it shows the emotions and state of the people in the society at that time. Therefore, it is one of the most important things in history no matter how trivial it may seem.

During medieval times, architecture really took off in the Slovakian region of Europe. Many castles that are still standing today were built, and art was coming into an all-time high. Tombs were being intricately made so that their loved ones had a beautiful place to spend their afterlife. This is most likely due to the religions that came about during this time.

During the Roman Empire period, conquests were made into Slovakia and it was conquered many times, but none of it ruined its individuality. During those time periods, Slovakian artifacts and architecture are still vastly different from Roman artifacts and architecture, which shows Slovakian pride.

As communism came to settle in, still, nothing changed. Slovakia was as strong as it always had been. The Czech Republic worked with Slovakia all the way through to try and make things work as a communist nation, but they never were to reap the benefits.

The dissolution of Czechoslovakia was what really gave Slovakia its own independence, and the country ran with it once it got it. This was probably the most major point in Slovakian history.

As of today, it has one of the deepest and richest cultures in the world and continues to put more work into that culture year after year. Slovakia is truly a destination for anyone who is a lover of history or a lover of nature. The country has more than enough of both to go around.

There is nothing better than visiting a beautiful country on a different continent. If you are looking for the perfect one to go visit, Slovakia is a great option. As much of the world is in turmoil in this day and age, Slovakia is thriving.

Amazing art is still coming out of its culture as well as great food and literature. Although much of its architecture happened back in the history of Slovakia, there are still great things being done in architecture there today.

History based on the architecture in Slovakia is greater than ever. There are tours both self-guided and professionally guided that are available through many of the castles and much of the land. These make for not just a fun type of vacation but also a very educational one.

If you are lucky enough to live in or around Slovakia, then you already know the basics of the greatness that it has to offer. Now you may know even more about the history of how this amazing place came to be. Use that information to grow your love for this amazing country.

Hopefully, this book gave an insight into who the people of Slovakia really are and what shaped them to be this way. The present is simply a conglomeration of the past, and it really shines brightly in Slovakia.

The History of Switzerland: A Fascinating Guide to this Wonderful Country in Central Europe

What's so great about Switzerland?

Well, the flag is a plus.

Introduction

Mountains. Neutrality. Watches. Secret bank accounts. Cheese and chocolate. In the modern world, these seem to be the things we think of when discussing the country of Switzerland. We love its products and dream of visiting its dramatic Alpine playgrounds. Of course, there is more to this small nation than a vacation spot or a political stance, but a surprising amount of Switzerland's fortunes (both monetary and otherwise) have been determined by its location. The natural barriers of two formidable mountain ranges, and its location in the figurative center of Europe, have always set Switzerland apart, and that separation has produced its unusual status throughout its history and into the era of the modern world.

Switzerland's population does not reach 9 million people, and on a list of the world's 194 countries and dependent territories, Switzerland is 132nd, followed in large part by protectorates and island countries. Yet modern Switzerland is a hub of world activity and a leader in economics and human development. Its cities are consistently lauded for their high quality of life – though such quality comes at a price, with some of the highest costs of living in the world. Switzerland boasts the highest nominal wealth per adult, and the world's eighth-highest gross domestic product. Swiss citizenship is a much sought-after status. Swiss men and women have the longest life expectancies in the world. How did such a small and cut-off land become so central (and not just in its location) to the events of the western world?

In this history, we'll look at the forces that formed this powerful and influential country.

Geography

Switzerland lies landlocked in the center of Western Europe. To the south is Italy, to the west, France. Germany is to the north and Lichtenstein and Austria are to the East. The little country is extremely mountainous, its geography divided between the great mass of the Swiss Alps, which spans the entire southern half of the country, and the Jura range, a sub-alpine mountain range that lies along the border between Switzerland and France. Between these two natural barriers is the Swiss Plateau, which lies east-to-west on relatively flat ground. Most of the country's 8.5 million population resides on the Swiss Plateau, where the country's major metropolises (Bern, Zurich, Lucerne, and Lausanne) are situated. This is not to say that the spectacular mountains go unpopulated; they are peppered with high-altitude cities, tourism, and industry. Today Switzerland is composed of 26 administrative cantons, and many of which have been in existence since before the Middle Ages.

Early History of Switzerland

Prehistory

The presence of humans in the area that would become Switzerland can be dated to 150,000 years ago. Farming settlements dating from 6000 to 5000 BC have been found at Gächlingen, a municipality that still exists in the far north of the country on the Danube River. Afterward, as was the case with most of Central Europe, the Hallstatt culture populated the area through the Bronze Age (from approximately the 12th to 6th centuries BC) followed by the Iron Age culture of La Tène (450 BC to the 1st Century BC - the Roman Conquest).

In 15 BC, Roman brothers Tiberius (a future emperor) and Drusus conquered the Alps, making them part of the Roman Empire. The region was divided into two Roman provinces, Gallia Belgica (later called Germania Superior) and Raetia. The first Roman settlement on the

Rhine, Augusta Raurica, had appeared by 44 BC. Augusta Raurica and several other towns grew quite large and prosperous in the first two centuries AD; the remainder of the surrounding plateau was largely utilized for agricultural estates. Today, Augusta Raurica is an important excavation site, where the remains of an amphitheater, aqueducts, town walls, a theater and a town forum with temples and an assembly chamber have been uncovered.

By the end of the 4th Century AD, despite its efforts to defend the territory, the Roman Empire was driven out of the area by increasing attacks from Germanic tribes, which then settled into the abandoned plateau.

Through the 4th Century the Swiss plateau and the Alps were divided between Alemannia and Burgundy, and finally the entire region was taken into the Frankish Empire when it defeated Alemannia and overtook the Burgundians. Thus, it remained for the next three centuries, until the Frankish Empire was divided in Charlemagne's Treaty of Verdun in 843AD, renaming the region into Middle Francia and East Francia. The two regions were reunited by the Holy Roman Empire sometime around 1000 AD. This led to various kingdoms controlling the area – houses such as Savoy, Zähringer, Kyburg and Habsburg, with the ambitious land-grabbing clan of Habsburgs annexing more and more of the land under their rulership.

In fact, Switzerland was the first Habsburg territory in the Holy Roman Empire and even is home to the Habsburgs original castle, Hawk Castle, or Habichtsburg Castle (1020 AD).

Geographic Advantage

Despite being a part of the Holy Roman Empire, the area that would one day become Switzerland enjoyed a certain autonomous privilege simply because of geographical isolation. With difficult mountain ranges both in the north and south of the territory, the cantons were too inconveniently located for any heavy-handed rulership.

Under the rule of the Holy Roman Empire, Switzerland's cantons were subject to "imperial immediacy," that is to say, they were "immediately" under the authority of the Holy Roman Emperor without the go-between of a duke or other intermediary. Theoretically this status was not to be coveted. For many territories, immediacy resulted in rather high expectations and demands being placed on a territory by the emperor, and without an intermediary, there was no effective way to compromise.

However, should the Holy Roman Emperor choose to focus attention elsewhere, the countries with imperial immediacy found themselves able and expected to exercise their own imperial powers, giving them a pleasing amount of autonomy. This was the case with Switzerland – it was simply out of reach, difficult to control, and had nothing of sufficient value to warrant the trouble required. The Holy Roman Emperor had far bigger fish to fry, and Switzerland was left alone.

For centuries, then, Switzerland's communities were mostly left to themselves to govern their own affairs. The people of the region became quickly accustomed to these freedoms and developed a fierce sense of protectiveness for their lands. The climate and terrain, rough as it was, in combination with this protectiveness, produced generations of hardy, daring and well-trained fighters ready to defend themselves and their small, resilient homelands.

The Gotthard Pass

The landscape of Swiss inaccessibility was changed by the completion of the Gotthard Pass. 13th Century Switzerland, through pasteurizing herds of cattle, enjoyed an unusual level of prosperity in its production of dairy products, and was eager to promote trade with Italy, which lay south of the most forbidding range of the Alps. The Gotthard Pass was the extension of an ancient local route located on the lowest point between the Alpine summits of Pizzo Lucendro and Pizzo Centrale. Still, the road afforded no real advantage until the completion of a wooden bridge that crossed the Schollenen Gorge, which had previously been inaccessible in springtime due to the violent rush of snowmelt waters. The Gotthard Pass extended from just south of Lake Lucerne, then wound southward through the Alps to emerge near Bellinzona, not far from the Italian border and only 108 km from Milan.

Now travelers could take the Gotthard Pass to its summit of almost 7000 feet and then travel directly south toward prosperous Duchy of Milan. For centuries afterward, Gotthard Pass remained the only feasible way through the Alps to Italy. Thus, beginning in the mid-13th Century, the Gotthard Pass opened trade between Switzerland and Italy. But more importantly, the opening of the pass created a far shorter route from

Germany to Italy, and in fact, established a new trade route between all northern and southern Europe. Suddenly, Switzerland became an extremely important piece of land.

The Swiss Confederacy Responds to Habsburg Interference

Now the Holy Roman Empire, led by Rudolf I of the Habsburgs, took notice of the potential wealth and advantages of Switzerland. In 1291, Rudolf I stepped in and took control of the important area of Lucerne by purchasing it from Murbach Abbey, the Benedictine monastery around which the village had grown.

In response, three of Switzerland's nearby rural cantons bordering Lake Lucerne, Uri, Schwyz and Unterwalden (sometimes called the "Forest Cantons"), made formalized agreements between themselves regarding mountain trade routes and other common interests. Uri, at the time, held the territory of the Gotthard Pass. The trio formed the Schweizerische, or the Swiss Confederation. These three cantons had long been rivals, as likely to fight one another as join forces, so this was not the first time that the question or treaties or agreements had been approached. But now, the urgency of the situation, as outsiders took control from them, prompted more effort for the cantons to make this agreement work.

The Federal Charter of 1291 is considered the founding document of the Old Swiss Confederacy. Over the next 100 years, further Swiss cantons joined this Confederacy, with the end of both the 14th and 15th centuries seeing dramatic increases in the Confederacy's size.

From this point forward, the Swiss people, accustomed to their autonomy, reacted violently to any attempts to encroach upon their country. The wars for Switzerland's independence continued for centuries, from small insurrections to large battles. Witnesses surviving these fights went home to spread tales of the fearsomeness of Swiss warriors.

The Warriors of Switzerland

Origins

The rugged landscape of Switzerland, the wildlife (including wolves and bears), and their own determination to maintain independence gave the Swiss people a predisposition toward skillful fighting and self-defense. They developed significant martial skills. What's more, centuries of self-reliance had turned them into a people who demanded their freedom and would settle for nothing less; their obvious pride and ferocity on the battlefield made them the terror of Europe. There were a few decisive battles that established and furthered this status.

In 1315, at the Pass of Morgarten, fighters from Schwyz faced down an Austrian army. Schwyz had struck against the Holy Roman Empire by plundering a monastery, which of course prompted a military response, and Austria sent 9000 troops, including 2000 mounted knights.

Mounted knights were, at the time, the height of military expertise and power. The Austrian force came under the command of Holy Roman Emperor Leopold I.

Schwyz was aware of the Austrians' approach. They had only 1300 men in their force, so the people retreated behind a series of manmade earthworks and wooden palisades. Leopold chose to attack via the Pass at Morgarten, the weakest point of the series. The Austrian army approached in a column, with its vanguard of mounted knights in the lead. The vanguard found itself redirected by enemy defenses and then set upon by a small and stubborn group of fighters blocking the route. Abruptly the rest of the Austrian army was at a standstill, and exposed, out in the open.

Schwyz fighters then cut off the mounted vanguard from the rest of the army, again by blocking the road, and a second group rained stones down on the mounted knights and then flew at them with axes and halberds, driving them into the marshes and cut them down. Most of the 2000 casualties of the battle were Austrian mounted knights.

This relatively small victory for the Schwyz, thanks in part to clever use of the terrain and the element of surprise, sent shockwaves throughout the empires. The guerilla warfare tactics of the Swiss people were unheard of. The chivalry of mounted knights supported the belief that battles should be fought almost tournament-style, with a particular etiquette. It was apparent that these rough canton-dwellers had no respect for chivalry. The tales of fearsome Swiss foes spread throughout Europe.

In 1385, Habsburg emperor Leopold III attempted to expand his lands into Switzerland. Once more, war broke out. Leopold's army faced off against Swiss forces on July 9, 1386 north of Sempach (in the canton of Lucerne). The Austrians again were surprised by the swiftness of the Swiss attack. By rushing their attack forward, the Swiss forces sought to keep the Austrians on terrain unsuitable for mounted attacks. Indeed, the Austrian knights were forced to abandon their horses. Swiss halberdiers, wearing light armor compared to the heavily protected knights, took many casualties at first.

Historically, Swiss warriors are seldom deterred or demoralized by poor odds – in fact, the more the odds line against them, the harder they seem to fight. And to an enemy, what could be more terrifying than an opposing force willing to fight to the death? A stubborn, angry and determined bunch, the halberdiers regrouped and pressed their attack toward breaking through the line of Austrian pikemen. Once through the barrier, they proceeded to slaughter another 2000 Austrians, a considerable victory considering their own casualties of merely 200. The Austrians were driven back again, and again, stories spread throughout Europe of the terrifying Swiss halberdier.

The Pikemen's Square

In 1422 at the Battle of Arbedo, the resiliency of the Swiss halberdier found its limitations. Territorial disputes over Bellinzona (near the south end of the Gotthard pass) led to war between the Duchy of Milan and the Swiss cantons.

About 2,500 Swiss confederate soldiers marched on the city of Bellinzona. In response, the Milanese army sent 16,000 troops (including 5000 cavalrymen). The Milanese general launched a surprise attack upon the Swiss, who quickly made a square formation and defended themselves. Once more, the Swiss warriors were able to thwart cavalry attacks, and the Milanese soldiers were forced to dismount. But at this point, the Swiss were simply vastly outnumbered. The Milanese persistently assaulted the Swiss until, having suffered about 500 casualties, the Swiss elected to cut their losses and retreat. Theoretically, as the Swiss forces were made of warriors from multiple cantons without the same training or commanders, chaos would have been a predictable result of such dire circumstances. Yet with precision and likeminded purpose, the Swiss broke through the Milanese line and retreated into the mountains. Strong discipline was added to the many traits that European forces feared from a Swiss army.

The Swiss themselves, however, considered this defeat as a lesson. The halberd was insufficient as its army's standard weapon. The canton of Lucerne had joined the Confederacy in 1352, and in its capital city of Lucerne, a council was held to determine a solution. It was here that the

Swiss decided to employ the use of long pikes and greatly increase the use of pikemen.

The long pike was unwieldly as a weapon, and in single combat was practically useless. To see it serve its purpose, it must be employed by a phalanx of men, each brandishing one of the long, sharp pikes as they all move in unison. The effective use of a pike phalanx requires a great deal of training and discipline, yet these seem to be the very traits in which Swiss warriors excelled.

In a standard Swiss pike phalanx, the men in the front four rows held their pikes at varying levels from ground to eye-level. The next four rows served two purposes: to replace pikemen lost in the front four, and to stand close enough together, with their pikes held vertically, to make a highly effective barrier against enemy arrows. By practicing this phalanx technique, Swiss pikemen formed a spiny, mobile barrier that could stop a cavalry attack dead in its tracks. Horses quite wisely refused to get anywhere near such a frightening deathtrap, and any knight who forced the way forward would find himself and his horse skewered.

That a defeat proved the value of these pike phalanxes is rather ironic, but even Swiss defeats had an air of purposefulness in them. In 1444, after the Treaty of Tours stopped the Hundred Years' War, the French king found himself with a mercenary army and nothing to do. He allied with Habsburg Emperor Friedrich III and sent 40,000 troops marching into the Swiss Confederacy, again in effort to expand territories. A reconnaissance force of 1500, which held 1200 Swiss warriors, was sent to block the army's path.

The two groups clashed at St. Jakob an der Birs, and the Swiss were clearly outnumbered once again; nevertheless, the stubborn and proud Swiss warriors insisted upon fighting; their commanders even ordered retreat and the warriors of the cantons refused. Up to the battle itself, retreat would have remained possible, and still, they threw themselves at these invaders to their lands. The Swiss fought to the last man, the battle ranging from weaponry and battlefield tactics until losses and confusion reduced the entire encounter to violent hand-to-hand combat. Even though they were defeated, the noteworthy fact was that Swiss pike formations held out for five hours against the superior forces, and the Swiss managed to kill approximately 4000 of the invading mercenary troops.

The Burgundian Wars

In 1473, yet again, a foreign ruler wished to enlarge his territories by snatching up Swiss cantons. This time, it was the Duke of Burgundy, Charles the Bold, who made a play to declare himself a king by expanding his lands to Italy, which, of course, meant taking the Swiss Confederacy into his territory. This time it was not only the Confederacy he angered but the Austrians and Alsatians, who united with the Swiss to drive the Duke away with at the Battle of Hericourt.

Charles did not give up; in 1476 he pursued a plan to cut straight through the middle of the Swiss Confederacy by first taking Bern. On their march to Bern, the Burgundians encountered the small town of Grandson. The Duke's army crushed the small resistance there and killed many of their Swiss prisoners by hanging or drowning them, an act that naturally enraged the Swiss. Charles the Bold, living up to his name, apparently had chosen to ignore tales of the danger of an enraged Swiss soldier.

A few days later the bloodthirsty Swiss Confederacy met Charles' forces in the Battle of Grandson. They employed their square pike technique, not only as a battle strategy but as a diversion, occupying Charles' efforts, decimating his cavalry, and whittling away at his forces and ammunition while the major mass of the Swiss Confederacy's army approached from the northeast. His forces were already badly battered when Charles realized that he had not yet met the entirety of Swiss forces. He fled the battle with his attendants, leaving behind a considerable amount of treasure.

There were two more fights, and the Swiss won both: Morat 1476, and Nancy 1477 – at the latter, Charles the Bold was killed. His death marked the end of the Burgundian wars.

The pike block's effectiveness demonstrated that the mounted knight was now antiquated. By the end of the 15th Century, over two thirds of European infantries were armed with long pikes.

Swiss Mercenaries

Their victory in the Burgundian Wars left no doubts in the minds of European powers: Swiss fighters were a coveted asset. European monarchs began hiring Swiss mercenaries to supplement their forces and to act as bodyguards. It was commonly believed that having a Swiss contingent within your forces could make the difference between victory and defeat.

During the 15th Century, soldiering was sort of a part-time occupation to supplement the Swiss farmer's income; something for him to do while he waited for harvests. With the passage of time, the number of Swiss farms began to decrease as cattle herding required more and more land for grazing. As a result, soldiering became a rather common full-time occupation. They were known for carrying two weapons: a traditional Swiss halberd and a golden-handled longsword.

A Swiss warrior's reputation as loyal, reliable, and ferocious on the battlefield was no exaggeration. Even more, monarchs liked the impartiality of the Swiss. Because they were hired, and not the king's royal subjects, they weren't embroiled in political arguments or subject to disagreeable taxes or laws, and they were therefore fighting without grudges against their employer.

By 1481, about 6000 Swiss mercenaries worked in service of King Louis XI of France, and by 1497, 100 Swiss guards acted as the French king's personal guards, or his "Garde de Cent Suisses" (Guard of 100 Swiss). These men not only watched over the king in his palace, but also accompanied him into battle.

The Papal Swiss Guard

The popes of the Renaissance were far more like kings than they were religious figures, operating with the same sense of politics, arranging marriages, making alliances with nations, and leading forces into battle. For decades, popes had held alliances with the Confederacy and had used Swiss mercenaries in battles.

Pope Julius II was sixty years old but remained an energetic military leader who desired to be both the ruler of Italy and to increase his hold over European power through his papal office. In these pursuits, he wanted to ensure his safety with a cadre of personal bodyguards. The Swiss had the advantage of being unaligned with any European power. Julius had also seen the Swiss in battle personally. He was witness to their prowess when France warred with Naples in the Italian Wars, in addition to serving as the Bishop of Lausanne for a time that let him become well acquainted with the Swiss people.

Julius's Swiss advisor was a cleric named Peter von Hertenstein, who had long been in the service of the papal authority. When Julius inquired about the acquisition of Swiss bodyguards, Hertenstein agreed to assist, and even recommended a relative, Kaspar von Silenen, as commander.

In 1505, Julius sent Hertenstein to Swiss lands with instructions to employ 200 Swiss guards; this expensive venture was funded by the famously wealthy Fugger family of Germany, which controlled the European copper market and a major portion of the European economy in the 16th century.

Upon his arrival, Hertenstein found the Confederacy's government less willing to cooperate than he had hoped. Swiss mercenary service had entered a stage of controversy, with great concerns over the sheer numbers of Swiss men who were in the employ of foreign powers. Only five years before, an unfortunate battle had pitched two contingents of Swiss soldiers against each other – one in the service of Louis XII of France, the other in service of Ludovico il Moro of Milan -- resulting in many losses.

Another problem was that "papal guard duty" did not appeal to the warriors of the Confederacy. It sounded quite dull, to stand around guarding an old man, compared to the fun of fighting bloody fights for kings with the promise of booty.

For these reasons, only 150 Swiss troops went to Rome in the winter of 1505 with Kaspar von Silenen, the first captain of the Papal Swiss

Guard. Pope Julius granted them the title of "Defenders of the Church's Freedom."

For the most part, Papal Swiss Guard duty is ceremonial. In May of 1527, however, Rome was sacked by mutinous troops of Charles V, the Holy Roman Emperor. Roman defenders, outnumbered, soon found the city walls breached. The militia retreated, and only 189 Swiss guards stayed at their posts in the Vatican, holding their ground the Campo Centro (the Vatican cemetery) and giving Pope Clement time to escape. The Swiss Guard cut down 900 enemy troops, losing 147 of their own as the remaining guards escaped with the Pope. The Papal Guard remains in service today, though through the centuries the size of the guard has changed and even, at times, been disbanded.

Requirements for serving in the Papal Swiss Guard are quite strict. Candidates must be men who are:

- » Citizens of Switzerland
- » Roman Catholic
- » Of good moral and ethical background
- » Between the ages of 19 and 30
- » At least 174 centimeters tall
- » In possession of a professional diploma or high school degree
- » Swiss military trained.

If a candidate meets all these traits, he can apply to the guard's recruiting office in Neuhausen where he will undergo a rigorous interview process. Plans have been proposed to allow the inclusion of women in the Swiss Papal Guard, but such plans remain in the "ideas" phase and no implementation of the inclusion of women has started.

Successful applicants go to Rome, and at once are put into a training program. They learn the traditions, behavior, and the occasional oddities of papal service. They work out at a gym and study martial arts. Tradition dictates that they practice halberd drilling, but since the assassination attempt against Pope John Paul II in 1981, the Swiss Guard has also trained at a nearby Italian firing range to learn care and service of guns.

Purportedly, the most difficult part of the job is standing motionless in the Italian sun wearing over 50 pounds of traditional armor. The stoic guards master psychological tricks to handle the task.

Defeat of Emperor Maximilian

Further cantons joined over the Confederacy over the centuries, increasing its power and expanding its reach from the Jura Mountains in the north to the Alps in the south. The Confederacy determinedly battled the Holy Roman Empire until in 1499, they defeated Emperor Maximilian I in the Swabian War, a dispute over the control of the Val Mustair and the Umbrail Pass in the Grisons. The Grisons were not part of the Confederacy yet, but Swiss troops were obligated to the Grisons by contract. Through a series of victories over the Habsburg allies, the Swiss won, basically, the Confederacy's figurative independence – simply in the fact that, although the Confederacy was still considered a part of the Holy Roman Empire, that Empire would no longer try to interfere with them, lifting imperial taxes and jurisdiction. Further cantons joined the Confederacy shortly thereafter, and Switzerland's area rapidly expanded in the early 15th Century, with another surge in size at the 15th Century's end.

Reformation in the Cantons

During the 15th Century, Switzerland fought not only for its independence from the Holy Roman Empire but from excessive influence of the Church. Several monasteries had already been put under secular management. While, in general, teachers were still priests, the administration of schools was in the hands of the cantons, not the church. Still, the Swiss populace could see the vivid contrast between the luxuries enjoyed by the Church and its priests and note its marked contrast to the standard of living borne by the population's majority. It did not escape their notice, either, that many of those priests, far from supervision, lived hedonistic lives nothing like the rules that the Church dictated. When stirrings of reformation spread through Europe, many in the Swiss Confederacy were ready for a change.

Huldrych Zwingli

Huldrych Zwingli served as a priest in Einsiedeln. His studies were in the renaissance humanist tradition, which contrary to modern views of "humanism," is a specifically religious viewpoint that simply wants to revert to the classical traditions and dispense with intermediaries between man and God (that is, to reduce or even dispense with the need for the Church and its priests). Therefore, as early as 1516 he spoke out against the injustice of the Church's hierarchies.

He was eventually called to Zurich, where he became a well-known revolutionary protestant, adding to his fame by speaking out against corrupt political processes and condemning the mercenary business (already falling out of favor, as previously mentioned). In Zurich, Zwingli's ideas were well-received. His most historically famous stance against the Church took place in the "Affair of the Sausages," (1522) when Zwingli openly defended locals who ate meat during Lent, saying that the Bible never dictated when Christians should, or should not, fast, nor what they should eat during Lent. Of course, this caused backlash from the Church but too late – the damage was done, and Zwingli's popularity grew immensely. In 1523, Zurich's city council took Zwingli's reformatory plans seriously enough to convert to Protestantism.

Within two years, the reformation swept through Zurich. The church in Zurich became secularized, with the state taking control of Church properties as well as the social works previously mandated by the Church. Churches were stripped of their opulent decorations. Priests were paid by the state and relieved of celibacy; convents disbanded. By 1528, the cities of Basel, Bern, Bienne, Mulhouse, St. Gallen and Schaffhausen had all followed Zurich's example, converting to Protestantism.

The Catholic powers were not silent on the matter. Catholic cantons quickly took power over the priests, snapping their lax behaviors back into shape so that the public could no longer point at corrupt priests as a symbol of church decay. Both production and possession of printed materials of the Reformation were outlawed. The study of Hebrew and Greek were banned, which prevented independent Biblical study.

Zwingli's reformation differed from Martin Luther's on points that may seem somewhat impenetrable to outsiders; their major point of disagreement was on the nature of communion and whether bread and wine were the literal flesh and blood or Christ or merely symbols of them. Reformer, pastor and theologian John Calvin of Geneva stood in the middle of this debate, trying to find a middle ground that would appease both sides of the argument by emphasizing that the sacramental symbols have great meaning but not individual power.

John Calvin

Meanwhile, in Geneva, Calvin was generating controversy with his developing theology, including doctrines of predestination and the sovereignty of God. Originally interested in priesthood, he broke with the Catholic Church in 1530 and threw in with the Reformation, where his beliefs were more obviously supported. Calvin's viewpoint of religion was far stricter and more demanding than the kinder, gentler Protestantism of Zwingli, but ideologically they were united against the Roman Catholic Church. (Later in this history, we will see how John Calvin inadvertently changed the history not only of religion but of the Swiss watchmaking industry.)

Reformation in Zurich was accomplished quickly and was popular enough to cause alarm in many of the Roman Catholic cantons. At the time, the Confederacy consisted of thirteen cantons; those in Alpine territories remained fiercely Catholic. The reasoning was not solely religious; they also relied strongly on the monies generated by mercenary work (which the Reformation disapproved of strongly). As early as 1524, the Alpine cantons formed the League of the Five Cantons specifically to fight the spread of the Reformation. In response, the Protestant-reformed cities created their own alliance, that went by several names, but which was basically the Christian Confederation. From 1524 through 1529, skirmishes erupted between the two groups, but it was not until a Protestant pastor was burned at the stake in Schwyz in 1529 that Zurich declared war on the League of the Five Cantons. The First and Second Wars of Kappel followed.

Battles, Spoken and Fought

Oddly enough, the First War of Kappel was staged, but unfought. Forces gathered from Catholic cantons with the intent of attacking Protestant cantons. Battle was avoided, though narrowly, when a resolution was reached without any bloodshed. The Second War of Kappel, however, brought over 7000 Catholic troops to attack Zurich. Zwingli's influence had caused the Protestant cantons to stop trading with Catholic cantons, and the embargo on food was pressing the issue, causing the Catholic cantons to physically move on Zurich. Zwingli, for himself, was eager to fight – unfortunately he was killed on the battlefield, thus halting the spread of his version of Protestantism to areas below the Rhine. The Catholics defeated the Protestants, and the Protestants were forced into a treaty.

The treaty demanded that the Protestant alliance dissolve. Catholicism was given priority in common territories, although most communities that had already converted to Protestantism could remain so. Reverting to Catholicism was enforced only in territories that were valuable trade route locations. Interestingly, cantons themselves were permitted to choose religions, so long as the Catholics maintained a majority in the diet (the governing body of the Confederacy).

Regardless of the treaty's terms, Catholic cantons did try on numerous fronts to bring protestant converts back into the fold with enticements rather than force. Their focus was on education and public works. The first Jesuit school was opened in Lucerne, with many others to follow, as well as a Catholic university for Swiss priests, a nunciature in Lucerne, and a Capuchin monk cloister, and a figurative military alliance with the Pope (which, being underfunded, had to operate in treaties rather than battles). In many cases, the resulting division of Catholics versus Protestants was resolved by simply having both groups represented in the cantons' individual governments.

With its own alliance dissolved, Zurich aligned itself with several southern German cities practicing Protestantism – however, when Germany went to war over religion, Zurich, along with other Swiss cantons, remained neutral.

Heinrich Bullinger, who succeeded Zwingli in Zurich, was a prolific writer and participant in the formalization of Protestantism, and he attempted to reconcile the two ideologies. In 1548, Bullinger assisted John Calvin in writing the *Consensus Tigurinus* (which attempted to resolve the schism between Protestants regarding communion). In 1566, Bullinger was instrumental in creating the two versions of the *Confessio Helvetica*, which expressed the commons beliefs of the Reformed Churches in Switzerland; the *Confessio* was adopted by many other protestant European regions. This written work, along with the *Heidelberg Catechism* (1563) and the *Canons of Dordrecht* (1619) were the foundation of theology of Protestant Calvinism.

Swiss Population Growth and the Peasants' Uprisings

While it remained protected from the outside countries, Switzerland suffered divisions inside by both religious conflict and violent class struggles. The Swiss peasant wars rose out of a tax dispute, when the rural folk of Switzerland took offense at taxation from the noble classes.

Switzerland suffered many plague surges (or about 31 plague years) within the cantons from 1500 to 1640. Viciously deadly smallpox outbreaks were particularly brutal on child mortality rates in roughly five-year cycles after 1580. Yet overall, the population managed to grow during the 16th Century by about 35%, or from about 800,000 persons to approximately 1.1 million.

The rise in population had several consequences:
1. Increased dependance on imports
2. Increased prices

3. Generational settlements of estates in the countryside led to smaller and smaller properties owned by families, until the land was insufficient to support those who lived on it.
4. The number of day laborers increased (that is, men who would work a day at a time for a day's wages)
5. Rural areas became increasingly financially dependent on cities.

Political power, however, was held by a few rich families, and as the 16th Century passed, these families began to see their roles as a hereditary right. Predictably, these families became insular, forming their own exclusive circles that allowed for no new voices to be heard.

Around 1525, dissention made itself known among the cantons, either arguments, public statements or outright fights in which both peasants the merchant-classes rebelled against this new order of nobility and their demands for taxes from the people. The Swiss people wanted a return to the old, common rights that the cantons used to enjoy. This conflict continued for decades, with revolts breaking out in various cantons and the uprising spreading from region to region.

Finally, around 1650, when it seemed that the self-proclaimed nobility planned to permanently ignore the population's demands, peasants and working classes from numerous cantons united in the Huttwil Treaty. Through this treaty, they declared themselves a political entity that was independent from city authority, and that it had full sovereignty in its territories over both political and military matters. Then, the peasant armies began to siege Bern and Lucerne.

The peasants were defeated by the cities' forces, and the Huttwil League was forcibly broken apart by an army from Zurich. Leaders of the insurrection were dealt with severely, many of them tortured, imprisoned or even executed.

Even so, ruling aristocrats were not foolish; they realized that they relied upon their people for production and taxes. Presumably following the torture, execution and other punishments, they instituted reforms, lowered taxes and appeased a number of the rebellion's demands. It is believed that this compromise prevented the complete absolutism that resulted in the French Revolution in Switzerland's neighboring country.

The Thirty Years' War

By the time the Thirty Years' War (1618 – 1648) erupted in Europe, Switzerland's mercenary contracts were either finished, or if they were not finished, they were instead neutralized by being in service to parties on opposite sides of the conflict. Even while the cantons were in religious conflict, they agreed overall about removing Swiss soldiers from foreign military involvement. Only the Swiss Papal Guard remained in effect.

Historically, the Thirty Years' War was thought to be a German civil war combined with aspects of the Reformation; more recently historians have linked the underlying cause to rivalry between the Habsburgs and the French Bourbons. Even now the points are debated right down to the accuracy of the name of the war.

To our viewpoint, however, the importance is that the Swiss Confederacy refused to participate. Borders and alpine passes were closed to foreign armies, and the Confederacy refused alliances with any of the involved monarchs.

There was only one exception to this strict neutrality, which was to allow the French army to cross the Protestant cantons to the Grisons, which was a sort of federation of loose communes with no centralized government. Though geographically neighbors to Uri and Ticino, the Grisons was not yet a Swiss canton and would not be until 1803. In the chaos of the Thirty Years' War, the Grisons suffered twenty years of war fought on its grounds.

The Peace of Westphalia treaties brought peace to the Holy Roman Empire and concluded the Thirty Years' War. At this convergence, Switzerland emerged as an independent nation recognized by all parties.

The Renaissance in Switzerland

Switzerland, poised directly between Germany and Italy, was swept up in the Renaissance but unlike those countries, did not have the financial capabilities to produce any large, noteworthy structures. Switzerland's contributions to the Renaissance were mostly those of artists, writers, doctors and thinkers. Switzerland's relative open-mindedness also made it a haven for those whose ideas were unwelcome in their home countries.

The city of Basel (canton of Basel-Stadt) became a center of intellectual freedom and learning during the Renaissance. Its university, founded in 1460, is the oldest in Switzerland and was an advocate of humanism, and therefore served as a safe place for notable political refugees driven from, or running from, their own homelands. This would not be the last time that Switzerland opened its borders to those fleeing oppression, as we will see.

Protestant and Huguenot refugees found sanctuary not only in Basel, but in Geneva and Neuchâtel, and a number of these refugees became important contributors to the Swiss watch industry and the iconic Swiss banking industry.

Important Swiss figures during the Renaissance included:

- Paracelsus, a physician, theologian and alchemist, who taught at the University of Basel. Credited as the "father of toxicology," Paracelsus pioneered many aspects of the Renaissance's medical revolution, including, but certainly not limited to, the use of chemicals and minerals in medicine (such as iron to treat anemia), introduced the ideas of keeping wounds clean and the concept of antisepsis, and was among the first to propose the idea that diseases were entities unto themselves (i.e., germs).
- Hans Holbein the Younger, a high renaissance painter and renowned portraitist who had great influence on Swiss artists, also spent considerable time teaching in Basel.
- Conrad Gessner of Zurich served as the City Physician, but it was his studies in linguistics, zoology and botany that made this true Renaissance man famous; he is considered the father of modern scientific bibliography (in fact he wrote a massive universal biography of, in theory, every book ever written), botany and zoology (his *Historiea animalum* was another huge accomplishment; it was also he who developed the concept of an animal species), and another book accounting about 130 known languages.

- » Matthäus Merian of Zurich, who operated a publishing house, produced maps that displayed early scientific cartography. He drew many city plans, published maps of countries and a world in a huge 21-volume set called the *Topographia Germaniae*.
- » A number of notable historians emerged at this time:
  - » Aegidius Tschudi wrote a history of the early Swiss Confederacy, which gave rise to the tale of William Tell and the valiant oaths taken by the early Swiss canton leaders. He was enormously influential though, after the 19th Century, many of his claims for historical resources were proven to exaggerated or even false, so his histories are to be taken with reservations.
  - » Konrad Justinger, Diebold Schilling the Elder, and Diebold Schilling the Younger were some of many notable artists and authors of Swiss illustrated chronicles, were where beautifully illuminated manuscripts produced for the aristocracy that detailed the politics and life of Switzerland prior to the reformation.
  - » Valerius Anshelm, a Reformation sympathizer, wrote his Swiss chronicles from the city of Bern. His works included a history of Bern, of Switzerland, and a Latin chronicle of world history.

Important printing centers formed in Basel and Geneva; their voluminous output greatly aided the dissemination of ideas. The first newspapers were generated here, though they were short-lived (censored and shut down by the nobility). The cities to Gall, Glarus and Bern also encouraged scholarship and education.

The Helvetic Republic

It seemed that Switzerland was minding its own business, creating cheeses, refining the watchmaking industry and basically getting along fine, when suddenly the Revolutionary French government invaded Switzerland in 1798 – sort of – conquered the country and established a new regime. Two Swiss cantons were allocated to France and to the Cisalpine Republic; the remaining cantons were abolished, the territories united under a constitution. It was the first time that the cantons were under a centralized government, which was called the Helvetic Republic. To the mind of the French revolutionaries, they were "freeing" the Swiss people from an outdated feudal system.

The invasion took place almost bloodlessly, with the French simply stepping in and seizing control, and most of the population unaware, or unwilling to believe, that such a thing could be happening. For some time, a debate had stewed among Swiss leadership. They could not agree on whether Switzerland should become a united republic or an aristocratic regime. Those who wished for a united republic were not averse to the intervention of the French revolutionaries.

This was not a common feeling, however. Finding themselves overtaken and turned into little more than a strategically placed French satellite state, the Swiss reaction was of serious opposition. For centuries they had controlled their destiny, and the people were outraged by this invasion and the destruction of their traditions. The progressiveness of the revolutionary ideas, such as this sudden "freedom of religion" was more shocking to them than welcome.

The Swiss struck back repeatedly at their invaders, attempting coups and inciting skirmishes throughout the land. The Nidwalden Revolt in September 1798 was particularly horrific, when the uprising was quelled by the French burning towns and villages in the canton, seriously damaging the infrastructure and killing around 400 Swiss. Then, when Russian and Austrian forces attacked the French (by invading Switzerland), the Swiss refused to fight for the new Helvetic Republic.

In 1803, Napoleon moved to appease the Swiss, calling a meeting of leading Swiss politicians. As a result, the Act of Mediation was established, restoring Swiss autonomy and reestablishing a confederation made up of 19 cantons.

Switzerland as a Federal State

In 1815, following the Napoleonic wars, the Congress of Vienna re-established Swiss independence and recognized Swiss neutrality. As a neutral territory, Switzerland formed a useful barrier between Italy and Austria – and it is worth mentioning that no one particularly wanted to scrap with the Swiss, who maintained a reputation as frightening, tenacious enemies. Three more cantons joined Switzerland at that time, but since 1815 the borders have remained unchanged save for small adjustments. Power was restored to Swiss nobility.

Despite Swiss disagreement with the Helvetican system of government, the more democratic society it had presented managed to change some Swiss minds about nobility. The Swiss people were no longer happy to follow the rules of the aristocracy. Civil war erupted and some Catholic cantons attempted to set up a separate alliance. The civil war in Switzerland was minor compared to that of other European nations, lasting less than a month and producing less than 100 casualties.

Nevertheless, it deeply impacted a society that had long held a strong nationalistic pride. Switzerland's cantons recognized that they could not take the path of their European neighbors; they must unite and strengthen their country, which meant including all political, religious and social groups.

Thus, in 1848, the Swiss produced a federal constitution that borrowed heavily from the American constitution, forming a centralized government though leaving self-government of local issues to the cantons. Two houses formed the national assembly, the "upper" the Council of States (two representatives from each canton) and the "lower" the National Council (representatives elected from throughout the country).

The constitution ended nobility in Switzerland. Switzerland also determined that troops would no longer be sent abroad to serve other governments with two exceptions: the Papal Swiss Guard, and a contract with Francis II, which obligated them to serve him through 1860.

The constitution provided that it could be rewritten completely, should such action become necessary. That provision has been utilized more than once. The Swiss constitution was rewritten in 1874, when a surging population and the Industrial Revolution made several modifications necessary. It was also heavily revised in 1891 to include elements of direct democracy, Switzerland's unusual type of democratic government.

Under the Alps:
the Gotthard Tunnel

A s we have seen, the Gotthard Pass was the preferred method of foot, horse and wagon travel *over* the Alps leading from Switzerland to Italy. In the late 19th Century, Europe recognized the need for a connecting railway between the North Sea and the Mediterranean. So, when technology was ready and the money was available, and it came time to tunnel *under* the Alps, Gotthard was once again chosen for its central point in the mountains. The cost of building the tunnel was divided among Switzerland, Italy, and Germany.

The Gotthard Railway Company (established 1871) was operated by Alfred Escher, a successful Swiss industrialist. After winning the bid, Swiss engineer Louis Favre was hired as the contractor. Surveys of the mountains showed the optimum route between Göschenen and Airolo, but the very layout of the Alps found ordinary surveying techniques and cartography insufficient to correctly lay out the tunnel's projected path;

complex geometric calculations were made and then double-checked by separate teams.

Boring began from opposite sides of the tunnel in 1871, with hopeful plans of meeting at the mid-point, the tunnel took ten years to complete. The construction required the use of dynamite, which had only been patented a few years earlier, on a large scale. Favre also used mechanized tunneling machines despite pressures to use manual labor.

Difficulties were expected and came as no surprise. Of the multiple problems that the tunnel construction suffered were the constant need for water (to cool the rock and machines) and compressed air (needed to supply energy to the machinery that transported the water). Huge pipelines were laid along the inside of the tunnel's path to accommodate these needs. Well over 200 workers were killed during construction, from rockslides, water inrushes, explosions, toxic fumes, and mechanical accidents, and also during an unfortunate attempt to strike that was violently put down by the Altdorf police force. At one point, the workers were stricken by an epidemic hookworm infection. While treatment of their infection led to significant advances in parasitology, the workers likely would rather have been parasite-free than contribute to such medical heroism.

Favre, who is credited with the tunnel's impressive engineering, unfortunately died of a heart attack in 1879, only six months before the tunnel's breakthrough – he was within the tunnel at the time of his death.

In 1880, the tunnel's two opposite borings connected with impressive accuracy; the innovate and careful surveying had paid off.

The tunnel opened for traffic on January 1, 1882 and was lauded as a monumental achievement. Swiss president Bavier declared, "The Swiss Alps have been breached." The private rail company Gotthardbahn operated the tunnel for a time using steam locomotives, but in 1909 the enterprise was absorbed into Swiss Federal Railways. In 1920, electric trains began to run through the Gotthard Tunnel and by the following year, all steam trains were replaced by electric ones. This significantly improved the pollution conditions inside the tunnel.

The 20th Century saw improvements in engineering to the extent that the Gotthard Tunnel became outdated. In 1980, the Gotthard Road tunnel opened and is now the path of about a million freight trucks every year. (An interesting side note: prior to the development of the road, Swiss Federal Railways offered "piggyback" services for vehicles, allowing cars and trucks to sit on the trains that passed through the tunnel.) The Gotthard Base Tunnel, another railway, opened in 2016. The Base Tunnel, 17 years in construction, is over 50 km longer than the original Gotthard Tunnel (making it the longest tunnel in the world) but because it runs a straight route at higher speeds, it is more energy and time efficient.

World War I

During the first World War, Switzerland was bordered on every side by warring nations. Germany and Austria-Hungary, Central Powers, vied against France and Italy, Entente Powers. Caught in between, Switzerland's neutrality was difficult to maintain. Germany had plans to violate Swiss neutrality and march straight through to outflank France's fortifications; it was only due to the mountainous terrain of Switzerland that Belgium, which reputedly also had less well-organized defenses, was selected to serve as the passageway to France.

Far from helpless, the Swiss Army at the time consisted of almost a quarter million troops with a nearly equal-sized support network. Early in the war, Swiss troops were stationed all along the Jura range and in the Unterengadin regions to keep France and Italy's trench wars from spilling over into Swiss territory. There were some violent encounters in these areas, with gunfire exchanged when foreign troops crossed the border.

Naturally, because Switzerland was largely divided between German, French and Italian-speaking citizens, there were internal conflicts and sides chosen, and Allied blockades caused economic difficulties. But despite these problems, Switzerland still managed to stay out of the war. When it became clear that its neutrality would be respected by all sides, many of the Swiss troops were allowed to return to their homes. They regathered when once more it seemed a foreign army would cross the country (this time, French forces) but this, too, failed to happen. By the end of World War I, only about 12,500 men remained in service.

While Switzerland remained neutral and mostly undamaged, its banking industry thrived while other European economies crumbled.

The country once again became a haven for political refugees and pacifists, and debate thrived among these modern thinkers about the ethics of war. From Zurich emerged two anti-war groups:

1. **The Dadaists**, inspired by the art movement, centered their protests about the illogical nature of conflict around abstract art, theater, and writings, and after the war they returned to their own countries to further the pacificism movement through artistic influence.
2. **The Bolsheviks** sprang from the Russian Social Democratic Labour Party. Vladimir Lenin came to Switzerland from Austria in 1914 and remained there until 1917, actively promoting his outraged stance that when Social Democratic Parties supported this war, they were forcing the working

class to basically fight for the sake of their class enemies. Lenin returned to Petrograd in 1917 to lead the October Revolution in Russia.

Switzerland opened its mountain resorts to serve as recovery facilities for almost 70,000 British, German, and French troops. The wounded soldiers were transferred from prisoner of war camps; they were either injured to the extent that their military service could not continue, or they had been imprisoned for more than 18 months and were suffering deteriorating mental health. This program was organized by the Red Cross, and the warring parties agreed to the terms.

In 1917, the scandal of the Grimm-Hoffman Affair disrupted the Swiss government and momentarily called the country's neutrality into question. Swiss Federal Councilor Arthur Hoffman sent socialist politician Robert Grimm to Russia to attempt negotiations for a separate peace deal between Germany and Russia. However, Hoffman had not consulted the remaining members of the Swiss government, even as Grimm presented himself as a full representative of the Swiss government. When the Allies discovered that such negotiations were taking place, Grimm was forced to return home and Hoffman had to resign his position.

Between World Wars

For about twenty years, Switzerland was an island of calm in the devastated European landscape. Even so, several important events occurred in the years between the First and Second World War.

» Burdened by the failing Germanic economies, Lichtenstein separated itself from Austria's influence. It instead signed agreements with Switzerland to guarantee the survival of its economy – the two little countries would thereafter share a currency and trade rules.

» Switzerland joined the League of Nations in 1920 but withdrew once more in 1938 when it seemed that war in Europe was inevitable.

» In 1934, the passing of the Swiss Banking Act allowed for anonymous numbered bank accounts to be established. This was, in part, to allow Germans (including German Jews) to move their money and assets out of the reach of the Third Reich.

» Considering growing European tensions, the Swiss began to prepare once more for war. Councilor Rudolf Minger led the rebuilding of the Swiss Army (with updated training regimens), procured a larger defense budget, and began a program of war bonds. At home, citizens were encouraged to have hold enough supplies for two months. Minger predicted, quite accurately, that war would come in 1939.

» The public propaganda policy of *Geistige Landesverteidigung* was heavily promoted; this was a concerted effort to prove Switzerland's independent national identity. Its primary purpose was to separate Switzerland from the fascist powers that surrounded it.

WORLD WAR II

Switzerland easily mobilized for a possible invasion at the outbreak of the war in 1939; the country was well-prepared for the contingency. Led by General Henri Guisan, the Swiss military fully mobilized more than half a million troops (including support services) within three days.

The neutral status of Switzerland during the Second World War was maintained by luck, the deterrence of their considerable military force, and concessions to Germany that delayed and/or prevented invasion. Because Swiss trade was blockaded by both Axis and Allied powers, cooperation with the Third Reich occurred in the form of trade and extended credit, though the rate of cooperation depended on extenuating circumstances: first, whether other trading opportunities were available; and second, the likelihood of a German invasion and the need to pacify the Third Reich.

Switzerland, for better or worse, found it safest to remain in a situation where Germany considered them more useful as a trading partner and neutral ground than as another abducted German state. In 1942, links with the Allied forces were severed by the German possession of France. Concessions to Germany reached their peak at this time. Generally, the Swiss press spoke out firmly against the Nazi Regime, which angered the Swiss government, which was trying to avert German invasion.

During the war, Switzerland served both Axis and Allied powers in several capacities:

1. The country served as a base for espionage from both sides. The United States set up its Office of Strategic Services ("OSS") office in Bern; it was from this location that the invasion of Italy was organized and directed.
2. Often communications between the Axis and Allied powers were mediated by Switzerland.
3. More than 300,000 refugees were interned within Switzerland, although some of the immigration practices came under criticism and scrutiny, particularly at points when Jewish refugees were refused admission. On its surface, this was a problem of definitions: the Swiss would only grant asylum to those persecuted for their actions, but not to those persecuted based on their ethnicity, race, or religion.

Both Axis and Allied powers violated Swiss airspace; Switzerland's Air Force had engagements from both Axis and Allied fighter plans, and many of its cities suffered bombings. Luftwaffe planes that slipped over the borders were either shot or forced down. The Allies actively bombed Swiss cities, resulting in both structural damage and fatalities. The Allies insisted that these bombings were errors, mistaking the Swiss towns for German or Austrian ones, but the Swiss felt that these bombings were deliberate retribution for Switzerland's trade agreements with Axis powers. After one particularly grim "accidental" bombing resulted in 50 dead Swiss citizens and the destruction of several manufacturing plants (which were, perhaps coincidentally, making parts for Germany), Switzerland issued a zero-tolerance policy for any planes invading its airspace. Eventually, English pilots who bombed Swiss towns faced court-martial, and the United States paid hefty reparations for structural damages.

During the war, the Swiss National Bank bought large amounts of gold from both the Allies and the Germans, in exchange for Swiss francs or other foreign currencies that could be used to purchase raw materials from other neutral countries. Millions of francs of this gold were stolen from the banks and citizens of occupied countries, and from victims of the Holocaust.

Toward the end of the 20th Century, the ethics Switzerland's policy of concessions to Germany during World War II came under serious attack. The Swiss government commissioned a study of Switzerland's interaction with the Nazis; the final report was issued in 2002 and is known as the Bergier Commission. One of the results of this report was to admit Switzerland's role in the sale of art looted by the Nazis. Switzerland, however, was not entirely free in its choices of trading partners. The country relied on trade for approximately half of its food and almost all its fuel supplies. Switzerland feared that Germany would withdraw the coal supplies it provided to them, for example, if Switzerland refused to transport the German coal meant for Italy. So, despite Allied pressures, these transactions continued.

Swiss concessions to the Third Reich indeed involved some distasteful bedfellows and, in hindsight, some poor decisions. It is hard to feel sorry for the bullied Swiss while their banks became filthy rich in stolen money. It is known that some Swiss officials were Nazi sympathizers; but naturally, others were not. In all fairness, we must view the actions (or inactions) of Switzerland for what they were: an attempt to stave off invasion, and perhaps to make the best of a frightening situation. In desperate times, actions taken are not always the noblest. Switzerland itself must live with its history, and in many ways, it continues to make amends, with its numerous organizations and contributions to the modern stage of promoting peace and prosperity throughout the world.

The National Redoubt

During World War II, invasion plans for Switzerland were developed by the German Army, such as Operation Tannenbaum. Had it not been for the Allied landing at Normandy and difficulties Germany faced in invading the Soviet Union, Switzerland would have almost certainly been overtaken by Germany and Italy, who planned to divide the country between them.

But invasion, planned or otherwise, might not have been as easy as rolling over the border. Switzerland had rethought its defense strategy. Rather than using a border defense, Switzerland turned its defenses to a plan of attrition and withdrawal to hidden fortresses within the Alps, an idea long in development, that was termed the Swiss National Redoubt.

The Swiss National Redoubt was a plan of considerable expense and controversial strategy: its purpose was to make the cost of invading Switzerland so high that it was not worth the effort. The Swiss Army would, in effect, surrender the visible portion of the country to invaders, but retain control of all that essentially could make the country run: the rail lines, the mountain passes, electricity.

The idea of the Redoubt had been in play since the 1880s, and in fact it used much of the same technology that was used to dig the original Gotthard Tunnel. With a Second World War looming large, the Swiss government expanded and refined the plans, and the jobs created by doubling down on building the redoubt were useful during the worldwide Great Depression.

The Alps were quietly and thoroughly outfitted with an enormous network of caverns that served as a well-defended hiding place, and guarded the vital passes through the mountains, making passage through the Alps impossible. With the country thus immobilized, it should be useless to aggressors. The Alps are honeycombed with military installations, including living quarters for anywhere from 100 to 600 troops, underground dams to produce electricity, hospitals, and airstrips, and supplies sufficient for an indefinite stay underground.

The Redoubt caused considerable controversy within the country, not only in its expense but in the fact that it basically left the heavily populated plateau at the mercy of invading forces while the government and military sought refuge in the Alps. This is probably why the majority of the Swiss people were not informed of the plan until the country was virtually surrounded by Axis powers and in imminent danger of invasion.

The Cold War

Swiss authorities recognized the possibility of entering the nuclear arms race. Switzerland had capable physicists at the Federal Institute of Technology. Defense budget limitations, along with ethical concerns, prevented such plans from going beyond the stage of talks. The Nuclear Non-Proliferation Treaty was a measure promoting the peaceful use of nuclear energy through international cooperation. The treaty was negotiated by the Eighteen Nation Committee on Disarmament, a Geneva organization sponsored by the United Nations. Switzerland, as the birthplace of the treaty, signed on in 1968 once the details of the Treaty were completed. Plans for developing nuclear weapons in Switzerland were ceased, at least formally, by 1988.

While Switzerland may not have developed its own nuclear arsenal, they were not inactive in preparing for possible Cold War outcomes. The National Redoubt, as established in World War II, was updated and adapted for the needs predicted in a nuclear war and the following nuclear winter. Electrical dams, shelters and defensive weapons were kept up to date deep in their Alpine hiding places.

To thwart invaders on the ground, the roads and bridges of the country were rigged with demolitions, which would permit the Swiss to destroy any important routes at a moment's notice. It is estimated that some 3,000 explosive charges were laid on Switzerland's thoroughfares.

Since the end of the Cold War, Switzerland has been decommissioning and gradually dismantling these preparations. They eventually removed the explosives from bridges and roads. Alternative uses have been found for the extensive networks of caverns drilled into the Alps. Many underground facilities have been purchased by companies who use the inherent benefits of Alpine caverns to their advantage; the conditions are perfect for the requirements of massive electronic data storage. Some of the caverns have even been opened as museums.

Still, Switzerland is far from a vulnerable country. The government funded the building of shelters in most Swiss homes, so that a surprising majority of older Swiss houses are equipped with bomb shelters. Among the barns and houses of little mountain towns, it is not unusual to discover a concrete bunker disguised as farm building, with a working air defense gun inside. And of course, Swiss men are required to spend time in the military and the reserves, so that roughly two thirds of Swiss men have military training and most retain guns, ammunition, and gas masks in their homes.

Switzerland and the European Union

The Swiss government has long desired to join the European Union, but the popular sentiment (led by the large conservative party) is against joining, and as a direct democracy, the votes of the people are taken at their value. To offset the potential disadvantages of non-membership, Switzerland has developed numerous relationships with the Union that comply with understandings membership would have achieved, and has also structured its economic practices to match those of the Union. Bern and Brussels have adopted trade agreements to offset the negative effects of separation (these include the free movement of persons throughout Europe, i.e., "passport-free" zones) and many other areas of cooperation with the Union. Among these are investing in poorer Southern/Central European countries, opening their electricity market, participation in project Galileo (the EU's Global Satellite Navigation System), and participation in the European center for disease prevention. Recent Swiss voting has reflected increasing support for these bilateral agreements with the European Union.

The Things She's Famous For

Now let's have a look at three export industries for which Switzerland is known worldwide.

The Swiss Cheese Empire

Humans have been making cheese for about as long as we've been drinking milk. Cheese-making techniques have developed and been perfected over our entire history. The Romans were especially known for their cheese technology using rennet (animal stomach lining) to craft sturdy cheeses that could be aged. As the Romans spread their culture throughout the world, they also brought their cheese-production techniques to the world's inhabitants.

The first historical record of "Swiss" cheese comes from the 1st Century Roman historian Pliny the Elder: he described "Caseus Helveticus," the cheese of the Helvetians.

Until the early Middle Ages, Switzerland was a self-sufficient country. The Alps were dominated by farms and herds of goats and cattle, and wherever milk was made it had to be preserved. It was turned into products that lasted longer, such as butter, quark and ziger (whey cheese). Much trial, error, and pure hard work over hundreds of years went into the creation of cheeses that could survive the transport time necessary to make cheese a valuable export.

In the early 15th Century, the Catholic Church, with its massive property resources and seemingly endless supply of monks to work menial tasks, took the initiative and put in the time and effort to experiment and see what techniques were most effective in the production of cheese. The Church also loosened fasting laws in the northern Alpine regions so that dairy products could be eaten during Lent and other church holidays. They experimented with different cooking techniques, types of milk, how long milk could be aged and stored. Once they got a hold of rennet, their magnificent cheeses could last much longer, and cheese became a part of European traveler's everyday lives. These monks kept stocks of cheese for guests.

Among the many cheeses invented by monks throughout Europe were Roquefort, muenster, and parmesan. The best-known Swiss cheeses are Alpine cheeses, such as Emmental, Gruyere and Appenzeller.

Neighboring Alpine regions all had (and still have) their own varieties. Their distinct character arose from cheese-making requirements and the different grasses on which the cattle fed throughout the summer. These cheeses made were shaped into "wheels" with a hard rennet rind so that they could stay fresh and hold a great shelf-life.

In the Confederation's early days, cheese was considered a principal food. It was even accepted as a form of currency: "Paid in cheese and money." Gruyere cheese was so profitable, its production facilities were raided by envious cheesemakers of neighboring Swiss cantons so the secrets of its cheese production could be discovered. Alpine herdsmen used to carry their wheels of cheese over the Alpine passes to Italy and trade them for spices, wine, chestnuts, and rice. Distinct local differences in cheeses emerged due to different mountain pasture sizes, various methods of production and methods of treatment - for example, cows that spent summertime in mountain pastures could produce larger cheese wheels.

By the 1700s, cheese was Switzerland's most valuable trading commodity, and it was sold everywhere around Europe. According to an actual 1793 travel guide: "Even in the regions which produce a lot of milk, it is hard to get good cream for your coffee or fresh butter, because the locals find it more profitable to make cheese out of their milk." People believed that long-lasting cheese (the sort that could survive travel) could only be produced in the Alps.

Then in 1805, Phillip Emanuel von Fellenberg experimented with his own dairy on his Hofwil estate and proved that good cheese could be made in the lowlands too. Then in 1815, Rudolf Emanuel von Effinger, lord of Kiesen castle, developed Emmental – the cheese with the distinctive holes. The Swiss were skeptical about this so-called "valley" cheese, but the flavor grew very popular and the ease of production was such that by 1832, valley-dairies popped up everywhere.

Emmental cheese's popularity was also boosted because it contained no lactose. The lactose was broken down in the production process. Most of the world is lactose intolerant, thus people loved Emmental. The Swiss cheese holes come from microscopically tiny hay particles that get unintentionally mixed into buckets of milk. These holes expand as the cheese matures. The process for making Emmental was expanded to develop other low and no-lactose cheeses.

For Switzerland, this was the great age of cheese. The canton of Bern alone exported almost 23,000 hundredweights of cheese in 1834. Dairies were so numerous in the Alpine regions that Swiss cheesemakers were forced to leave Switzerland to find markets elsewhere that weren't so crowded and had more room for the necessary agriculture. Swiss cheesemakers became almost as valuable an export as was the cheese itself. The United States welcomed thousands of cheese-making Swiss immigrants.

By 1875, fortunes had been invested in the cheese trade, but supply was beginning to outpace demand. Just as many dairy farmers made cheese quickly, cheaply, and incorrectly as those who made a quality product. In other cases, dairymen sold inferior product to locals while saving their higher-quality cheese for exports. Products like milk and butter, as bemoaned by the tourist pamphlet, were so difficult and expensive to find that the market for cheese fell into ruins. Family businesses were destroyed as "trust" in cheese production failed.

To resolve this cheese catastrophe and regain their reputations, the cheesemakers of Switzerland united in reform. They agreed to decrease the quantity of cheese but increase the quality. Dairy schools were opened to give cheesemakers the opportunity to improve their craft. Cheesemakers were taught the importance of livestock stabling and were given in-depth knowledge of feeding cattle. Cheesemakers had to be certified to sell product on the market.

In 1913, fears over war in Europe made the Swiss concerned about supplies and possible food shortages. The Swiss government wanted sole authority over who could or could not export Swiss cheese, so it created The Association of Swiss Cheese Export Firms. Later, the ASCEF became the Swiss Cheese Union. The Swiss Cheese Union expanded their reach into quality control as well as export rights monitoring.

Over the course of the 20th Century, rigorous standards were introduced into the world of Swiss cheese. The variety of cheeses allowed for production were limited to fourteen types. Of those, even fewer were endorsed for manufacture and export, such as Emmental and Gruyere.

But where money can be made, corruption can flourish. The Swiss Cheese Union became far too big and controlling for its own good. It had arms in Swiss government, bombarded newspapers with cheese advertisements, and even took bribes to provide certain sellers with special treatment and opportunities. In 1999, the World Trade Organization disbanded the Union.

Today, Swiss cheese makers are back on top. Switzerland has more than 475 varieties of cheese. According to industry figures, the people of Switzerland alone ate 186,756 tons of cheese, averaging about 22kg per person per year. The top-produced variety of Swiss cheese is Le Gruyere, of which more than 28,500 tons was produced in 2015. Mozzarella is second, then Emmentaler, séré (the Swiss-French word for fromage frais) and Raclette. The continued production and exportation of cheese supports the strong economic backbone of Switzerland.

The Fine Chocolatiers

Until the Industrial Revolution, chocolate was predominantly available in the form of a drink, and accessible only to the wealthy.

By 1806, the Swiss town of Vevey was busy with factories: some for tobacco; some for milk production; and seven small factories open for chocolate production. The chocolate of the time was practically unrecognizable compared to the substance we know today. It was bitter, grainy, gritty, and unpleasant. These unsweetened chunks of cacao were liquefied into hot beverages, and often prescribed by druggists as tonics and elixirs, at a very high cost. The wealthy indulged in chocolate, believing it to be a symbol of status and that consuming it improved one's energy and well-being.

After developing a taste for chocolate at Italian fairs, enthusiast François-Louis Cailler lived in Italy for four years to learn the crafting of chocolate. He then set up his own factory near Vevey in 1819, feeling that the product's potential was untapped. He invented a machine-pressed chocolate that allowed for mass-production. He tried to establish a chocolate-selling business model, and in doing so learned that making chocolate had a lot of setbacks. Cocoa beans had to be imported from South America. He never knew how many beans he could get or when they would arrive, and they were quite costly, as were sugar and the production processes. Solid chocolate was bitter and crumbly so Cailler continued producing chocolate in liquid form to sell to wealthy customers. Still, Cailler became the first recognizable chocolate entrepreneur of his kind, paving the way for other chocolate innovators.

In the canton of Neuchâtel in 1826, Phillippe Suchard opened a two-man factory named Chocolat Suchard. His factory utilized a nearby river to generate hydropower for his mills. He invented a mixing machine for cocoa that added fair amounts of sugar. Then, his grinding mills used heated granite plates and granite rollers to grind cocoa paste. Suchard's commercial process made chocolate far tastier, but the substance still lacked an acceptable texture, it was undesirably crumbly and gritty. Cocoa paste was also pricey to produce. Nevertheless, a huge order for chocolate from the King of Prussia bolstered Suchard's struggling business and brought attention to the product throughout Europe.

Swiss businessman Charles-Amadeé Kohler established his own factory in Lausanne, 1830. Kohler had the idea to mix hazelnuts into chocolate (hazelnuts even in the modern era continue to be Switzerland's most popular chocolate mix-in). Hazelnuts improved chocolate's flavor-profile, yet the form of chocolate remained unmanageable.

Let's turn back to the Cailler factory near Vevey. By 1867 Cailler's daughter was married to Vevey candlemaker Daniel Peter. The increasing popularity of oil lamps was damaging the candle business, so Peter and his brother-in-law, Cailler's son, bought the chocolate factory. Peter too saw potential in chocolate but knew that the substance needed further improvement, and hopefully, a way for their product to distinguish itself among competition. Peter searched for any opportunity to improve his own product. A neighbor also interested in food production provided some valuable input to the process; his name was Henri Nestlé.

Nestlé wanted to make his own baby-food formula and thus experimented with powdered milks produced from the abundant population of Alpine cows. Powdered milk was a step in the right direction, improving the flavor of chocolate immensely, but the mixture required a high water content that caused substance separation and was susceptible to mildew. The inventors decided to substitute condensed milk for powdered.

For seven years of trial and error, chocolate hopefuls Peter and Nestlé continued their work in Vevey and figured out just the right mixture of chocolate and condensed milk until they eventually invented milk chocolate with a creamy, smooth character.

Their milk-chocolate was so successful that Daniel Peter and Henri Nestlé created the Nestlé Company in 1879.

That same year, Swiss manufacturer Rudolf Lindt invented conching machines. These conching machines were the final piece of the puzzle that led to truly great chocolate with the delightful property of melting in the mouth. In terms of chocolate, texture is every bit as important as taste. Conching is a technique used on milk, in which its fat content is emulsified, and the cream doesn't separate. It involves intense mixing and aeration of hot liquid chocolate, sifting through its contents and eliminating unwanted bitterness and acidity. It is roughly the equivalent process of milk homogenization and pasteurization.

Lindt's conching machine design was sold to other chocolatiers in the 1890s, and such machines were soon utilized by The Nestlé Company and then by any other chocolate entrepreneur who wanted to stay in business. The Nestlé Company created the first real bar of milk chocolate, often called "Peter" bars. It was solid and sturdy could be bitten through it and the chocolate would "melt in your mouth." The Nestlé Company made sure that bars of chocolate were inexpensive, turning chocolate from a privilege for the wealthy into an enormously popular affordable treat, with marketing directed toward women and children. Today, The Nestlé Company still has Daniel Peter's original milk-chocolate recipe book.

Between the 19th and early 20th Century is when the popularity of Swiss chocolate spread beyond its borders and marked Switzerland's ascension to chocolate royalty. Chocolate advertisements deliberately emphasized the fact that good chocolate comes from Switzerland. Advertisements shows the Alps and their cows that produce great Alpine milk.

Even beyond Lindt and Nestlé, Switzerland is home to many small award-winning chocolate houses. While less widely known outside Switzerland, they produce some of the finest chocolate in the world. Chocolate has been one of the country's top exports since the 1900s.

A Question of Time: Swiss Clocks and Watches

Clock and watchmaking did not originate in Switzerland. France and Germany, separately, were the countries that innovated timepieces first. The first geared clocks were created around the start of the 14th Century. These pieces were large and therefore stationary. In the mid-1600s the first pendulum clock was developed and is still used today in some instances such as in traditional grandfather clocks. Germany developed a miniaturized clock small enough to be worn and to qualify as a "watch," somewhere between 1509 and 1530, an item affordable only by the extremely wealthy. Despite a commonly quoted line from *The Third Man* (1949) that playfully mocks Swiss neutrality, the Swiss did not invent the cuckoo clock; cuckoo clocks were originally a product of the Black Forest area in Germany.

The Reformation saw the intense persecution of protestants, such as the Huguenots of France, who fled to Geneva, bringing their watchmaking skills along with them. Coincidentally, John Calvin was leading the Reformation in Geneva and declared that wearing jewelry was a sin of pride and was thus forbidden. The numerous jewelers, goldsmiths and enamellers of Geneva scrambled to find a way to make up for the loss of income and cleverly realized that watches could be considered necessary tools rather than jewelry. They threw in their efforts into watchmaking. With the technical knowledge of the Huguenots and the craftsmanship of Geneva's jewelry artisans, watches of significant quality were created.

With this influx of skilled workers, and the booming demand for watches, Geneva soon became known for its timepieces. The industry was so prosperous that the area became glutted with watch manufacturers, causing many such businesses to seek new territories for their factories in the Jura mountains.

In the 18th Century, Britain dominated the pocket watch industry, a consumer demand that emerged with the popularity of waistcoats. To accommodate growing needs for improved tech, inventions including the tooth cutting machine, the balance spring, chronometers, and lever escapement improved the accuracy of timepieces. Switzerland contributed innovations as well, including the "perpetual" watch (created by Abraham-Louis Perrelet), a predecessor of the self-winding watch. The pendant winding watch was developed by Adrien Phillipe, one of the founders of Patek Philippe. Swiss-born inventor Abraham-

Louis Breguet in 1801 invented the tourbillon, an exquisite watchmaking device that counters the effect of gravity drag on timepieces. Even in the modern era, a tourbillon is an expensive addition to a watch. French watchmaker Jean-Antoine Lépine invented his namesake calibre, notably thinner than previous models, which allowed the development of smaller and thinner pocket watches.

The Swiss were quick to incorporate advantageous designs into their timepiece production. But it was the flexibility and the decentralization of Switzerland that gave its biggest advantage in the world of time. The Swiss streamlined watch production. Early innovation is credited to goldsmith Daniel Jeanrichard (of the Neuchâtel canton), who applied the division of labor to watchmaking, increasing both efficiency of productions and standardization of the products. By 1790, Geneva was exporting approximately 60,000 watches each year.

This process was called *établissage*, but in simple terms it is the assembly-line production of watches, with the caveat that parts may be made elsewhere and then delivered to the line for inspection and then incorporation into the assembly. For example, to supplement their income in the winter, Swiss farmers worked making watch components for the firms in Geneva. Their flexibility combined with their streamlined work process (which the French and British refused to adopt) meant that Switzerland could mass-produce watches and jump ahead of its competition.

To illustrate the point, in 1800, both Switzerland and Britain produced about 200,000 timepieces. By 1850, however, Britain continued to produce slightly more than 200,000, whereas Switzerland produced well over two million.

The only drawback was that, in mass-production of timepieces, the Swiss manufacturers were not focusing as intensely on quality. The American production of watches rose just as the French and British markets fell, and American timepieces were of noticeably higher quality than the mass-produced Swiss watches. Though there were still some Swiss watch companies who were making high-quality pieces, the market was flooded with cheap, lower-quality Swiss watches.

In 1868, American Florentine A. Jones moved to Switzerland to open the International Watch Company. He brought with him the American optimized production process, keeping it all in-house, which ensured the reliability of the watches over those produced by établissage. Many Swiss companies (Longines, for one) quickly saw the advantages and followed suit, combining the qualities of optimized production with the beauty and craftsmanship of traditional Swiss timepieces. As a result, production remained high but the quality of the product improved.

The next wave of inventions in watchmaking were machines (by Pierre-Frédéric Ingold and Georges-Auguste Léschot) that could produce identical and interchangeable watch parts, another huge leap forward in watch tech, as watches could now be more easily repaired, and parts were almost a guaranteed fit.

Wristwatches have an interesting history. The small portable German timepieces of centuries before were precursors of the idea, but actual wristwatches were introduced in World War I, as pocket watches could not be effectively carried by soldiers. Inventive soldiers began tying their watches to their wrists with leather straps. Watches that could fasten to wrists were soon produced; for a brief time, they were called "trench watches" and some even had protective casings to stop shrapnel damage. Genuine trench watches are highly valuable collectors' items.

Today, watches are Switzerland's third-largest export, or 1.5% of the gross domestic product. Watch manufacturing employs almost 60,000 people. Switzerland is home to about 700 watch manufacturers, most of them located in Geneva and the Jura Arc. The market has fluctuated over the years, as one might expect, with technological advances and competition from other nations (such as the rise of Japanese quartz technology, which was countered by an aggressive marketing campaign of the Swatch brand, and, currently, the popularity of Apple watches). Switzerland invented the first wristwatch, the first water-resistant watch, the thinnest and smallest wristwatches, the first quartz watch in 1967, and the world's most expensive watch, then LED and LCD displays, new watchmaking materials, and watches that require no batteries.

In 1971, to protect the integrity of its watch exports, Switzerland defined the legal standards by which a watch brand could be labeled as "Swiss." These standards met with some disagreement among Swiss watchmakers and therefore were revised in 1995.

- » The regulations first define the difference between a watch and a clock (the difference is in their dimensions of movement)
- » The regulations then define circumstances under which those dimensions of movement may be considered Swiss, which include that:
    - » The movement is Swiss
    - » 60 percent of the watch's value is accounted for by Swiss components
    - » The movement was cased in Switzerland
    - » The manufacturer's final inspection takes place in Switzerland
- » Foreign-made watches that use Swiss parts can claim to contain Swiss movement but cannot be called Swiss watches.

Watches made prior to 1971 were not required to meet these standards, and therefore may either fail to meet the qualifications of a Swiss watch or, alternately, may far exceed the requirements.

Modern Switzerland

What is Direct Democracy?

Whereas most western countries practice representative democracies, Switzerland's political system uses components of direct democracy at all government levels. In a direct democracy, every citizen's vote counts. Citizens can propose constitutional changes through popular initiative or ask for operational referendums to be held on laws. A certain number of supporting signatures must be obtained from other Swiss citizens (or 50,000 signatures for referendums; 100,000 for amendments) and then the issue will be put to the vote.

This system of voting puts more power in the hands of individual citizens, but also involves quite regular voting requirements. For example, Swiss citizens have voted 31 times on 103 federal questions and many more questions at the cantonal and municipal levels, between 1995 and 2005. Citizens are called vote on any type of issue at any political level. Simple majority vote is enough to win elections at municipal and cantonal levels; federal/constitutional level requires double majority votes to pass, meaning that a majority of individuals *plus* a majority of cantons' votes are required. Therefore, a constitutional amendment cannot be passed by a majority of personal votes in favor, if a majority of the cantons do not also agree.

In many ways direct democracy is an enviable system that puts the decision-making directly into the hands of a country's people, particularly in view of the relative ease of subversion and corruption in a representative system. However, it is important to distinguish that Switzerland's relatively small population makes direct democracy possible; one-to-one voting increases in difficulty and expense proportionately to increases in population numbers. Switzerland also has tough citizenship requirements, which reduce the number of available voters. Increasing technological capabilities may make direct democracy a more feasible possibility in the future for larger countries desiring to make a change.

On this subject, Switzerland was the last of the Western republics to grant the right to vote to women, and the right was granted piecemeal, first by some (but not all) cantons in 1959, at the federal level in 1971, and then finally the last holdout cantons in 1990. Once they achieved the federal level of suffrage, women rose quickly in Swiss politics. Switzerland's first female president was Ruth Dreifuss, elected in 1999.

In the modern era, Switzerland's executive power is shared by a committee of seven with a rotating, ceremonial president. The committee is strongly in favor of finding consensus.

Citizenship in Switzerland

Because of Switzerland's low crime rate (one of the lowest in the world, in fact), wealth, progressive nature, healthy environment, politics and neutrality, Swiss citizenship is highly sought-after and therefore, not easy to obtain. But in the past twenty years, citizenship laws have undergone some dramatic changes.

There are three paths to becoming Swiss:

1. **Birth**. However, a child is not granted citizenship merely for being born on Swiss soil. A child is granted Swiss citizenship only if:
    a. his/her married parents include at least one Swiss citizen
    b. his/her unmarried mother is Swiss.
    c. his/her unmarried Swiss father acknowledges paternity before the child turns legal age.
2. **Marriage to a Swiss citizen**. Note, this is not automatic. If one marries a Swiss citizen, one can "fast-track" naturalization. The spouse *must* be a Swiss citizen at the time of the marriage for these rules to apply. Foreign spouses of Swiss citizens must have lived in Switzerland for a total of five years to apply for fast-track naturalization.

3. **Naturalization**. If one has no blood ties to Switzerland through birth or marriage, one must live in Switzerland for at least ten years (or six childhood years).
    a. Knowledge of a national language is required.
    b. A residential permit is required.
    c. Criminal offenders or people on welfare are theoretically excluded.
    d. If these conditions are met, an applicant's request is "green-lighted"; however, at this point the canton in question begins its approval process, and the rules of obtaining citizenship differ from canton to canton.
    e. Applicants are expected to be well-integrated into Swiss society, law-abiding, and no danger to Swiss national security.

Swiss people are permitted to hold multiple nationalities, though this rule is restricted to select countries. Switzerland also permits renaturalization to those who lost their citizenship through legal forfeiture. The ease of obtaining a Swiss citizenship increases dramatically if one can prove descent from Swiss parents or grandparents.

Switzerland as a World Center

Switzerland has diplomatic relations with most countries. Because of its neutrality, it has been able to serve as an impartial intermediary between nations. This, along with the relative ease of doing business within the country, has led to Switzerland being an unparalleled gathering place for world organizations.

Not only a huge number of world organizations, but also many large corporations headquarter in Switzerland. Corporations that elect to use Switzerland as their home base must have at least one Swiss citizen on the board of directors.

Among the world organizations that make their home headquarters and/or hold their annual forums in Switzerland are:

1. The Red Cross and the Red Crescent, aid organizations that are independent of each other but operate under the same seven principles: humanity, impartiality, neutrality, independence, voluntary service, unity, and universality. (Geneva)
2. The World Trade Organization (WTO) (Geneva)
3. The International Federation of Association Football (FIFA) (Zurich)
4. The International Ice Hockey Federation (IIHF) (Zurich)
5. The International Olympic Committee (IOC) as well as the Olympic Museum and the Court of Arbitration for Sport (Lausanne)

6. CERN, the world's largest laboratory (Geneva). The facility is dedicated to particle physics research.
7. The Paul Scherrer Institute (canton of Aargau). This important research facility has developed amazing technologies from Velcro to the scanning tunneling microscope, a Nobel prize-winning creation.
8. The International Telecommunication Union (ITU) (Geneva)
9. The World Health Organization (WHO) (Geneva)
10. The League of Nations (Geneva)
11. The European headquarters of the United Nations (the Palais des Nations – although Switzerland did not join the United Nations until 2002); the country is also host to the United Nations Human Rights Counsel, and the United Nations High Commissioner for Refugees (Geneva)
12. The International Labor Organization (ILO) (Geneva)
13. The World Economic Forum holds its annual meetings (Davos)
14. Bank for International Settlements (BIS) (Basel)

Swiss Military Today

Switzerland, being landlocked, has no navy, but as it also shares lakes with the borders of other countries, it does employ armed military boat patrols. Due to the country's neutrality, the Swiss military does not serve in wars, but they are often called upon for aid and peacekeeping missions. Its Land Forces and Air Force are composed of conscripts: men typically are conscripted at the age of 18 and about two-thirds of them are found fit for service. If they are not suited to service, alternate service exists. Women are permitted to volunteer for service. In 2003, the size of the Swiss army was reduced by popular vote to about 200,000 troops, with 120,000 of those on active duty and 80,000 in reserves. Soldiers keep their military equipment, including all their weapons, and so many a Swiss closet would yield some surprising contents. 29% of Swiss citizens are legal gun owners and the majority of these are guns issued by the Swiss army. However, the army no longer issues ammunition. The Swiss engage in a great deal of recreational shooting and many children belong to gun clubs.

Twice, a referendum has been proposed to eliminate the Swiss military altogether, but both times it has failed by fairly overwhelming majority vote. The second such vote was held just after the September 11, 2001 terrorist attacks on the United States, which probably explains a great deal of the resistance against eliminating military power.

The Swiss Economy

One of the world's strongest and most stable economies, Switzerland is ranked as the world's wealthiest country per capita across several ranking systems. The country is lauded for its "ease of doing business," global competitiveness and innovation. Strangely, while Switzerland itself is referred to as largely free of corruption, its banking system is criticized, even by the Swiss people themselves, as almost irredeemably corrupt.

Home to several huge multinational corporations, Switzerland's most important economic sector lies in manufacturing. Its most produced products are health products and pharmaceuticals, precise scientific instruments, chemicals, and musical instruments, while its leading exports are chemicals, electronics and machines, and precision instruments (including watches). Next, Switzerland's service industry holds an important economic position, promoting banking, its international organizations, insurance, and tourism.

Taxation is relatively low, however, though comparisons of the tax rates do not include the budgets of cantons and municipalities. Nevertheless, the Swiss federal government's main source of funding comes more from the value-added tax than from direct federal tax.

Just more than 5 million people in Switzerland are employed; they have a highly flexible job market and very low unemployment rates; it was measured at merely 2.3% in 2019 after hovering around 3% for several years prior to that. Switzerland's population has approximately 8.2% living below the poverty line, and another 4.3% qualify as the working poor, meaning that their jobs are low-paying (roughly one in every ten Swiss jobs qualifies as such). Foreigners make up about 25% of the population of Switzerland. Of the available employment in the country, women and foreigners are the most likely to hold jobs that are considered to pay at the "poverty" level.

Mysteries of the Swiss Bank Account

The legendary "Swiss Bank Account" carries iconic status in the popular culture. What is means, simply, is that whether you have ten dollars or ten million dollars in a Swiss bank account, no one (including your nation's tax authorities or your ex-spouse) can access the information. Your balance, your deposits, your withdrawals, everything simple and complex about your bank account, is kept secret. The accounts are numbered, not named.

Switzerland's powerful banking complex actually developed through its merchant trade role in the 18th Century, and even then, client confidentiality was of importance. The Swiss practiced banking secrecy to protect, and draw, the interests of wealthy Europeans. Disclosure of their assets was forbidden, which can of course protect one from any number of pesky taxes, tithes, or expectations. Prominently, Catholic French Kings putting their holdings into Geneva accounts, so that they were not subject to Protestant banks. Then, in the 1780s, Swiss bank accounts began the practice of insuring deposits, which increased their banks' reputation for financial security. Confidentiality of bank customers was held in much the same way as the secrets of the confessional, and even today, disclosing client information is considered a criminal offense.

In 1934, banking secrecy was codified. The Federal Act of Banks and Savings Banks was passed to protect the assets of those persons persecuted by the Nazis; however, this secrecy goes both ways. Not merely the persecuted but the persecutors – and anyone else looking to avoid divulging how much money they have – can take advantage of the system. Financial crime and tax evasion are common and obvious uses for these mysterious secret accounts. Swiss bank accounts are havens for arms dealers, dictators, mobsters, corrupt officials, and tax evaders.

Numerous times, there have been international efforts to seek regulations in Swiss banking and to repeal or lessen secrecy laws; investigations try to probe legal ramifications such as how much the secrecy laws contribute to money laundering. Switzerland's political forces, however, minimize and resist any such efforts. Of course, any "opening" of the information on these massive bank accounts would ruin Switzerland's most profitable business. Despite claims of disapproval from citizens and the world, banking remains dominant in the Swiss economy.

Estimates from the Swiss Bankers Association (SBA) in 2018 put Swiss bank holdings at about $6.5 trillion U.S. Dollars (which equals approximately 25% of all global cross-border assets).

Speaking in Switzerland

There are four national languages in Switzerland:

Language Location Spoken Percentage of Population

German* Mainland, Eastern 62.8

French Western 22.9

Italian South 8.2

Romansch Canton of Grisons .5

*German is spoken in two dialects: Swiss German (more informal) and Standard German (formal, for business uses).

Nearly two-thirds of the Swiss population speaks more than one language. The government issues documents, communications, and translations into German, Italian and French but Romansch translation of official documents is not required, despite Romansch being an official language.

An interesting linguistic phenomenon occurs here. German and French spoken in Switzerland have developed to contain peculiarities called Helvetisms. These words, which did not come from native German or French, are formed in the melting pot of combined Swiss cultures and the mixing of languages, such as some Italian slipping into German. Modern French and German dictionaries include Helvetisms as part of their languages' vocabularies.

Bilingualism is strongly encouraged. Swiss school pupils are required to learn at least one of the other languages of Switzerland.

Education and Sciences

Pre-college education is controlled by the cantons, therefore across Switzerland, in both public and private schools, the age requirements for school children, the cost and quality of the schools, and the language curriculums are varied. Once they have completed elementary school, students are typically divided into groups depending on their learning capacities: students who are gifted are put into advanced classes; those who need more dedicated learning are given educations adapted to their needs.

Higher learning is serious business in Switzerland. The twelve universities in Switzerland, many of them ranked among the world's top schools, are also controlled at the canton level. While Basel is the home of the oldest university in Switzerland, Geneva is home to the world's oldest graduate school, the Institute of International and Development Studies. There are two federally funded institutes and many applied science universities.

Some of the world's most famous scientists are affiliated with Switzerland (meaning they were born in Switzerland, or studied and worked in Switzerland); among them:

- » Werner Arber, Nobel Prize Medicine, 1978; for discovery of restriction enzymes and their application to molecular genetics
- » Felix Bloch, Nobel Prize Physics, 1952; for nuclear magnetic precision measures

- Daniel Bernoulli, the mathematician who found the dynamical equation of fluids
- Albert Einstein, Nobel Prize Physics, 1921; for his groundbreaking contributions to the field of physics
- Charles Guillaume, Nobel Prize Physics, 1920; recognized for his work in precision measurements
- Walter Rudolf Hess, Nobel Prize Medicine, 1949; for mapping of diencephalic function in the brain
- Carl Jung, the founder of analytic psychology, whose work influenced not just the study of psychology but of literature and religion.
- Emil Theodor Kocher, Nobel Prize Medicine, 1909; for his work in physiology and pathology of the thyroid gland
- K. Alex Muller, Nobel Prize Physics, 1987; for discovery of superconductivity studies
- Paul Herman Muller, Nobel Prize Medicine, 1948; for discovery of DDT as a contact poison
- Jean Piaget, a founder and major figure in child psychology
- Tadeus Reichstein, Nobel Prize Medicine, 1950; for work with hormones in the adrenal cortex
- Heinrich Rohrer, Nobel Prize Physics, 1986; for invention of the scanning tunneling microscope (uses particularly in nanotech)

Energy and the Environment

Switzerland uses 56% hydroelectricity and 39% nuclear power, which leaves them with a network nearly free of CO_2 emissions. Swiss green energy initiatives are striving to remove nuclear power from the grid (although the referendum has been rejected in national votes) and to cut the nation's energy use by at least 50% by the year 2050.

Switzerland's environmental record is one of the best in the nations of the developed world; the Global Green Economy Index ranks Switzerland among the top 10 green economies worldwide. The people are active recyclers (with 66 to 96 percent of recyclable materials recycled, depending on the canton). It is interesting to note that Switzerland's well-organized recycling system, which utilizes volunteers and railway transport, began in 1865 with the building of the first modern paper manufacturing plant in Biberest. Illegal disposal of garbage in Switzerland is met with heavy fines.

Culture, Media, and Entertainment

The constitution of Switzerland guarantees the freedom of the press and the right to free expression. Switzerland's cultural diversity and multiple national languages, plus its early advances in the availability of printing, account in some part for the fact that historically the country has had the greatest number of newspapers published in proportion to the population's size. News is produced around the clock by the Swiss News Agency (SNA) in three of the country's four languages. The Swiss Broadcasting company (recently renamed as the SRG SSR) oversees television and radio programming but cable networks provide most of Switzerland with access to foreign programming.

Early Swiss literature is mostly German, and it was not until the 18th Century that French became fashionable enough to enter the literary market. Switzerland boasts several German and French speaking authors known worldwide; their Italian and Romansch authors are more modestly popular. Of course, most adults of a certain age remember reading the incredibly popular children's classic novel *Heidi,* by Johanna Spyri, the tale of a Swiss mountain girl who strives to be reunited with her grandfather. Swiss poet Carl Spitteler won the 1919 Nobel Prize in Literature for his contributions to poetry; his masterpiece work is *Olympian Spring.*

Because of the three major cultures that combined to make Switzerland, the resulting Swiss culture is notable for its very diversity, and the Swiss have a wide range of customs. Swiss cooking, just for example, is varied over the cantons, with each developing its own individual traditional dishes. Folk art is diligently practiced and kept alive by organizations devoted to it, through wood carving, embroidery, yodeling and dancing, accompanied and the undeniably Swiss musical instruments of the alphorn and the accordion.

About 1000 museums are spread throughout the country. Important cultural festivals are held annually including the Paléo Festival (a rock-and-roll concert), the Lucerne Festival (featuring classical music), the Montreux Jazz Festival, the Locarno International Film Festival and the Art Basel (and international art fair with showings also in Miami and Hong Kong.

The Romansch culture is somewhat culturally and linguistically isolated, and with the increasing pressures of globalization is struggling to maintain its unusual cultural identity.

Sports

It comes as little surprise that mountaineering, skiing, and snowboarding are extremely popular in Switzerland, seeing as the terrain for such sports is ideal. Both the residents of Switzerland and gaggles of tourists gather to play on the Alpine slopes. The Swiss professional football association is the Swiss Super League and Switzerland is home to the highest football pitch in the world: Ottmar Hitzfeld Stadium, 6,600 feet above sea level. Naturally the numerous large and beautiful lakes of Switzerland make it an ideal place for sailing.

The Swiss enjoy watching televised football, skiing, ice hockey, and tennis. Switzerland is the birthplace of Roger Federer, generally considered one of the greatest tennis players of all time.

Though several successful race drivers have come from Switzerland, motorsport racecourses have been banned in Switzerland since 1955's Le Mans disaster, the worst accident in racing history, when debris from a crash flew into the crowd, killing 80 and injuring more than twice that many.

Switzerland has a few traditional sports, including schwingen, a form of traditional wrestling that originated in rural cantons, and which is considered by some to be the national sport. Hornussen is an amusing Swiss variation combining principles of both golf and baseball, and Steinstossen is an ancient game (rather like the stone put) that was played in the Alps from prehistoric times.

Life and Tourism in the Alps

The Swiss Alps hold the highest mountains of all the Alpine range. The Swiss have built several hydroelectric dams in the Alps and created a fair number of artificial lakes; notably with the effects of global warming reducing the size and runoff of Alpine glaciers, the Swiss are examining alternative solutions and problem solving in their future energy production. The Alps are divided into three "zones":

1. The subalpine zone, located below the tree line, ranging from heights of about 1200-2300 meters depending on which area of the Alps one considers. This is where most towns, people and areas of production are located.
2. The alpine zone, above the treelined, also varies according to location. Some villages can be found here. Below the permafrost limit, which is at about 2600 meters, meadows can be used for grazing.

3. The glacial zone, where snow and ice are permanent. Aside from scientific observatories, no settlements will be found in these areas.

Many of Switzerland's tiny Alpine towns were established in the Middle Ages and continue the traditions of their ancestors, farming hay and grass to feed their cattle through the winter, their cattle supplying the milk for cheese, with each hamlet having its own distinctive flavors of Switzerland's most popular export. The mountain people have an interesting outlook, combining their respect for tradition with the conveniences of modern tech; for example, they must meet guidelines in cheese-production if they want to export the product, but they still follow traditional recipes and techniques.

The towns are too small to warrant official services, and the men are busy working on the farms, so the local housewives serve as the well-trained volunteer fire department, running drills monthly and keeping themselves trained. The towns are made of Alpine wood, and a single fire could be devastating.

Though visitors are made welcome, they should not expect luxuries. The residents of these little towns have no wish to become homes to extravagant mountain lodges. Just for example, the little town of Gimmelwald had itself declared an Avalanche Zone years ago to avoid expansionism. Nearly all these small villages are linked to public transport systems, which are well established in the Alps.

There is one notable exception to their old-fashioned ways: the Swiss farmers supplement their income through the winters by operating nearby lifts and transports that bring tourists into the heights of the Alps. The winter season runs from about November to late May but of course the weather is the final deciding factor on when the season will start and end. Major winter sports destinations include Bernese Oberland, Graubunden and Valais; in many cases tourist towns are traffic-free and only public transportation is available.

The Alps are obviously known for winter sports but in the summertime, the mountains are also set up for enjoyable and manageable hiking and cycling trails. Difficult altitudes are achieved by lifts and cable cars, then miles of paved trails have been established to allow for sightseeing on foot or bicycle. Bike rentals are popular and biking routes well-marked. Because most of the ascents are achieved by car or lift, the bike trails are flat or downhill. The trails are partitioned into manageable lengths and equipped with gondola stations, little cabins that provide food, hot drinks, inexpensive accommodations, so that hikers are not required to carry supplies along with them. The trails are so well-developed that it is possible to hike the Alps from France to Slovenia. Hikers get to meet a good number of friendly, belled cows and goats along the way. Additionally, there are lots of campgrounds, and typical of Switzerland's pride in its cleanliness and amenities, these are well-groomed, with stores and good facilities for the campers.

The traffic-free town of Interlaken is the springboard for multiple ways to view the beauty of the Alps and the surrounding lakes. Some of these options are quite adventurous, including skydiving, paragliding and hang gliding. From Interlaken, one can easily find one's way to the mountain resorts that serve famous Alpine peaks Eiger, Monch and Jungfrau. Trains from Interlaken can take tourists along magnificent mountain views. It is also a well-known destination for backpackers, offering many accommodations specifically for the needs of that brand of tourism.

Mountain climbing is another popular Swiss activity. With more than 250 summits exceeding 3,600 meters, a climber could not ask for more choices in ascents.

Life in Switzerland's Great Cities

The Swiss enjoy the highest per capita income in the world, averaging $88,000 per person, but this privilege comes with one of the highest costs of the living in the world as well. Major urban areas are very expensive places to live. City systems are organized and reliable. The trains and buses run on time in Switzerland – usually down to the second.

The Swiss are hard-working, time-conscious people, but they do not often fall into the traps of overwork. It is more appropriate to say that they "work to live," meaning that they work smarter, not harder, and then thoroughly enjoy their time away from the job. Few businesses remain open during weekends and evenings or have seriously restricted hours. The Swiss take their leisure time as seriously as they take their work. They are proud of their clean cities, streets and rivers and take special care to keep these things pristine.

Generally, the Swiss are quite practical in the way they deal with social problems. For example, when a city is faced with both excessive traffic and rising unemployment, they develop a bike rental system that creates new jobs. In the case of drug abuse, the Swiss government subsidizes safe needles, and public restrooms install blue lights (an interesting trick – it keeps one from being able to find a vein for injection). Drug use is considered a health problem rather than a crime and is dealt with as such.

Most Swiss people live in urban areas (about two-thirds of the population). This is a rather dramatic change that has occurred just over the last century. Before, Switzerland was mostly rural, a country of little Alpine hamlets, mountain herders and plateau farmers. But starting in 1935, urban development took over the Swiss plateau, which has become quite densely populated. Despite some concerns about overcrowding, Swiss cities are renowned for their high quality of life. Swiss cities embrace their clean rivers, with much of the social life occurring on the riverfront, and show great pride are care for their "old town" areas which typically line those same rivers.

Here we'll examine the most populous and famous Swiss cities:

Basel

Basel is still known for the centuries old and highly acclaimed University of Basel. However, Basel is also the leader of Switzerland's pharmaceutical industry. Novartis and Roche, along with several other drug companies, are headquartered there. Basel's companies are strong players in the life-sciences industries. Basel is often considered a cultural capital of Switzerland, and is home to forty notable museums such as:

- » The Kunstmuseum, established in 1661, which was the first publicly accessible art collection in the world
- » The Fondation Beyeler, Switzerland's largest art museum
- » The Museum of Contemporary Art (Basel), which was the first contemporary art museum in Europe

Basel continues its centuries-old commitment to the promotion of humanism. Basel, Zurich, and Geneva are all rated among the top ten most livable cities in the world.

Geneva

Like Zurich, Geneva is a global city, though its fame is due more to its international organizations rather than the thrumming business world of Zurich. Known as the Capital of Peace and Freedom, Geneva is home to 35 international organizations and 250 international non-governmental organizations. It is somewhat unusual in that most world cities that host such staggering numbers of international organizations tend to be capital cities, whereas Geneva is not.

Though generally it is known more as a hub humanitarian, political and peace centers, Geneva, too, ranks high as an important financial center on the world stage. Geneva's population is moderate, at slightly over 200,000 persons, and the cost of living there is quite high.

Bern

The unofficial capital, or "Federal City" of Switzerland, is built on a peninsula in the turquoise Aare River. Bern appears stately, but its attitude is laid back and casual. The city is decorated with eleven colorful Renaissance fountains of local heroes and events. One of its most famous sights is the Zytglogge, a medieval clock tower of moving puppets. Bern's city center, many of its medieval buildings still standing, has been designed by UNESCO as a World Heritage Site. In the summer months, citizens love to swim in the river. A popular outing is to hike upstream and then float back to downtown on the current.

Why is Bern considered an "unofficial" capital? Following the inclusion of the final cantons of Valais, Neuchâtel, and Geneva to full membership in 1815, the purposes of a "capital" city for the sake of congressional meetings was given in two-year rotating terms to Lucerne, Zurich and Bern. Eventually Switzerland's Federal Assembly dictated that Bern should function as the Federal City while other important institutions were granted to other cities. As ever, the Swiss believe in compromise. Zurich was given the Federal Polytechnical School, Lucerne the Federal Insurance Court, Lausanne the Federal Supreme Court, and Bellinzona the Federal Criminal Court, just to name a few. Regardless, in the new constitution of 1999, Switzerland did not name a capital or Federal City, and the Swiss Federal Council seems reluctant to pursue the matter; the last measures taken were the formation of a committee to, basically, weigh the pros and cons of such a declaration for Bern – almost twenty years ago.

Lausanne

Overlooking Lake Geneva, Lausanne is made up of two sections: the Waterfront and Old City (which is listed in the Inventory of Swiss Heritage Sites). It is often called "The San Francisco of Switzerland" because of the many steep hills throughout the city streets. Lausanne is a mecca for shoppers, with many of the finest and most exclusive shops in the world lining its thoroughfares. It is the smallest city in the world to have a rapid-transit system.

Lausanne has attracted a fair number of writers over the years, both those seeking refuge and those looking for inspiration, including Hemingway, Gibbon, Shelley, and Byron. T.S. Eliot is said to have composed most of *The Waste Land* while in Lausanne).

It is also known as an "international sport" city, hosting about 55 international sports associations in addition to the International Olympic Committee.

Lucerne

Lucerne is a notably artistic city. The beautiful Chapel Bridge (the oldest covered bridge in Europe) crosses the Ruess, and inside the bridge one can find a series of paintings depicting three centuries of events from Lucerne's history. Swans live on Lake Lucerne. The dam there controls the level of the lake to avoid flooding in the surrounding towns, and little steamer boats take people back and forth to the various lakeside villages.

It is within sight of Mounts Pilatus and Rigi and therefore a popular destination for tourism.

Each year near winter's end, a carnival called Fasnacht breaks out in the Old Town streets. It is comparable to Mardi Gras (also having a basis in Catholicism), and is full of costumed characters, parades, indoor parties, and dances, singing and music. The event lasts almost a week and draws tens of thousands of visitors.

Zurich

The world city of Zurich dates back Roman times, and in Old Town Zurich, some buildings date back to the 12th Century. But by the 19th Century it was a major economic center. Despite its size and financial power, Zurich has surprisingly few tall buildings – many of its districts maintain height restrictions on the buildings.

A major transportation hub for roads, air traffic (its airport serving 60 passenger airlines from around the world) and railways, Zurich is the center from which almost 3,000 trains a day take almost half a million people all over Europe. The largest city in Switzerland, Zurich is home to 1.5 million people and more than 150,000 companies. The people are known for their wealth and for working hard to get it. The city's employees are highly motivated and show a low level of absenteeism. Zurich promotes professional training and education and produces skilled labor at every level. It is ranked as the city with the highest quality of living in the world, but also as the most expensive city in the world.

Hard workers they may be, the people of Zurich are also invested heavily in the arts, classical and contemporary music, opera, theaters, and ballet, combining a respect for tradition with curiosity about new innovations, therefore pushing the envelope to find new forms of expression in these artistic arenas. A couple of interesting Zurich attractions are Europe's oldest vegetarian restaurant, Hiltl, which serves an incredible variety of vegetarian entrees smorgasbord-style. One can also visit the Beyer Clock and Watch Museum, an amazing display of timepieces from 1400 BC to the present.

Conclusion

Switzerland's climate, geography and location have determined its position – pardon the pun – in the events of the world. However, it is the fierce resilience of the proud Swiss people that have made it the world power and mediator that it is today. The Swiss are willing to sacrifice, even fight to the death, but show an amazing preference for compromise most of the time, believing in unification and consensus if possible.

Neutrality is Switzerland's unusual calling card, a position that subjects it both envy and criticism. While the subject of controversy in its historic choices, and the subject of suspicion in terms of its secret bank accounts, Switzerland has no more skeletons in its closet than any other European nation, and in many ways, it pays for, or at least offsets, its indiscretions with concerted efforts toward the betterment of mankind and the planet Earth. Switzerland continues to play a leading role in setting the examples for world peace, humanitarian organizations, and forward-thinking environmental and scientific innovations.

As if this were not sufficient to garner admiration, Switzerland remains one of the most beautiful countries in the world, surrounded by the majesty of its mountain ranges, its landscape flowing with clean rivers, and graced by vast lakes.

Its cities are remarkable and its people unconquerable. The Swiss are justifiably proud of their magnificent homeland.

REFERENCES

Videos

Animated History of Switzerland (2019). *Suibine*. Via YouTube.

How Switzerland Managed to Remain Neutral with WWI and WW2 Raging Around Them. (2018) *Today I Found Out*. Via YouTube.

Interesting Facts about Switzerland. (2016) *Coolvision*. Via YouTube.

Rise of the Swiss Warriors and Mercenaries. (2019). *KingsandGenerals*. Via YouTube.

Switzerland's Great Cities (2008). Rick Steves Europe.

Switzerland's Jungfrau Region: Best of the Alps (2003). Rick Steves Europe.

Websites

www.myscience.ch

www.nobelprize.org

www.swissinfo.ch

www.chocosuisse.ch/

www.eda.admin.ch/aboutswitzerland/en/home.html/en/switzerland/swiss_specials/swiss_chocolate/switzerland_and_chocolate/

www.salondeschocolatiers.com/en/

www.alpenwild.com/staticpage/history-of-chocolate-in-switzerland/

www.houseofswitzerland.org/swissstories/history/six-reasons-why-swiss-chocolate-such-success

https://medium.com/a-dose-of-curiosity/how-did-switzerland-become-known-for-chocolate-d41f912f28

www.easyvoyage.co.uk/travel-headlines/a-brief-history-of-swiss-chocolate-77496

alpinehikers.com

blog.bus2alps.com/2018/12/20/swiss-bliss-the-history-of-switzerlands-chocolate/

whatscookingamerica.net/History/MilkChocolate.htm

www.cheesesfromswitzerland.com

https://foodsforliving.com/2018/01/03/featured-content/

www.eda.admin.ch/aboutswitzerland/

www.thelocal.ch/20170321/15-facts-you-may-not-have-known-about-swiss-cheese/

www.firstclasswatches.co.uk/blog/2015/07/the-history-of-the-swiss-watch-industry-part-one/

www.livwatches.com/blogs/everything-about-watches/the-complete-history-of-the-swiss-watchmaking-industry

www.fhs.swiss/eng/origins.html

https://theculturetrip.com/europe/switzerland/

www.assetsure.com/jewellery/watch-insurance/history-of-swiss-watchmaking/

www.hautehorlogerie.org/en/encyclopaedia/history-of-watchmaking/

https://blog.crownandcaliber.com/swiss-watchmaking-factories/

www.ablogtowatch.com/interview-a-brief-history-of-the-swiss-watch-industry-america/

www.watchswiss.com/perpetual/history-of-time/

Wikipedia.org Entries: Anshelm, Valerius; Banking in Switzerland; Basel; Calvin, John; Charles the Bold; Geneva; Gessner, Conrad; Gotthard Pass; Hans Holbein the Younger; Helvetica Republic; Interlaken; Justinger, Konrad; Lausanne; List of Swiss Cheeses; Lucerne; Merian, Matthaus; National Redoubt; Papal Swiss Guard; Paracelsus; Red Cross and Red Crescent; Reformation in Switzerland; Renaissance Humanism; Swiss Alps; Switzerland; Switzerland in the World Wars; Ticino; Treaty on the Non-Proliferation of Nuclear Weapons; Tschudi, Aegidius; Zurich